INTERCULTURAL ARCHITECTURE
THE PHILOSOPHY OF SYMBIOSIS

Yokohama wood-block print, c 1865.

KISHO KUROKAWA

INTERCULTURAL ARCHITECTURE
THE PHILOSOPHY OF SYMBIOSIS

ABOVE: Kisho Kurokawa, Hiroshima City Museum of Contemporary Art, Hiroshima, 1988. *OPPOSITE:* Kisho Kurokawa, National Bunraku Theatre, Osaka, 1983.

The American Institute of Architects Press • Washington, D.C.

Author's note

I would like to express my gratitude to a number of people involved in this project, first and foremost to Charles Jencks for agreeing to write the foreword and for many stimulating discussions on architecture. I also wish to thank my publisher Andreas Papadakis for his enthusiasm and support. I am deeply indebted to my office staff for their research and work in obtaining illustrations, to Jeffrey Hunter for translating, and to Joan Lee in London for her editorial work. Warm thanks are also due to the staff at Academy Editions, Vivian Constantinopoulos and Andrea Bettella, and to Lucy Warner for proof-reading.

Published in the United States of America in 1991 by
The American Institute of Architects Press
1735 New York Avenue, N.W., Washington, D.C. 20006

First published in Great Britain in 1991 by
ACADEMY EDITIONS
an imprint of the Academy Group Ltd, 7 Holland Street, London W8 4NA

ISBN 1-55835-035-7 (HB)

Printed and bound in Singapore

Contents

Foreword
Charles Jencks

This is a unique book that looks at contemporary culture, architecture and a new aesthetic – that of symbiosis. Symbiosis, a concept of mutuality developed in ecology and biology, is seen by Kisho Kurokawa as the most intelligent philosophy to adopt in a world culture where fashions, trends and cultural movements all rapidly become international. It is a philosophy of 'both-and' rather than 'either-or', a practice of mix-and-match rather than creation from scratch, an ethic of inclusion rather than exclusion. As such it is one of the most essential statements of Post-Modern culture to date. Perhaps it is no surprise that it comes from a Japanese architect subject to so many contradictory tendencies – those from his Eastern home, Western contacts and an ever-changing technology.

What also makes this book unique is Kurokawa's hybrid sensibility and wide-ranging interests. Here is an architect conversant with French philosophers, the media world and traditional Japanese aesthetics; a designer who will build a 16th-century tea house next to his computerised high-tech office; an individual who overcomes the divide between the two cultures by thoroughly understanding each side of the split.

His philosophy reaches most mature expression in the Contemporary Art Museum of Hiroshima, a subtle blend of meanings from the East and West. This building complex sits on a wooded hill-top looking over the city that has given its name to the tenor of the 20th century. One's first impression of the Museum is its modesty and ambiguous understatement. Only a couple of aluminium pitched roofs can be seen hovering above the tree-line because 60 percent of the museum has been sunk underground. These pitched forms gleam in the sunlight like the fuselage of a 747, but their shape also recalls the traditional Edo storehouses of the 17th century. Unlike Kenzo Tange's buildings, which Kurokawa criticises for being alienating and one-dimensional, it blends together meanings from different periods and cultures. 'An architecture of symbiosis', he calls it, which is so suggestive that one feels lost in the dream of a novelist.

Actually Kurokawa is something of a writer with 30 books to his credit, among them this title that became a minor Japanese bestseller in 1988. His life's work reads like the print-out of multiple entries in Who's Who combining accomplishments in television, city planning, politics and the architecture he has now very successfully practised for 30 years. In the 70s he was voted Japan's third most popular person (after the Emperor and Prime Minister),

Kisho Kurokawa, Hiroshima City Museum of Contemporary Art, Hiroshima, 1988, bird's eye view from the south.

while today his Promethean success has led to a certain amount of suspicion and envy, especially within the architectural profession. 'The Japanese bang in the nail that sticks out', Kurokawa reflects, but like the noted film director, Kurosawa, with whom he is sometimes verbally confused, he continues to follow his singular and creative path.

The most striking image of his Hiroshima Museum is the entrance rotunda. This shape surmounts a broad stairway and it recalls many contrary forms: again those Edo structures now bent into a circle; a Western dome open to the sky; a glistening spaceship which has been sliced apart, and the flash of the bomb and its mushroom cloud. The last two images may be unintended – certainly Kurokawa didn't mention them to me as we stood in this plaza overlooking the city. But he *has* incorporated stones which were scorched by the blast. So when one sees, on arrival, the gleaming knife-cut of aluminium slicing through the blue sky – an explosive flash – and then turns around to discover this cut is also oriented to where the bomb fell, the allusion has great force. It is made stronger for being suggested, not represented.

Kurokawa has also achieved here one of the key goals of Post-Modernism which has eluded so many other architects: to bring different periods of architecture together in a non-totalistic way. The past, suggested by the fractured stone at the base of the elevation, the present represented by the white architecture of the middle, and the future implied by the aluminium top, are layered and juxtaposed so that each era is dimly suggested and partly in conflict with the next. Such juxtapositions of memory contrast with the depthless present-tense of Modernism and High-Tech architecture, the monologic of living on one plane of existence while talking neither to the past nor future, But this is not a Hegelian synthesis and suppression of previous periods, nor is it the schizophrenic chaos or anarchistic collage of the past. Critics such as Terry Eagleton and Frederic Jameson accuse Post-Modernists of plundering history, whimsically quoting from different epochs to distract a mindless audience. But the fragments and historic themes are here for many reasons, some of them functional, contextual and symbolic. Meanings are layered coherently and cross-referenced to make chronological, constructional, thematic – and, yes, psychological – sense. It's not the 'consumption of styles', but their coherent superposition. East and West are not resolved in some totalistic synthesis, but played against each other staccato-like to keep their identity and autonomy.

Kurokowa's allusive architecture and writing are both important for the wide breadth of reference, a recollection of countless images which are bound together by association and contiguity. The texture of thought is important because it suggests so many things without naming them, keeping interpretation open and renewed. At a time when Post-Modern architecture has often become too literal, this suggestiveness is to be welcomed; and at a point when most other writers on architecture are backward-looking or futurist, this intercultural philosophy is to the point.

Prologue

A great conceptual revolution is under way across the world, but is taking place so quietly that it has gone largely undetected. It is not the birth of a new ideology, like Capitalism or Communism; nor is it the advent of a new philosophy to replace that of Kant or Descartes. Yet the new currents of thought that are arising around the world will have a greater effect on us than any ideology or systematic philosophy. They are changing our way of life and our ideas of what it is to be human. This great, invisible change I identify as the philosophy of symbiosis.

Criticism of Japan – 'Japan bashing' – has been popular recently. American congressmen and representatives smashing a Toyota product with sledge-hammers is perhaps the quintessential image of Japan bashing. But the same impulse can be easily observed in Japan itself, where, as the proverb states, 'The nail that sticks out is hammered down'. Japanese society inherited a long tradition of human relations cast in a feudal mode, which dictates that those with special talents, with unique personalities, or those who achieve sudden success are attacked and ostracised by their peers. In an isolationist or protectionist era, when it is sufficient to guard the status quo and shun all external influences, individuality and achievement are despised as destabilising factors, and they are feared for the bad effects they may have on the established order. The fact that most Americans engaged in Japan bashing are protectionists further testifies to the truth of this claim.

The elimination of the spirit of protectionism, both in trade and in group loyalties that exclude all outsiders, is a universal struggle and a universal goal. But to pursue that goal also means that we are plunging into an age of confrontation: between benefit and harm, between personalities, and between cultures. It will no longer do simply to hammer down the nail that sticks out. We can no longer solve anything by attacking those who are unique or extraordinary. We are living at the start of an age of symbiosis, in which we will recognise each other's differing personalities and cultures while competing; in which we will co-operate while we oppose and criticise each other.

Will the traditional Japanese reverence for harmony, the emotional and spiritual commitment to consensus, function effectively in this age of symbiosis? If we define harmony and consensus as undercutting all individuality and exceptional ability, as forcing all to bend to the will of the group, then that tradition will find itself at sea in the age of symbiosis. Nor is there much hope for a harmony that is served by cowering before the strong and failing to put

ABOVE: Anti-Japan demonstration on Capitol Hill. *OPPOSITE ABOVE*: Mitsuigumi House. *OPPOSITE BELOW*: Kisho Kurokawa, Nagoya City Museum of Modern Art, Nagoya, Aichi Prefecture, 1987. Not to be regarded as products of compromise, these two buildings respectively incorporate elements from different cultures. Mitsuigumi House is an example of late-Edo architecture, showing the assimilation of Western architecture which was to expand in the Meiji Restoration, and displays many Western elements whilst maintaining an overall Eastern image. Kurokawa's Museum is an affirmation of a multivalent energy creating a new hybrid style which retains the spirit of Edo-period Japanese architecture in a contemporary 20th-century building.

forth one's own position forcefully.

When the positions or standards of cultural value are in disagreement, it is not necessary for one side to defeat the other and force his values on his opponent. They can instead search for common ground, even while remaining in mutual opposition. The success of this approach depends upon whether one has any desire to understand one's opponent. Even two cultures so different from each other that understanding is impossible will find that the sincere desire to understand the other makes co-operation possible. Symbiosis of this sort, a symbiosis that includes elements of opposition and competition, is a common feature of the animal and plant kingdoms, which is why I have selected the word symbiosis rather than peace, harmony or coexistence.

The 'Death of God' and The Icon

One of the great revolutions of the Modern age has been the 'Death of God'. Up to now, society has taught us that all humankind is equal before God. For those with religious faith God was the absolute and, at the same time, the one who instructed humanity in its proper course. Even after the masses ceased to believe in an absolute God, mass society created substitutes for the deity: heroes and ideal human beings, or 'superstars'.

There comes a time when each of us notices that his life has not proceeded exactly as he had wished. To compensate for this disappointment, he may transfer unrealised dreams to a hero, an athlete, a superstar or an idol of some sort. At the same time, this ideal image, or icon, becomes his goal. Society until now has been composed of this God, this ideal, this icon, on the one hand and, on the other, the great body of humankind – Heidegger's *das Mann*. But in the present age, God, the ideal and the icon are dead. We have lost the icon as our goal, we have lost our heroes and our superstars. Though stars may still be born, they soon fall to earth, and they are consumed in the blink of an eye.

A society that still has a goal, still has an icon, is a society supported by the concept of progress. Progress is defined as approaching closer to that society's goals, to the human ideal, the social ideal, to the heroes and the stars. For most of the nations of the world, Western society and Western culture have continued to be the ideal and goal. As a result, developing countries have made every effort to approach, even if little by little, the ideal that the West represents. Progress has been identified with Westernisation.

Societies that cherish this ideal refuse utterly to recognise the value or meaning of other cultures. For them, modernisation is Westernisation. It is the conquest of one culture by another.

Japan, in particular, from the time of the Meiji Restoration in 1868, consciously chose this path. With progress as its rallying cry, the nation has spared no pains in its grinding efforts to modernise. Years ago, Tokyo, and especially the Ginza area, was regarded as a major symbol of this belief. Enraptured by the icon of the Ginza, towns across the archipelago dubbed the main streets of their shopping arcades as the local Ginza, and little Ginzas

ABOVE: View of Ginza area. *BELOW:* Little Ginza in Urawa, Saitama Prefecture. An example of modernisation in Japan which gave rise to smaller 'Ginzas' everywhere else in the country.

sprouted all over Japan as quickly and thickly as bamboo shoots after rain.

And so, is it that Japan set out in pursuit of Western society and, eventually, surpassed it? This would be a ridiculous point to argue as it is impossible for a society to either overtake or not overtake another society of a completely different nature. We cannot speak of superiority or inferiority among cultures. Each of the different cultural spheres in the world treads a different path – it is not as if they were all on one large athletic field, racing against each other.

Recently in Japan we often hear the claim that it has overtaken the West and no longer has any goal to aim for. This is a great mistake. True, the philosophy of society up to now, with its faith in the ideal, the icon, has crumbled; and we find ourselves in a world without icons. Without an ideal, the concept of progress becomes meaningless; but now that superstars have faded, it has become possible for each of us to play the role of hero.

A Mirror Society

The film stars of the old days, whose names were synonyms for the ideals of female and male beauty, have passed from the scene and today's stars are on an ordinary human scale. When we see everyday-acting entertainers on our living-room television screens, we might believe we are stars too. Since an absolute and other God, a star as an image of human perfection, no longer exists, we must provide a dwelling for God and for stars within ourselves. This is the beginning of a mirror society in which we define ourselves through the activity of observing others and also see ourselves. Since we cannot find peace of mind in God, we are forced to find it in looking at others. The present is an age when we are all greatly concerned with those around us.

Modern society offers great opportunities for each of us to emphasise our individuality and create a unique identity. We have taken the first step into an age of discrimination which values signs and symbols. The possibility that many unique individuals may flourish in symbiosis, that we may see the birth of a symbiotic society that respects every different cultural sphere is on the horizon.

I have purposefully used the word 'possibility' because the road is not an easy one. A mirror society easily degenerates into a conformist, absolutist society. This danger is particularly strong in Japan, where the strictures of the feudal village – which rejected nonconformists and those of exceptional talent – remain strongly entrenched in people's minds. A mirror society is in danger of becoming conformist to avoid being ostracised.

When one corporation succeeds in a certain venture, the rest follow in a thundering herd. Many Japanese businessmen, on the pretext of socialising, go out drinking night after night with their colleagues to communicate the message: 'I am just like you. We're the same sort. No need to worry that I have any special talent, any real individuality'. They are preserving the peace of the village. And by the same token, they are jealous and spiteful of anyone who does show special talent, anyone who succeeds.

ABOVE: Akashiya Sanma. *BELOW*: Ken Naoko. Japanese television personalities.

The danger of a backward-looking mirror society spans the world of the university, business, government and the arts. Those who dare to violate the strictures of conformity are denounced by their colleagues and have the value of their achievements challenged. This is the accepted practice in Japan.

The age of heroes and superstars is finished. Recognising and evaluating the individual worth of others is a fundamentally different activity from the process of creating heroes and superstars. From the fair and proper evaluation of different cultures, different talents, and different personalities is born the critical spirit, and a society of symbiosis is created.

The End of Universality

In the age of symbiosis the ideals of universality and equality, which have passed unchallenged, will cease to apply. Until now, the most widely accepted form of universality has been technology. It was widely believed that technology, which brought wealth and happiness to the masses, would unify and homogenise the entire world, regardless of the differences in development or culture among nations. Cars, nuclear power plants, and the glass and steel of Modern architecture were supposed to make people in the deserts of the Middle East, the tropical cities of Southeast Asia and the loess plains of China happy, and make them the same.

We no longer believe this is true: technology does not take root when it is cut off from culture and tradition. The transfer of technology requires sophistication: adaptation to region, to unique situations and to custom. When the technology of one culture is introduced into another with a different lifestyle, it is often difficult to ensure that the technology will take root. Even if in the future, atomic fusion is perfected and becomes economically viable, is it necessarily a good idea for such power plants to spread across the globe as the universal means of power? Probably not. If the per capita income of the Chinese were to reach the level of the Japanese, would it be a good idea for China to become a mass automobile society? Probably not. Each cultural sphere should cultivate its unique technological systems to create its distinctive lifestyle.

The 21st century will be one in which fusion, fission, steam and water-generated electrical plants will exist in symbiosis. This will not be so because some regions are too poor to introduce nuclear fusion generators, but because different people will select different technologies to create their own lifestyles.

The Mix-and-Match Age: Jekyll and Hyde

In contrast to the first half of the 20th century, during which the concept of progress implied improvements in the quality of materials and standard of living, in the future, creativity will be the concept that expresses the richness of our standard of living. Though we will no longer have a unified goal toward which we progress, people will make the discovery of fluid, mix-and-match goals their aim. While Paris fashion reigns as the model of style, other designers need merely imitate it to create their own fashions. But in an age of mix-and-match, fashions from many different times, sexes and uses are combined and juxtaposed. Unlike an age fond of hierarchy, when conventions of time, place and occasion reign, in the mix-and-match age we can find delight in reading the sensitivity that has dictated the choices in each combination.

This will be an age where people can pursue many different activities at the same time. It will be a time of a broad and flexible 'Jekyll-and-Hyde' sensitivity that can freely juxtapose the sacred with the profane, a Paris mode with farmer's overalls; a creativity that can, through subtle combinations, bring us novelty. It will, in other words, be the age when a richly-creative, schizophrenic personality reigns supreme. Sincerity and insincerity will live side by side, the distinction between work and play will fade, formal and casual will lose their meaning in fashion – such will be the lifestyle.

Whether it will be more enjoyable to live in this new age of symbiosis remains to be seen. The world will be a harder place though it will be 'hard' in a way different from our interpretation of that word. The age of the individual, an age of pluralism and diversification, during which each person will express his individuality and be responsible for making his own choices, will bring the joy of discovering what is different and unique. Each of us will need to make continual efforts to acquire the skills that will allow us that pleasure. Unless we cultivate our sensibilities, it will be difficult to make new discoveries or to be creative. Compared to an age of conformism when we could be lazy, we have no choice but to take the first steps on a path that may be difficult but which leads to a richly creative life.

BELOW: Kisho Kurokawa, Yuishikian, Tokyo, 1984, view of hearth area. With this tea room in his own home Kurokawa has re-created the Shosuitei tea room by the Edo period tea master Kobori Enshu, by way of the Kan'unken tea room. A place to retreat and think (reflected in its name: the Hut of Consciousness Only), it stands in antithesis to the architect's modern study. LEFT: Kisho Kurokawa's study in the same apartment.

Hanasukiya
The Aesthetic of Symbiosis

A Re-creation of Kobori Enshu's Yuishikian

In my own home, I enjoy a life in which the most advanced technology exists in symbiosis with tradition. My apartment is perched on the 11th floor. Next to my study, where my IBM 5560 sits, I have constructed a traditional Japanese tea room, which I have named Yuishikian – the Hut of Consciousness Only.[1] My personal computer is part of a communication network designed by a friend, Richard Farson, president of the Western Behavioral Sciences Institute in La Jolla, California. It is directly linked over the Venus P satellite network to some 50 men and women in the worlds of scholarship, politics and finance. Yuishikian, on the other hand, is my place to retreat and think, and to receive and entertain guests and friends from Japan and abroad with the hospitality of the tea ceremony.

Yuishikian is the re-creation of a particular tea room that once existed but has disappeared, a symbol that represents a formative, crucial and yet forgotten model of Japanese aesthetics. This model is profoundly linked to the basic principles of the Japanese aesthetic, *wabi* and *sabi*.[2] But we will discuss this in greater detail further on; I will first of all describe the tea room that served as the model for my Yuishikian.

This particular tea room was in Takimotobo, a residence for Buddhist monks, constructed at the Iwashimizu Hachimangu shrine in Kyoto by the scholar-monk Shokado Shojo.[3] Shojo's tea room was, in turn, a reconstruction of an earlier tea room, the Kan'unken,[4] built in the first decades of the 17th century, but destroyed by fire in 1773. Shojo studied the tea ceremony under the great tea-master Kobori Enshu, and his Kan'unken was an exact duplicate of Enshu's Shosuitei, the tea room in his Fushimi residence.[5] Both consist of four mats and a *daime*-sized mat.[6] My Yuishikian, then, is a re-creation of Kobori Enshu's most representative tea room, the Shosuitei at Kobori's Fushimi residence. I spent 17 years reproducing this tea room. Why did it take so long?

Originally, tea rooms were constructed of materials that could be found easily and near at hand. Rare and expensive materials were avoided. A log or branch from a nearby grove of trees, a stone by the roadside, were collected and incorporated into the final design. The original spirit of tea-room architecture is the same. It is an architecture built by gathering things close at hand – trees and fallen branches in the immediate environment, the half-decayed boards of boats. As a result, the tea room seems not to have been designed but built through a process of natural accretion. But of course the

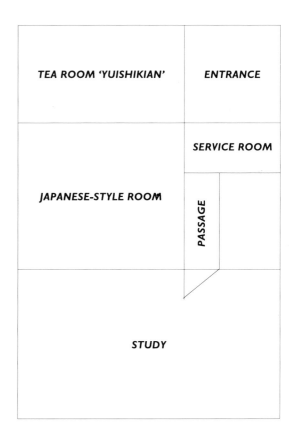

Plan of Kisho Kurokawa's apartment.

aesthetic perceptions of the tea masters were operating in the selection process. Their ability to discover the beauty of such commonplace objects, unremarkable to the average person, was crucial. And they possessed the skill to incorporate these objects into the design of a tea room. Though the tea rooms contemporary with Kan'unken and Shosuitei did not employ rare or luxurious materials, obviously many problems arise when one tries faithfully to reproduce the same tea room some 300 years later.

Tea room plans provide a detailed account of the original structures. In the 18th-century plans I was working from, not only are the materials and dimensions noted, but the way in which the natural timbers bend and twist, and the details of finishing the materials are all clearly recorded. Yet when one actually attempts an accurate reconstruction, one finds that crucial information is still missing. The challenge is to acquire that information in the process of the construction.

To clarify the missing details I studied diaries and accounts of tea ceremonies held in this tea room. In his Matsuya Kaiki, (1741),[7] Matsuya Hisayoshi describes a tea ceremony that he attended at Enshu's Shosuitei. In addition to a detailed account of the tea utensils and the food and sweets served, he also describes the tea room. His remarks gave certain details not provided by the extant plans of the tea room.

I knew from the plan that the tea room had a basketwork ceiling with a bamboo frame, but the material from which the ceiling was woven was not identified. According to Matsuya Kaiki, it was made of reeds. The plan told me that the tokonoma post was made of kunogi. It took some time to identify this wood. Was it a sort of tree that no longer existed? Or was it now known by a different name? Was kuno an orthographical mistake for kuri, or chestnut? I considered various possibilities, but in the end an acquaintance in Kyoto who is familiar with ancient manuscripts told me that kunogi was a dialect variation of kunugi – a kind of oak.

According to the plan, the back and sides of the tokonoma were papered with antique paper, but what sort of paper? I looked for a model to the Joan tea room.[8] This was designed by Oda Uraku and its tokonoma was papered with the leaves of old almanacs.[9] Searching for almanacs from the early decades of the 17th century, I frequented rare book and antique shops. It took over ten years to acquire enough paper for my tokonoma walls. In one place in the tea room, a gently curving log is called for, and I had to pester my carpenter to go searching in the mountains for just the right one; it took more than ten years to find it.

The height at which a flower container is hung from a decorative hook or nail in the tea room is quite important as well, but this was not indicated in the plan, and it was no mean feat to determine the authentic height. A plan called 'Enshu's Four and One Daime-sized Mat Tea Room at Fushimi Roku Jizo', by a certain Ensai (otherwise unknown), tells us that the hook should be three shaku two bu and five rin (about 91cm) from the floor. But when we tried

Plan of the Takimotobo residence at the Hachimangu shrine by Shokado Shojo which includes the Kan'unken tea room (CENTRE). Kobori Enshu's four and one daime-sized mat tea room at Fushimi Rokujizo; cutaway axonometrics (ABOVE AND BELOW). Minimal space of a tea-ceremony house: about 2x4metres, used as a model for the Yuishikian.

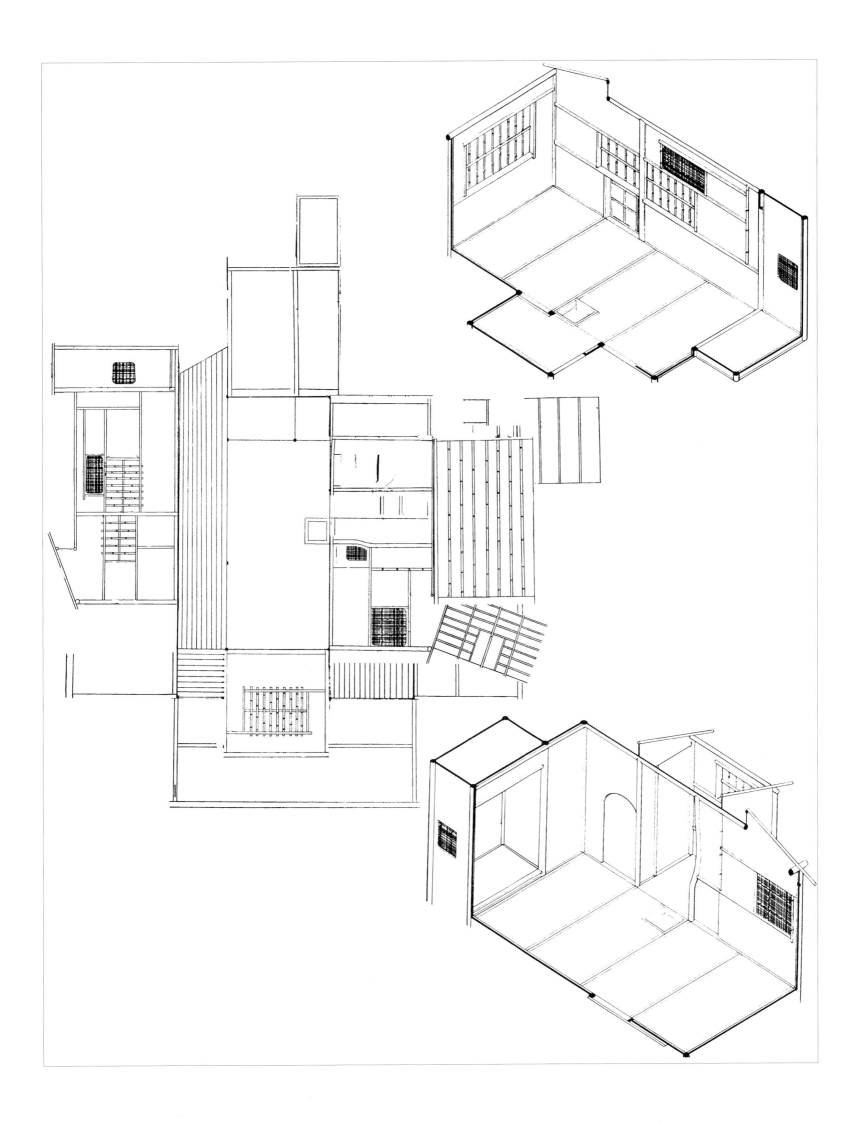

hanging it at this height it seemed inappropriately low. I checked the source again and found that some regarded the note on this plan an orthographic mistake for three *shaku* two *sun* and five *bu* (about 98cm). Still, even this height seemed far too low and so out of harmony with the tea room as a whole that on this particular detail I made an exception and followed the example of the Yuin teahouse,[10] setting the decorative hook at three *shaku* seven *sun* (about 112cm).

Following this process of careful consideration of historical sources and inspection of available materials, and relying on the skills of the mere handful of tea room carpenters to be found in all Japan, it took me 17 years to complete Yuishikian. And since there is no space in central Tokyo to build a tearoom, I constructed it as a rooftop garden to my apartment, harmonising it with the rest of the garden area, so that, when completed, my Yuishikian nested among the apartment buildings of the central city.

Why did I take so much trouble to recreate this particular tea room with such painstaking accuracy? As a symbol of the aesthetic vision I call *hanasuki.*

Wabi implying both Splendour and Simplicity

I offer the term *hanasuki* in place of *wabisuki* because I believe that *wabi* as a concept has come to be interpreted in too narrow and one-dimensional a fashion. Traditionally, *wabi* has been thought of as silence as opposed to loquacity; darkness as opposed to light; simplicity as opposed to complexity; spareness as opposed to decoration; monochrome as opposed to colour; the grass hut, not the aristocrat's palace. Even in school texts, *wabi* is defined as an aesthetic of nothingness.

But isn't the true and essential Japanese aesthetic one in which silence and loquacity, darkness and light, simplicity and complexity, spareness and decoration, monochrome and polychrome, the grass hut and the aristocrat's palace exist in symbiosis? In *wabi* a superbly decorative principle, a special splendour, is to be found – like the undertaste in fine cuisine, that lingers and perfumes each subtle dish.

Nambo Sokei[11] finds the essence of Takeno Joo's[12] tea ceremony in Fujiwara no Teika's[13] poem in the *Shin Kokin Shu:*[14]

I gaze afar

And ask for neither cherry flowers

Nor crimson leaves;

The inlet with its grass-thatched huts

Clustered in the growing autumn dusk.[15]

The blossoms of spring and the red leaves of autumn are a metaphor for the gorgeous *daisu*-style tea ceremony of the aristocrat's mansion.[16] When we gaze at them deeply, we arrive at a realm where not a single thing exists – the rush-thatched cottage on the shore. Those who do not first know the blossoms and the leaves can never live in the thatched hut. Only because we gaze and gaze at the blossoms and leaves can we spy

Wooden masks for Noh performances, with Tokuwaka's *Hannya*, the female demon (*OPPOSITE*) and Sanko's *Okina*, an old man (*ABOVE*). These depict the symbiosis of heterogeneous elements, encapsulated in the aesthetic of *hana*. So, while playing an old man, for example, the actor should portray the old man's characteristics whilst retaining the youth of *hana*; and while wearing the mask of a demon the actor should retain an element of humour.

out the thatched hut. This is to be regarded as the essence of tea.

What Nambo is saying is that only one who knows the splendour and gorgeous beauty of the blossoms of spring and the red leaves of autumn can appreciate the *wabi* of the roughly thatched hut on the lonely beach. This is not an aesthetic of nothingness by any means. It is an aesthetic of a double code, in which we are asked to gaze at the roughly thatched hut while recalling the gorgeous flowers and leaves. It is an ambiguous, symbiotic aesthetic which simultaneously embraces splendour and simplicity.

Murata Juko, who is known for his pursuit of the most severe state of Zen[17] says in *Yamanoue Soji Ki* : 'Juko described his ideal as a splendid steed tethered to a grass hut'.[18] *Wabi* is not simply a grass hut; it is the scene of a beautifully caparisoned, powerful horse tied to a humble, elegantly simple straw hut'. The goal of this aesthetic is an ambiguous code in which two symbols simultaneously contradict and overlap.

The Splendour of *Wabi*

The novelist Tanizaki Jun'ichiro wrote in his essay *In Praise of Shadows (In'ei Raisan)*:

> Sometimes a superb piece of black lacquerware, decorated perhaps with flecks of silver and gold – a box or a desk or a set of shelves – will seem to me unsettlingly garish and altogether vulgar. But render pitch black the void in which they stand, and light them not with the rays of the sun or electricity but rather a single lantern or candle: suddenly those garish objects turn sombre, refined, dignified. Artisans of old, when they finished their works in lacquer and decorated them in sparkling patterns, must surely have had in mind dark rooms and sought to turn to good effect what feeble light there was. Their extravagant use of gold, too, I should imagine, came of understanding how it gleams forth from out of the darkness and reflects the lamplight.[19]

We see here that Tanizaki is by no means simply praising shadows alone. His aesthetic, too, is a double code – the absolute opposition of the gorgeous golden decoration and the shadows of the night. In his dramatic phrase, 'the brocade of the night itself', we detect the lineage of an aesthetic of *wabi* that is very far indeed from a philosophy of nothingness.

The ambiguity of this aesthetic of *wabi* is even clearer when we arrive at the related term, *sabi*, as propounded by the haiku poet Matsuo Basho.[20] Mukai Kyorai, Basho's leading disciple in the art of poetry, described the master's verses as 'unchanging flux';[21] this symbiosis of 'flux' or impermanence and changeableness with an 'unchanging' quality that transcends the flow of time and achieves eternal existence, lies at the core of Basho's idea of *sabi*.

Kyorai writes in the treatise known as the *Kyorai Sho* that '*Sabi* is the colour of a verse; it does not mean a sad and lonely verse. It is like an aged warrior who arrays himself in his gorgeous armour and throws himself into battle. Though he dons brocade robes and serves at a banquet, he is still old. It is the

The tea master Sen no Rikyu.

LEFT: The tea master Murano Shouo. *BELOW:* The tea master Toyotomi Hideyoshi.

LEFT: En'an tea room, Kyoto. This three-mat room, by Rikyu's disciple Furuta Oribe, is one of the sources of Yuishikian. BELOW: Oda Uraku's Joan tea room, Oyama City, Aichi Prefecture, interior view.

combination of a flower-bearer and a white-haired crone'.[22] In other words, the withered, sad state of old age is not *sabi*. On the contrary, *sabi* is the sight of the old man in his glorious armour, fighting bravely; or seated at a splendid banquet in his fine raiment. The aesthetic of *sabi* is produced in the contradiction of two symbiotically existing elements, the splendid brocades and the old man's quietly elegant appearance.

Thus, the interpretation of these two core principles of traditional Japanese aesthetics, *wabi* and *sabi*, as spare, restrained and anti-decorative concepts is badly skewed. In order to restore the present vulgarised and corrupted version of *wabi* to its original meaning, I have invented a new term: *hanasuki*.

Zeami, who brought the art of the Noh theatre to perfection, wrote in works such as *Fushi Kaden* and *Kakyo* that *hana* – flower – was the life of Noh.[23] The aesthetic of *hana* is one of the symbiosis of heterogeneous elements, of disparate moods or feelings. In *Fushi Kaden* Zeami instructs the actor who portrays a demon to perform in an enjoyable way, combining the qualities of frightfulness and enjoyment. In the role of an old man, the actor should don the mask and costume of an old person and 'portray an old man while still possessing the Flower'.[24] When one performs Noh during the day, he tells us, he must act with the dark energy of night inside himself. Zeami's aesthetic is a characteristically Japanese one of symbiosis that has much in common with the original meaning of *wabi*. I invented the term *hanasuki* because I am convinced that Zeami's aesthetic of the flower is identical with the true meaning of *wabi*.

Yuishikian as an example of *Hanasuki*

Yuishikian, which I constructed as a symbol of the aesthetic of *hanasuki*, has 12 windows and is an extremely bright tea room. Kobori Enshu favoured tea rooms with many windows: the eight-windowed Konjiin tea room at Nanzenji was a favourite. My 12 windows can be regarded as stage lighting for the host's mat. By opening and closing different windows from season to season, the interior can be illuminated in a variety of ways. If I leave the door to the garden open, that view and all its light become part of the tea room interior as well.

In front of the *daime*-sized host's mat the four long mats are lined up in a row. This simple yet bold layout emphasises the theatricality of the host's mat. The tokonoma is framed by a white juniper post on one side and the *kunugi* oak, with a bark resembling red pine, on the other. The juniper is roughly finished in a square shape by hand chiselling four corners, but leaving the bark on its four sides. The bark has been left on the oak post, which disappears into the upper wall. The combination of materials with such a range of expression produces a great dynamism.

The roof and the placement of the windows add variety to the design, making Yuishikian a highly decorative tea room. But I did not sacrifice the simplicity and calm that are characteristic of tea room architecture. This is what makes Yuishikian a model of *hanasuki*.

Why has the idea of *wabi* become so perverted that we are forced to invent

Oda Uraku's Joan tea room, Oyama City, Aichi Prefecture, round window and exterior view. Here we see the aesthetic of hana suki at its utmost – combining the simple and the sumptuous, being and non-being, silence and eloquence – in the waist-high windows, the arched hearth partitions and the round window cut through the sleeve wall.

a new term, *hanasuki,* to convey its original meaning? I can offer two answers to this question. The first can be traced to the confrontation between the great tea master Sen no Rikyu and his master, the feudal warlord Toyotomi Hideyoshi (1536-98).[25]

Hideyoshi has been described as either the son of a farmer or the son of a foot soldier. Whichever he may have been, he had no time to acquire learning and cultural polish in the years of his rise from a humble station to the position of ruler of all Japan. Even if he had been blessed with the time and the opportunity, in my opinion he lacked by nature a sensitivity to the arts and learning.

Sen no Rikyu served Hideyoshi as an artist in residence and his teacher in the art of the tea ceremony. In their relationship we can detect the conflict between authority and art, the ruler and the creator. Though Hideyoshi was the supreme ruler of all Japan and brooked no opposition from anyone, in the art of tea Rikyu was his superior. Given Hideyoshi's nature, it is quite likely that he resented this great man of the world of art, a realm even Hideyoshi could not rule. After hearing Rikyu speak on *wabi* tea, which placed great emphasis on simplicity and humility, Hideyoshi asked Rikyu to design a tea room entirely papered in gold leaf, as if to taunt his master. And in fact he actually held a tea ceremony in such a tea room.

I believe that Rikyu was forced to articulate an extreme form of *wabi* as an antidote to Hideyoshi's equally extreme tendency toward ostentation, that he pursued this radical *wabi* as rigorously as a Zen monk pursues the way of enlightenment in the special context of this struggle between the ruler and the artist. These particular circumstances are what led Rikyu to develop *wabi* into an aesthetic of nothingness, of death.

In this contest between political and artistic authority, Rikyu may at first seem the loser: Hideyoshi eventually forced him to commit ritual suicide. But in the struggle, Rikyu refined and distilled his aesthetic ideal until he arrived at the nearly inconceivable extreme of simplicity: a tea room of one-and-a-half mats.

Rikyu was a genius, the great formulator of the aesthetic of *wabi* tea. But a more balanced concept of *wabi,* a *wabi* of *hanasuki,* can be detected in the tea ceremony practised by Rikyu's disciples.

Rikyu's leading disciple was Furuta Oribe.[26] The simple addition of a single mat to Oribe's three-mat tea room, En'an, results in the four-and-a-half mat tea room by Enshu.[27] Furuta's tea room then, is one of the sources of Yuishikian. The deep eaves over the earthen area by the corner entrance, the displaced external post construction, the abundance of windows, including a small floor-level latticework portal staggered with another higher portal and a flower-viewing window – Furuta's design displays a wealth of detailing and testifies to a sensitivity attuned to the symbiotic interplay of simplicity and grandeur, silence and drama: a skylight is cut through the roof of the entrance eaves to offer a view of nearby Mount Atago.

Another important follower of Rikyu was Oda Uraku. His Joan tea room is

Katsura Detached Palace, Kyoto, exterior views showing the simplicity of the building. The spare, plain style was read by Taut and Gropius as an ideal image of Modern architecture.

Katsura Detached Palace, Kyoto, with details of decorative metalwork of the staggered shelves in the first room of the Chu Shoin (*LEFT*) and velvet baseboard wall covering of the Shoiken (*CENTRE*). Here the contrast is achieved between the plain, refined beauty of the outside and the highly decorative elements of the details within the pure space, lending an ambiguity to the whole work. The interior view of the Palace (*BELOW*) depicts the Shoin, or aristocratic residential, style of architecture. The lattice doors create an intermediary space.

also a classic example of inventive and original *hanasuki:* a round window is boldly cut through the sleeve wall at the left end of the main facade and a triangular floorboard inset beside the tokonoma brings a fresh new touch to the three-and-a-half-mat plan, not to mention the decorativeness of the arched, cut-out wooden hearth partition, old calendar pages pasted around the base of the walls, and the bright atmosphere created by the row of waist-high windows.

Finally, when we consider Yuishikian's model, the Shosuitei tea room designed by Enshu (Oribe's disciple) we come to the unavoidable conclusion that Rikyu could not have taught only simplicity and spareness.

Bruno Taut at Katsura Detached Palace

The reason that the traditional interpretation of *wabi* has been far too narrow and shallow can be found in Rikyu's articulation of the concept in an extreme form, as an antidote to Hideyoshi's ostentation. I also believe that it can be traced to the encounter of Bruno Taut and Walter Gropius with the Katsura Detached Palace and their well-publicised response to it.[28]

The attention of Japanese architects was first drawn to their own tradition by the remarks of these Europeans, who praised Katsura and the Grand Ise Shrine as models of Modern architecture and then promptly returned home to the West.[29] Japanese architects meekly followed their lead; they accepted the judgement that their native aesthetic tradition was one of nothingness, silence and simplicity. But it is important to note that the judgements Taut and Gropius passed on these works of Japanese architecture were made entirely from within the context of Modern architecture.

The Modern architecture aesthetic was born from industrialisation and mass production; its straight, spare, non-decorative line is that of the mass product. Taut and Gropius read Katsura Palace as an icon, an ideal image of Modern architecture. But they overlooked several important features of the palace: the decorative metalwork of the staggered shelves in the first room of the Chu Shoin; the dramatic checked pattern of the tokonoma of the first room in the Shokintei arbour; the side window of the tokonoma of the second room of the Shin Shoin; the round window in the transom of the Shoiken retainers' quarters and the velvet baseboard wall covering the elegant door-pulls of those same quarters. These details are astonishing in their rich decoration, and they stand out even more sharply, embedded as they are within a space that is so pure and simple.

We can see then how one-dimensional was the appreciation of Katsura Palace by Taut and Gropius. Their rejection of the Toshogu shrine at Nikko as an example of the bad taste of the shoguns is further evidence of their failure to grasp the totality of the Japanese aesthetic tradition.[30] The shrine at Nikko must have seemed to these modernists terribly extreme, while the Grand Ise shrine and Katsura Palace are contemporary works. Yet only when they are placed side by side can Japanese architecture of that age be appreciated in its

wholeness. What understanding is there to be gained by totally rejecting one and interpreting the other in a highly selective and clearly self-serving way? Perhaps this is just another manifestation of the doctrine of expediency that is at the core of Modern architecture.

As the sculptor Okamoto Taro has suggested, the Japanese tradition embraces two aesthetic currents that exist together in symbiosis.[31] One is bold and dramatic, the other a simple, non-decorative and extremely refined beauty. He traces the first to the ancient Jomon period and the second to the subsequent Yayoi period.[32] There is nothing strange about the fact that both Toshogu shrine and the Katsura Palace were built in the same Edo period, and there are no grounds for dismissing the former as an embarrassing lapse in taste by the Tokugawa shoguns. The vigorous, even violent decorativeness of Jomon culture finally flowered in the gorgeous castle architecture of the *Azuchi-Momoyama period* (1568-1600), which has continued to nourish Japanese culture to the present day.

There may be those who believe they have discovered the source of Japan's aesthetic tradition when they visit the temples of Kyoto, with their unadorned, unfinished wood. But we must not forget that when Todaiji and Toshodaiji were first built, their pillars were painted crimson and their rafters glowed vermilion, gold and green.[33] They were a rainbow of rich primary colours. Except for certain Zen monasteries, the temples of Japan were all originally as colourful as the Toshogu shrine is today. I regard the decision not to restore those colours as they faded naturally and to accept their new, quieter, but very different beauty as an indication of the great range of Japanese aesthetic sensitivity. The reaffirmation of Japan's symbiotic aesthetic is not only of importance as a reinterpretation of traditional Japanese aesthetics, but I believe that this sensitivity of symbiosis has replaced Modernism and will be the aesthetic of the 21st century.

ABOVE: Todaiji Shrine. When first built, this shrine was painted in rich, bright colours which faded naturally, rather than being repainted after a period of time, thus allowing for a different, quieter beauty. *BELOW:* Toshogu Shrine, Nikko. Dismissed by Taut and Gropius as a blatant flaunting of the Tokugawa shoguns' bad taste, this shrine should instead be regarded as an example of the multivalent nature of Edo architecture, able to co-exist with simple, non-decorative works.

Grand Ise Shrine, Ise, Mie Prefecture, aerial view and detail. Another shrine read by Taut and Gropius as an exemplar of Japan's undecorated and austere sukiya architecture, yet, at the same time, rejecting different but equally important styles of the same period.

Osaka City Public Hall, 1916. An image of Meiji period architecture shows the difference between incorporating Western culture into the Japanese and rejecting Japanese culture altogether.

Transcending Modernism

For half a century, beginning in the 1920s, the following three elements have characterised what we know as the modern world: 1) universalism based on industrialisation; 2) a division of labour based on function; and 3) elimination of classes. Industrial products such as watches, automobiles and airplanes were great luxuries when first invented, but our industrial society now provides these things in great quantity and at reasonable prices to the masses, fulfilling its great dream of producing the blessings of a material civilisation and eliminating the gap between rich and poor. As a result, today almost all of us can buy anything from a watch to a personal computer with our pocket money.

This great wave of industrialisation gave birth to the International Style. This is the Modern architecture we are all so familiar with, the great boxes of steel, glass and concrete. The International Style liberated architecture from past modes through the use of new materials and revolutionary technologies, creating a universal architectural model that spread to all countries and cultures. For me, the International Style resembles Esperanto since it sought to create a common architectural language for all humanity.

But this universal model is in fact based on the values and ethos of Western civilisation. Again, the resemblance to Esperanto is clear, for Esperanto was a universal language based on Western languages. Modernisation turned out to be industrialisation, based on the value system of the West; and the developing nations, in their pursuit of modernisation through industrialisation, have all quite naturally pursued Westernisation with equal keenness.

By ignoring the climate and traditional culture of the site, the International Style imposes a single style throughout the world. As part of the process of modernisation unfolding in the People's Republic of China, an all-glass hotel called the Changcheng Fandian has been constructed in Beijing. But with Beijing's climate – cold in winter and hot in summer – the operating costs of an all-glass multistorey structure are enormous. Such local maintenance problems are typical of buildings in the International Style. It is not enough to carry the latest in building technology into a developing country and put together a building from it; if replacement parts and proper repair services aren't available, the new building will soon be severely crippled: elevators stop running and spare parts cannot be found.

When Toyota decided to sell its cars in the United States, it began by establishing a customer-service network of several hundred outlets. Without a proper maintenance system, sophisticated technology is soon reduced to utter uselessness. When high technologies are introduced into developing countries, they must be adapted to the culture and climate of the site. The need for a symbiosis between technology and the cultural tradition must be appreciated.

It is time, too, to correct the mistaken Western conception that universalism is divinely ordained; we should abandon Esperanto-style thinking. Internationalism can be achieved by deepening our understanding of our own language while engaging in exchange with other languages. If Yukio Mishima or Yasunari Kawabata had written their classics *The Temple of the Golden Pavilion* or *Snow Country* in Esperanto, they could not have created the literary depth that they achieved in Japanese. It is precisely because they wrote in their richly suggestive vernacular that they achieved literary success. But need we conclude that a literature that could only have been written in Japanese can only be understood and appreciated in Japan? Quite the contrary. People around the world are reading Mishima and Kawabata, Tanizaki, Abe Kobo and Oe Kenzabrou – in translation. Through translation, literature of quality in Japanese becomes literature of international quality.

I must make perfectly clear, however, that in rejecting the universalism and internationalism that presupposed the superiority of the West, I do not advocate a static traditionalism or narrow racialism. I believe instead that the coming age will be a time when the different regions of the world will re-examine their own traditions. On the international level, each region will confront the values and standards of other regions and, while mutually influencing each other, each will produce its own distinctive culture. Rather than internationalism, I call this interculturalism.

The Weakness of Purebred Culture

As a culture matures, it becomes more and more centripetal, and conservative forces aimed at preserving its purity come strongly into play. It rejects all dissonant, opposing and heterogeneous elements and constructs its own distinct hierarchy. In this process, the culture's identity is sharpened and refined. Such a refined, highly distinctive culture – a purebred culture as it were – is surprisingly unstable, and this is particularly so when it has grown tremendously. Unlike a 'mongrel culture', which contains many heterogeneous elements, a purebred culture is unable to adapt to changes in its environment. One of the reasons European culture is undeniably on the wane is that since the time of the Greeks and Romans, Europeans have been excessively concerned with preserving the orthodoxy of their culture, excluding all the surrounding cultures of the Islamic world and Asia.

The weakness of the pure-blooded and the strength of the mongrel can be seen in business organisations as well. If a company limits itself to one product and concentrates entirely on strategies for its production and sale, it will acquire very sophisticated skills and know-how concerning that product. If that product is automobiles, for example, the company is capable of becoming an unchallenged giant in that industry. But if, due to external circumstances, the

Changcheng Fandian Hotel, Beijing; an all-glass, International Style building constructed on the value system of the West.

automotive industry as a whole falls upon hard times, the company will collapse – victim of the transportation revolution, an upset in the balance of petroleum supply and demand, or trade friction.

In the past, coal-mining was the leading industry in many outlying regions, but now it is disappearing – and taking the coal-mining towns with it. Textiles is on its way out as a major Japanese industry. A look at the present state of the national railways system, the petrochemical industry, steel and shipbuilding shows how technologies that are organised centripetally around a single product are susceptible to the passage of time and, for all their size and strength, deteriorate easily when conditions change.

To acquire the necessary flexibility and adaptability, many industries today are sub-dividing and diversifying. The companies Toray and Kanebo are excellent examples: originally textile manufacturers, their main products are now cosmetics, clothing, sporting goods and pharmaceuticals. The break-up and privatisation of the Japanese National Railways is another example of the benefits of diversification.

The Age of the Minor

The mongrel has the flexibility to incorporate heterogeneous, even opposing elements. Such an organisation is youthful; but as it ages, it begins to reject the heterogeneous. The key to youth and life lies in whether the mainstream of a culture can still incorporate non-mainstream elements. The re-evaluation of the so-called minor elements that is much talked about among French philosophers of the new school can be taken as a warning to contemporary society of the truth of this fact. The subtitle of *Kafka* by Gilles Deleuze and Felix Guattari is *Pour une littérature mineure* (Towards a Minor Literature), indicating the importance of minor traditions in the authors' minds.[1] They frequently speak of 'Literature with a capital L'. The source of this idea is probably Jacques Lacan's '*Autre* (the Other, the subject) with a Capital A'.[2]

Because the absolute subject contains plurality and free space within itself, we must respect minorities and heretics and allow a state of tension between the part and the whole. The key concept behind these authors' attempts to re-evaluate minor literature is that a 'simple conglomeration of individuals cannot be called a group. A group first comes into existence when heterogeneous elements assemble and exist at the same time'. In other words, to create a group it is necessary for elements that exist as extremes at a given time, the minor elements, to be incorporated into the purified mainstream.

Deleuze and Guattari make frequent reference to the concepts of links and the rhizome, models of systems that are not organised in either a vertical or a horizontal hierarchy, but display intersection and fluidity.

Liberation from all dialectic, dualism and binomial opposition is what these authors seek. In order to transcend dualism, they offer the new terms (insisting that they are not systematised sufficiently to rank as *concepts*) rhizome, multiplicity and machine. The rhizome is the antithesis of the tree, which, for them,

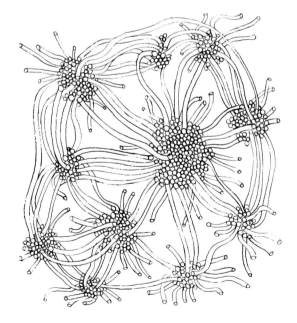

Image sketch of rhizome by Kiyoshi Awazu.

is a model for the hierarchy of dualism. First there is the central trunk, from which branches sprout in order. This hierarchy is firmly established; a branch, for example, never sprouts a trunk. A rhizome, by contrast, is an interwoven complex that defies division – an intertwining of many heterogeneous things, out of order, without a centre. It is always dynamic and changing, producing bulbs here and there as it mingles and twists back on itself.

Deleuze and Guattari distinguish their machine from an unmoving rigid mechanism. Their machine is an assemblage of various independent and heterogeneous elements with a living, fluid existence.

I believe that the advent of an information society will provide us with the chance to deconstruct and rebuild the social 'tree' structure of our present rigid industrial society. If we are not careful, however, the network of our information society may take shape as an ever greater 'trunk', or centralised structure. The test in the years ahead will be whether we can create a fluid and living rhizome instead.

Incorporating 'Noise' into our Lifestyle

René Girard in his book *Mensonge romantique et vérité romanesque* (1961), says that when one structure is completed it begins to close itself off.[3] The completion or realisation of a culture, society or nation is followed by this closing, as it becomes more and more difficult to incorporate things from outside.

The same is true for a human individual. After building a personal life by entering adulthood and marrying, a person's defensive instincts begin naturally to operate. He selects and rejects information accordingly, and builds a closed structure around himself. This structure is his lifestyle, his personality, or his society. In other words, as a person matures he tends to close himself off and, in the interest of avoiding danger, avoids intercourse with those heterogeneous elements that are actually necessary to achieve further maturity. But according to Girard, the fundamental nature of human thought processes is differentiation, which is born of crisis, or what Girard calls 'the theatrical factor'.

In order to preserve both our physical and spiritual youth and continue to receive proof that we are alive it is necessary to incorporate heterogeneous elements – 'noise' – into our lifestyle.

Girard's theory of the scapegoat is another way of saying the same thing. According to Girard, the creation of a scapegoat – that is, the elimination of heterogeneous elements from the hierarchy, or structure of authority – is a means of preserving that hierarchy. For that reason, heterogeneous elements ('noise') that shake the structure of authority, or stability, are most important.

In the second volume of his work *L'espirit du temps*, the French sociologist Edgar Morin discusses the concepts of crisis and event and writes of 'order from noise'. The economist Jacques Attali, too, has written on this topic in his article 'L'ordre par le bruit' ('Order from Noise') that appeared in the special 1976 issue of *Communication* on the topic of crisis.[4]

Crisis and 'noise' as defined by Morin are elements that stand in opposition to, or are heterogeneous to a system. This is not a heterogeneity that can be quoted, absorbed and harmonised in a peaceful fashion, but refers to the event or process that upsets the hierarchy and makes it feel endangered, forcing it into a new level or a different dimension. 'Noise', in this sense, is related to a critique of Claude Lévi-Strauss' theory of Structuralism.[5]

Lévi-Strauss examined myths and family structures of peoples in various cultures and illuminated the connections and relations between them. In other words, he organised them. But his model rejected the unknown factors and elements that remained outside of his organised structures or were difficult to organise into structures – in other words, 'noise'.

To exclude 'noise' from a society or culture is to send that society or culture on its path of decline. By refusing to be bound by a single standard of values, by cleverly incorporating elements from other cultures into one's own, one makes possible a reconfirmation of one's culture. This will be the internationalism of the new age.

Japan is a small nation situated next to a large one, China. The Japanese have always cultivated the ability to survive by incorporating elements of Chinese civilisation into their own. On the other hand, its farming villages were governed by a rigid communalism, and those who did not obey the rules of the village, or who were unique, were labelled strange or mad and, to maintain the village order, were driven away. Outsiders were allowed to join the village unit only after the most careful consideration. One of the reasons Japan has survived to the present is this dual structure, the fine balance the Japanese have maintained between a hermeticism that preserves the social order and an openness to new elements.

That wonderful sense of balance can be seen in the rapid swings of the country between an open and closed nation in the years before the complete opening up of the Meiji era. Though Japan was technically closed to the outside world for several centuries, trade and communication with other countries continued. Chinese publications – many of them translations into Chinese of European works – provided the Japanese with sufficient acquaintance with the West, and trade routes were never completely closed.

Japan's problems began, rather, after the country was officially opened to the world, from the Meiji era on. The race to modernise in the form of a complete Westernisation resulted in efforts to reject Japanese culture up to that time. This is not the same as incorporating Western culture into the Japanese as noise. Since Meiji times, study abroad in the United States or Europe has been regarded as crucial for a complete education. Western food, architecture and clothing have become the norm, and the Japanese have lived by a Western standard of values.

This tendency to look exclusively to the West is still with us. To be recognised abroad or to be active abroad means to the Japanese Europe and America. There is still no awareness of recognition or activity in the broader world that includes the regions of Islamic culture, China, Southeast Asia,

Australia, Eastern Europe and the Soviet Union.

Japan must adopt new government policies that place the Islamic world, China, the countries of Asia and Eastern Europe on a par with the West. Yet we must guard against letting the new importance we give to the many regions of the globe lapse into a provincial regionalism. Some advocate an insular regionalism, insisting on carrying out all projects solely with the resources of the region involved, refusing foreign capital investment and the help of outside specialists, but this type of isolationism can only result in decline.

We would do well to remember the case of Kyoto. While preserving Japan's ancient cultural traditions, the city was a pioneer in a major public works project to supply industrial water and was the first Japanese city to have streetcars. It reached out to talented people from other cities in Japan and abroad to achieve these things. Kyoto is able to preserve its traditions today precisely because it took such positive and liberal steps and embraced the future with open arms. This is exactly what we mean by incorporating noise into the established order.

This concept of 'noise' has something in common with Yamaguchi Masao's concept of the periphery.[6] A culture that focuses its interest on the centre may intensify its own purity, but its outlying regions are fated to decline. Let us direct our attention to the heterogeneous elements around us, the strange, suspicious and quirky, idiosyncratic things. Let us be alert to them, and cultivate a broad magnanimity. Unless we say goodbye to our distinct brand of communalism – the lifestyle of the farm village – that leads us to ostracise anyone with individual or special talent, Japan has no future.

Time-sharing and the Rabbit Hutch

The second guiding principle of the modern age is division of labour based on function. The social policy of segregation by function reaches its extreme form in the analysis and distribution of industry and architectural and urban space by function. The social rule of 'time, place and occasion' is another form of division by function. Houses contain bedrooms, which are used for sleeping; dining rooms for eating; living rooms for entertainment; and halls to connect these separate facilities: this is the way of Modernism. And since according to that way of thinking, the sole function of the bedroom is sleeping and the sole function of the dining room is eating, every home must have a considerable amount of space.

Japanese houses have been described as rabbit hutches. They are indeed small, but this has a distinct advantage. Because of the versatility of tatami-floored rooms, Japanese houses have escaped a thoroughgoing division of space by function. The multipurpose tatami-floored room becomes a bedroom when you pull the futon mattresses out of the closet and spread them on the matting. When you place a low table in the centre of the room, it becomes a dining room. Set floor cushions here and there and you have a room to receive guests. Place a flower arrangement and hang a scroll in the tokonoma, and you have a tea room. By changing the signs – the décor – one room takes on many different meanings. This multipurpose space makes time sharing possible and in this way we triumph over the limitations of a relatively small space.

This strategy of time-sharing shows a way to transform the densely overpopulated city of Tokyo. The central business district of Tokyo is nearly 100 per cent utilised during the day, but from midnight to dawn it is a ghost town. Surely lockers and other systems could be devised that would make it possible for two businesses to use the same building around the clock. Hotels, for example, have nearly doubled their guest turnover and their profit by transforming themselves from mere places to sleep to centres for banquets, conferences, business meetings, places to nap during the day, and even sites for romantic assignations. Once we cease to regard a place or thing as wedded to a single function and adopt a flexible, time-sharing system, we increase efficiency and require far fewer facilities to meet a wide variety of needs. By restoring even a small degree of plurality to our present classification and segregation by function, we can create new riches and a new life-style.

The startling rise in property prices in Tokyo in recent years is a major problem, and will be the undoing of the Japanese economy unless it is checked. In Chapter XII present a plan for the complete reconstruction of the city that I believe is necessary. Rather than redevelopment of the present city by tearing this down and rebuilding that, I propose the construction of an island in Tokyo Bay that will restore the proper balance between demand for land and its supply. This plan involves cleaning up Tokyo Bay and preserving Tokyo's historic Shitamachi area, while restoring the old forests of Musashino in the city's western suburbs and building looping canals as fire breaks, in a symbiosis of development and restoration.

If the problems of land costs and the threat of fire were solved, I believe that Tokyo could be the most fascinating and futuristic city on earth. One reason is that Tokyo is already a time-sharing city. There can be no denying that houses in Tokyo are small; but the city itself provides every sort of 'second home' conceivable, for even the most arcane tastes. Tokyoites may not be able to invite their friends or colleagues to their home for a party or dinner after work, but the city is filled with fine restaurants, bars and clubs where they can entertain their friends. A Tokyoite may not have a games room in his home, but he does not lack for mah-jong, pachinko and billiard parlours, computer-game centres and sing-along clubs. He may not have his own tennis court or pool, but there is no shortage of sports clubs, golf courses, driving ranges and tennis courts in the city.

These facilities take the place of your own private living room, games room, your own pool and tennis court – they are your second homes. Since they provide space efficiently, by the hour or other period of time, they are time-sharing second homes. Considered from this point of view, it is precisely because of this time-sharing system that Tokyo offers cuisine from nearly every country on earth and such a tremendous variety of entertainment spaces. We can see how a group (or a wealthy individual) could purchase or rent a one-room apartment in the city and make it into an actual second home – a study, a hobby room or a place to entertain guests – while building the family home in the suburbs, where land prices are more reasonable.

What is lost to Functionalism and Dualism

Application of Modernism's division by function has not been restricted to the home but has extended to urban space in general. In the Athens Declaration of the C.I.A.M. (Congrès Internationaux d'Architecture Moderne) conference in 1933, the city was analysed and divided into areas for work, living and recreation, with transportation facilities between these different functions.[7] The present systems of land-use planning and zoning, dividing the city into colour-coded functional areas, are based on this way of thinking. But not everyone has assented to this functionalism, promulgated by Le Corbusier.[8]

Jan Mukarovsky, a member of the 1930s structuralist group in Prague, criticised Le Corbusier's simple functionalism as follows: 'The existence of the whole is the source of the life-energy of all individual functions, and no human action is limited to a simple function'.[9] But with the increasing industrialisation of our society, segregation based on simple functionalism has spread around the world. The segregation of functions is, above all, easy to grasp – like explaining a machine by describing its parts. In addition, functionalism was a convenient weapon for dismantling the academism and feudal elements that remained so strongly rooted early in this century. The lions of Modernism rejected the state of the city of their day, where pluralistic functions accumulated over the ages existed in an overlapping state, as anti-modern. They made the purification of functions, open green spaces and fresh air their slogans and embraced Le Corbusier's 'shining city' as the vital new breeze of Modernism that would sweep away the confusion of the past. The image of the city of the future as a place of multistorey buildings and huge empty plazas which has spread to Brasilia and Chandigarh and all modern cities of the world dates from that time.

This principle is evident in the zoning system that segregates residential from industrial areas, the designation of the city centre as a business district and the suburbs as residential districts. Social welfare policy is conceived along the same lines. The handicapped and the elderly are accommodated in special segregated facilities away from the centre of the city and treated as wards of the state, cut off from normal human relations with the community and the family. It is crucial to retrieve and reclaim what has been sacrificed in a wide range of spheres to these principles of Modernism and Modern architecture, segregation and dualism. The whole of existence, the essentially indivisible chaos of life, the complementary nature of functions, the intermediary zone that has been lost through segregation, the ambiguity lost through clarity – all of these elements are missing from Modernism and Modern architecture.

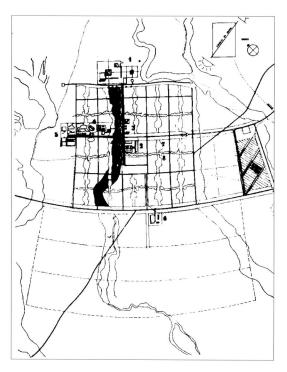

ABOVE: Master plan of Brasilia by Lúcio Costa, 1957. BELOW: Master plan of Chandigarh by Le Corbusier with Maxwell Fry, Jane Drew and Pierre Jeanneret, 1951. Both these cities were an attempt at a particular function – examples of Modernism to sweep away the confusion of the past.

The Pyramid Model of Aristotle, Descartes and Kant

Of course, the simple functionalism by which each part and each space has a single function is not just a product of Modernism; it is the very basis of Western Rationalism, and can be traced back to the ancient Greek philosophy of architecture.

In his *Metaphysics*, Aristotle declared that 'the primary features of beauty are *taxis, symmetria* and *horismmenon*, and they can be expressed mathematically'. *Taxis* is order or hierarchy. The word *symmetria* derives from *syn*, meaning common, and *metreo*, meaning measurement; it means dividing an object into equal measures or quantities. *Horismmenon* means a limit. The philosophy of ancient Greece was to lift man from chaos through the exercise of reason in categorising, analysing, defining and limiting phenomena.

The categorisation and analysis of nature by the faculty of reason is a central attitude of Western culture in every age. The religious, mythological dualism which postulates good and evil gods, a good god of light and the evil material world, the creator god and his creation, is derived from this. Similarly, the philosophy of Descartes, which divides all of finite existence, dependent upon God's will, into spirit and matter, and the philosophy of Kant, who distinguishes the thing itself from phenomena, freedom from necessity are based on Western analytical dualism. This same philosophy has permeated the social structures, the cities and the architecture of all industrialised nations. But how great is our loss as a result! The relentless pendulum swing between humanity and technology, science and religion, good and evil, the part and the whole that has afflicted modern society is a direct result of this unrelenting binomial opposition.

A Pluralism that incorporates Binomial Opposition

The dualism – binomial opposition, the analytic method – that has played such an important role in Western modernisation is deeply entrenched in our ways of thinking and living. As a result, when we wish to refute dualism, we inevitably fall into the contradiction of creating a new binomial opposition. In discussing the concept of symbiosis, too, we are most often forced to produce a binomial opposition in our attempt to transcend all dualism. This is without a doubt the greatest weakness of the concept of symbiosis.

Maurice Merleau-Ponty's philosophy is often described as a philosophy of multivalence or ambiguity.[10] Alphonse de Waelhens, in his foreword to Merleau-Ponty's *The Structure of Behaviour (La structure du comportement,* 1941), compares Sartre and Merleau-Ponty: 'In the end, Sartre strengthened the Cartesian dualism of mind and matter, while Merleau-Ponty remained endlessly concerned with the subtle connections between the two.'[11] One paradigm Merleau-Ponty considered was the case of a man confined to a prison cell: the prisoner's perception (mind) of a meal placed outside the cell changes drastically depending on whether his body (matter) can pass through the bars. The state of the body is the basis for the state of the mind (*cogito*); or the mind can project itself out of the body and be out of synch with it.

Critics of Merleau-Ponty – Lacan, for example – claim that to divide being into matter and mind and set them up as two opposing entities is already to fall into the Cartesian dualism. By the same reasoning, as long as the arguments for the concept of symbiosis against dualism resort to creating oppositions (symbiosis versus dualism), there can be no escape from it.

The concept of symbiosis is basically a dynamic pluralism. It does not seek to reconcile binomial opposites through dialectic, nor does it follow Merleau-Ponty in searching for a unified principle that transcends two opposing elements. At times it is a binomial opposition; at times Merleau-Ponty's unified principle; and it can also be neither. It can only be described as a dynamic, pluralistic principle that can take many different forms.

Post-Modernism that assimilates Binomial Opposition

Man is flesh, man is spirit, man is a unity of flesh and spirit. Man is something that is neither flesh nor spirit – as, for example, the consciousness referred to in the Buddhist philosophy of Consciousness Only, referred to as the *alaya* consciousness.[12] The 'neither flesh nor spirit' here is an intermediary space, a central concept of the philosophy of symbiosis. The intermediary space that is neither assimilates both flesh and spirit, the two elements of the binomial opposition; it is not a third element itself.

In intermediary space, we can postulate two elements in combinations of differing proportions – for example, flesh and spirit, in ratios varying from 10:1 to 1:10. In other words, an infinite number of elements in a plural system can be postulated. But, in fact, the concept of intermediary space is easier to understand if we abandon these opposing elements and describe it instead as the creation of dynamic relations between an infinite number of freely combined proportions of flesh and spirit.

Deleuze and Guattari's concept of the rhizome contains this element of dynamic relationships. In the past, new ideas and revolutionary philosophies have established their value and truth by refuting all previous philosophies. By creating a new binomial opposition, they discredit and refute their predecessors. But the philosophy of symbiosis, while refuting its opposing element (philosophy, theory, or social system), which had previously been the mainstream, also assimilates it. Modernism, for example, is the element that the philosophy of symbiosis must oppose most of all. But rather than completely rejecting Modernism, symbiosis must simultaneously assimilate it.

Post-Modern architecture, in the narrower sense of the term, (we might also call it 'historicist' architecture), which made its appearance as a rejection of Modern architecture, has fallen into the same old binomial opposition or pattern of dualism. Modern architecture, with its emphasis on function, rationality and efficiency, must be criticised at the present moment. But a new horizon will only be opened up by a dynamic, free philosophy that assimilates Modern architecture while criticising it.

Asserting Japan's identity in a Nomadic World

The philosophy of symbiosis is dynamic, free and light; it is the philosophy of the nomads of the new age.

In a society of settlers, people live at fixed sites within a certain territory and create boundaries and neutral zones to avoid conflict. In such a society of mutually closed groups, peace means not violating the boundaries of others or interfering in their internal rules. This is a world of coexisting protectionist societies.

But today we live in the society of *homo movens,* who has learned the value of movement, exchange and discovery. Our world transcends differences in ideology, culture and levels of economic and technological development. A society of symbiosis is a pluralistic world where each person can display his own individuality, where many different cultural spheres exist together. In this situation, the expression of a unique national character, a people's identity, becomes extremely important.

Imagine that in a part of the world peopled by nomadic tribes, an unknown band suddenly appears in the middle of the desert. They give no sign of their intentions. Without a doubt, they would be driven away as a band of brigands or demons. In the nomad's world, it is crucial to clearly indicate who you are, why you have come, and that you mean no harm. Japan today is like a band of silent black-robed horsemen that suddenly appears in the desert. There is nothing more unsettling than a silent group that simply stands there, smiling slightly. The group may even seem to be demonic. One of the reasons for Japan-bashing is the unsettling effect of Japanese behaviour.

The Japanese tradition of prizing silence and regarding clever speakers as lacking in substance has produced a nation of slow, silent craftsmen and silent, hairsplitting researchers and academicians. It has gone so far that an artist or scholar in Japan who is articulate is regarded as a performer, and his achievements suspect. We must put an end to this. Japan's educational system is far behind in teaching young people to express themselves clearly and to explain themselves and their views. Ambiguity is, indeed, a special and important characteristic of Japanese culture; but the inability to express oneself has nothing to do with the ambiguity I speak of.

Japan must present her culture more clearly to the peoples of the world and make the goals of the Japanese nation clear — this is an urgent necessity. Our goal is a world in which the many different cultures recognise one another's values, compete with each other, and while opposing each other in their unique identities also live in symbiosis.

Leaving the Pendulum Phenomenon behind

European history has been marked by extreme swings of the pendulum between Rationalism and non-rationalism. Since the Industrial Revolution, with its philosophy of mass production, the sudden appearance in England of

William Morris' Arts and Crafts Movement emphasised the importance of craftsmanship and handwork.[13] The universal popularity of Art Nouveau and Jugendstil design at the end of the 19th century employing curving lines of plants and other natural forms, was part of a reaction against the Industrial Revolution, another pendulum swing. Antonio Gaudí is regarded as having conceived of the structure of architecture in an extremely rational manner, yet his architecture shares much with Art Nouveau and Jugendstil and was in its own way a reaction against, or pendulum swing back from, the Industrial Revolution as well.

At the beginning of the 20th century however, architects such as Peter Behrens, Tony Garnier and August Perret advocated Rationalism, and swung the pendulum back to that extreme with the Bauhaus and Modern Architecture Movements.[14]

This pendulum phenomenon was imported into Japan. The Japanese who advocated rapid growth in the 1960s were suddenly opposed to rapid growth and technology in the 1970s. Japanese journalism performed a sudden about-face and unleashed a zero-growth campaign, printing daily articles and editorials labelling all technology evil. The simple, ordinary life, lived at an easy rhythm, became the approved lifestyle. In the 1980s, Japan became ever more directly involved in international society, and rapid growth was no longer a subject of debate; it became difficult even to maintain the current rates of growth, faced with the vicious circle of oil price shocks, the emerging NICs economies, the high yen, trade friction, reduced government budgets and a cooling of domestic demand. Now the most advanced technologies, such as biotechnology, new media, computer communications and superconductors, are looked to in hope for a revival of the economy.

What we see here are two extremes – an extreme faith in the virtues of technology and, at the same time, an extreme rejection of the value of technology. This dualistic, pendulum phenomenon only confuses and unsettles our thinking; it produces few positive results. And the swings of the pendulum seem to be wider in younger, less mature nations. When chauffeured by a bad driver, we are rocked back and forth by his sudden acceleration and braking; a good driver makes these transitions smoothly and effortlessly.

The time has come for us to transcend dualism and leave these extreme swings of the pendulum behind us. Since human beings are by nature an ambiguous form of existence, incorporating contradictions and oppositions, we have no grounds for disdaining or faulting that which is intermediate, which cannot be divided into opposing dualisms. On the contrary, I am convinced that this intermediary zone will prove to be a fertile field of human creativity as we face the future.

Centralised Authority in Industrial Society

The last characteristic principle of the modern age, the elimination of social class, is based on a pyramid hierarchy in which part and whole are clearly

Horta, *Maison et atelier Horta*, Brussels, 1898-1900, detail of staircase.

distinguished and the whole is valued above the part. In architectural terms this takes shape as: 1) the superiority of the structure to the interior; 2) the superiority of the infrastructure to the substructure; and 3) the superiority of public space to private space. All of these are examples of the whole taking precedence over the part, resting on a higher level than the part in a pyramid-type hierarchy. Since housing is a part of the city, it is only planned after the public spaces and facilities, the squares and roadways that make up the city's infrastructure, are in place. Housing is secondary and subsidiary.

The same can be said with regard to works of architecture and the various spaces of which they consist. The part is always subsidiary to the whole, in a hierarchy of levels. Nor is this way of thinking restricted to architecture or urban planning. Industrial society subscribes to a strategy of the concentration of efforts in the name of efficiency, with the corollary of priority to big science, big technology and big industry. The components that make up these areas of human activity are subsidiary to the whole, as an industrial hierarchy of sorts is created. This structure of industrial centralisation has merely replaced the old structure of feudal centralisation. Modernism's hierarchy of levels, its insistence on the superiority of the macrostructure, reigns at the expense of plurality and the variety of the parts, their humanity and subtlety of perception. As we move into the information age, the modern industrial structure will radically change. Small and medium-sized manufacturers will outstrip their huge rivals and the service industries rather than manufacturing will lead the industrial world. The present pyramidal hierarchy, in which large enterprises form the superstructure and parcel out work to medium and small enterprises, will be replaced by an entirely new industrial network.

The Holon: Equality of the Part and the Whole

There is considerable interest across a wide range of fields in a non-dualistic view of the part and the whole, or philosophy of symbiosis. One articulation of this view was offered by Arthur Koestler, who formulated the concept of the *holon*.[15] Koestler has coined the term *holon* by combining the Greek root *holos*, meaning whole, and the suffix *on*, for 'part' or 'particle'. The word simultaneously signifies the part and the whole. Koestler is a critic of reductionism, which reduces a phenomenon to its parts for analysis. In that process, he insists, the essence of the phenomenon – the harmonious sum of its parts – is inevitably lost, and the thing falsified. In his essay, 'The Tree and the Candle' Koestler describes the properties of the holon using two examples. A burning candle serves as a metaphor for the concept of an open system, since the candle, while retaining its own basic form, takes oxygen from the atmosphere around it and in turn releases moisture, carbon dioxide, water and heat. He cites a tree as a living example of levels of hierarchy, an intermediate structure because it represents the whole system for all units smaller than itself but at the same time it is only another unit in an even larger system, the forest.

Koestler points out that biological and social structures as well as human activities and linguistic systems all exhibit these two properties of openness and hierarchy. He calls this the open hierarchy, which he regards as the fundamental characteristic of the *holon*.

Tokyo: Holon of 300 Cities

In my book *Toshigaku Nyomon*, I called Tokyo a conglomeration of 300 cities. I think that all cities should actually be considered conglomerations of smaller cities. We are accustomed to thinking of a city as a single, unified entity simply because it is an independent administrative unit with prescribed boundaries. But the simple act of tracing an administrative boundary does not make a city single and unified. In fact, the smaller cities that make it up each possess their own histories, and physically they merge and separate, changing shape to match the local topography. If we realise that the greater city is made up of independent areas, each with its own identity, linked to the others in fluid relationships, it is clear how Tokyo is a conglomeration of 300 cities. When we have accepted this way of looking at things, we see that the smaller parts that form the larger city need not be subjugated to the whole in a 'tree' hierarchy, but that the parts and the city (the whole) form a *holon*.

A few years ago, I chaired a planning committee to establish a code for scenic views in the city of Nagoya. The unique thing about the regulations we proposed was that we did not urge the creation of a unified view for the entire city but suggested instead that scenic views be designated in more than 100 places throughout Nagoya. These locations were chosen as representing the cultural and natural life of the city, its inhabitants, and its environments; we called them Autonomous Scenic Zones. Each was a unique expression of the life of Nagoya City, and we allowed them to retain this uniqueness and variety. The concept was revolutionary when compared with the typical modernist approach, which would be to establish universal standards and then apply them uniformly to all individual cases. Our work in Nagoya produced another *holon*, of the individual Autonomous Scenic Zones and the city as a whole.

A Revolutionary Concept: the State and the City-State

The philosophy of the *holon* can also be applied to the relationship between the state and other self-governing bodies. When Prime Minister Masayoshi Ohira was still alive, I sat at his policy research council and had many opportunities to discuss various ideas with him. One day in a discussion of relationships among the state, the prefectures and the cities, the prime minister said suddenly, 'Mr Kurokawa, why not eliminate the prefectures entirely and just get by with the state and its cities? In place of the prefectures, we could have a general communications processing agency.' The prime minister's ideal was to increase the autonomy of Japan's cities, in the direction of city-states. Our report was entitled 'A Plan for a National Garden City-State'. Rather than a nation centred around garden cities, we meant a garden city-state at a national level. From the standpoint of the hallowed concept of the subordination of self-governing bodies such as cities to the state, this view of the state and the city-state as equal entities is indeed revolutionary and *holonic.*

The philosophy of *holonism* is bound to exert a strong influence on theories of industrial and business organisation as well as on architecture and artistic creation. The top-down method where a general framework is followed by a part-by-part breakdown of the components fails to give sufficient consideration to the final details. On the other hand, there is no guarantee that the whole will reach successful completion if we proceed from the bottom up, by piling detail upon detail to build the totality. The truly creative and *holonic* approach is to give equal weight and consideration to both top-down and bottom-up approaches.

In my own designs, I begin with extremely general, macro considerations, such as the urban planning, the surrounding environment, and various social factors. At the same time, I begin to imagine and sketch very specific parts and details: the shape of the door handles and their feel in my hand, the curve of the hand rails on the stairs, carpet patterns, the furniture and the textures of the walls. This double and parallel approach, working on the whole and the details simultaneously leads to a *holonic* style of architecture. Non-Japanese architects and architectural critics have described my work as a combination of bold spatial structure and eloquent, handcrafted details. This evaluation pleases me, particularly because it shows an appreciation of the *holonic* relationship I have striven to create between the parts and the whole.

Koestler's essay, 'Janus', is named after the two-faced god of Roman mythology who, on the one hand, forces humanity into the various levels of the hierarchy but, on the other, urges them onto a transcendent and whole reality. For in Koestler's part and whole there is the drive towards the symbiosis of man and God. Koestler also postulates three levels of reality: sensual awareness, followed by conceptual awareness, and finally the mystical awareness of 'oceanic feeling', a world that transcends both sense perceptions and concepts. Koestler claims that this oceanic feeling is similar to the synchronicity described by Carl Jung and Wolfgang Pauli. I interpret the idea of synchronicity to mean the symbiosis of past, present and future; Koestler, however, while referring to Jung and Pauli's synchronicity, enlarges it to mean the symbiosis of body and spirit, consciousness and the unconscious, and man and God.

Towards a Merging of Mysticism and Science

Recently, the continuity between religion and science has also become apparent. As the physicist David Bohm has proclaimed, 'Even life can be made from matter'.[16] An extremely interesting discussion between Bohm and Rene Weber, was included in Weber's book *The Holographic Paradigm and Other Paradoxes.* In their conversation, entitled 'The Physicist and the Mystic – Is a Dialogue Between Them Possible?' they noted how, up to the present, physics has applied itself to discovering the unity of part and part, yet no trace of the unity of the part and the whole has been uncovered. For the first time, physics is broaching this issue.

We see here that the same problem that attracted Koestler is drawing the attention of the science of physics. Quoting Einstein's remark that 'the most beautiful of all things is God', Bohm and Weber claim that mysticism, once the province of religion and art, is beginning to evolve a point of contact with science and physics. A new dynamism that transcends the dualistic categorisation of science and religion as distinct fields is making itself felt. The defeat of Modernism is a great common theme of our age; but Japan has the additional task of freeing itself from the ideology of Westernisation. To Japan's great advantage, it has a tradition of Buddhist thought that articulates a philosophy of symbiosis which transcends the limits of dualism. This tradition, cultivated over long centuries, is inherent in Japan's culture and way of life.

An Identity of Opposites

Suzuki Daisetz's philosophy of the identity of opposites is the fundamental principle by which the part and the whole, or contradictory opposites, are revealed as existing in relation to each other.[17] The *Vajracchedika Sutra* contains a verse which can be translated, 'A is non-A, therefore it is called A.' And this is the source of the philosophy of the identity of opposites:

'The oriental individuum is not an independent individual as in the West. It contains no self-existent core, but exists by virtue of emptiness (*sunyata*), which transcends the individuum. Though the individuum and that which transcends the individuum are contradictory, they exist together without the loss of the individuum's identity. "Identity" (*soku*) means that two things are not different. "Non" means that two things are not the same.'

The identity of opposites creates an ambiguity of meaning, a floating multivalence, through simultaneous affirmation and rejection on a conceptual level. The entities A and non-A are in fact a single entity. Since two contradictory entities are a single entity, Suzuki Daisetz calls the mutually embracing relationship of the part and the whole the philosophy of the identity of opposites. Human beings exist as a part of the universe; at the same time, the universe is enfolded in the consciousness of human beings. Zen teaches that the universe and humanity are mutually inclusive, and it is easy to find other expressions of this antidualism or non-dualism in Asian thought.

In the world of the oriental individuum, where the part and the whole are accorded the same value and the individual and the meta-individual exist together, neither losing their own nature nor contradicting each other, there is no pyramidal hierarchy in which the part is subjugated in its unity with the whole.

The Edo philosopher Miura Baien devised a sympathetic philosophy of the unification of opposites, which he set forth in a trilogy: the discourses on metaphysics, corollaries and morality.[18] It has been shown that Miura Baien invented the dialectic a half century before Hegel.[19] More important than any comparison with Hegel however, is the recognition of Baien's inspirations in

Asian thought, particularly Indian philosophy. His philosophy is typical of the Asian tradition in that it resolves dualism into monism and represents a symbiosis of analysis and unification, the part and the whole. In his dialectical analysis, Miura Baien's philosophy indeed seems close to Hegel's but it is clear from the name he used, the unification of opposites, that he ultimately sought a unified, whole world. We can interpret his thought as a philosophy of apprehending all seeming opposites as a single totality, a philosophy of the symbiosis of part and whole. We do not know whether Miura Baien ever studied the Buddhist philosophy of Consciousness Only, but his thought bears a close resemblance to it. I am convinced that the philosophy of Consciousness Only will be the source for the thought of the 21st century. While Western thought has reached the dead end of dualism, Buddhism and its philosophy of Consciousness Only offers Japan a means to assume the intellectual leadership of the future.

Tsukiji Hotel, by Kisuke Shimizu, late 19th-century print by Kuniteru. A dramatic combination of heterogeneous and hybrid elements, this tradition culminated in the Eastern-Western architecture from the late Edo through the early Meiji period. The building is composed of an Islamic-style gate, a hipped, Western-style roof, weathercock, bell-shaped and round windows in the tower, crisscross lath and plaster outer walls, and red-lacquered sash and frame construction. Its particular beauty is the product of Eastern and Western cultures and their symbiotic synthesis.

Edo: Precursor of the Age of Symbiosis

A Highly Developed Modern Society

Much has been published on the rich and varied culture of Edo as the flowering of classical Japanese life. In the early 1960s, I predicted that Edo would be widely reappraised, and I studied the city from a variety of perspectives. I have emphasised the importance of Edo's Shitamachi, or central, 'downtown' area;[1] the value of streets and alleys as opposed to squares; the city's *sukiya*-style architecture in relation to its population density; the automatons of the Edo period; the philosophy of Miura Baien. I have collected and studied the woodblock prints of the last years of the Edo period, with special attention to the typically Edo-period colour known as Rikyu grey.

In 1981 I designed the Arts of Edo Exhibition at the Royal Academy of Arts, and in my introductory talk at Oxford University, I suggested that 'the Edo period – or more broadly, the three-century span of purely Japanese culture from the mid-16th to the mid-19th century – holds the roots of all that is Japan today'. The major Japanese art traditions that survive today – the way of tea (*sado*), flower arrangement (*ikebana*), the Noh and Kabuki dramas, *sukiya*-style architecture – all can be traced back to the latter half of the 16th century and all gained popular acceptance in the Edo period. They flourished until the 'reforms' of the Meiji era brought a wholesale rejection of everything associated with the past. Certainly the new government, but also the populace, sought to disassociate itself from the feudal past in the push toward Westernisation, even if that meant depreciating 'pre-Modern' life and culture.

With the opening of Japan to the West, Japanese architecture suddenly started copying Western architecture outright; Japanese took to wearing Western clothes. This seems to support the view that modern Japan began from the Meiji era. We often hear that Japan rose from being a backward country to an advanced industrial state in a little over a hundred years, and that the leaders of developing nations should look to Japan as a model for their next hundred years of growth. Such explanations, however, overlook a number of important facts.

As is gradually becoming clear, the Edo period saw grand achievements in mass culture and was far more 'modern' than has been appreciated. Ronald Dore notes in *Education in Okugawa Japan* that by the end of the Edo period (1868), 43 percent of boys and ten percent of girls between the ages of six and 13 attended school – higher percentages than in England at the time. Edo was the largest city in the world, with a population of well over a million. In scientific scholarship, Yamagata Banto proposed a steady-state theory of the solar system in his *Instead of Dreams (Yume no Shiro,* 1820),[2] while Shizuku Tadao translated John Keill's commentaries on Newton's *Principia* only very shortly after they had reached France.[3] By the early 19th century, cartographer Ino Tadataka (1785-1818) had drawn accurate maps of the Japanese islands.[4] Moreover, in the 1770s, philosopher Miura Baien had set forth his dialectical system in three *Discourses on Metaphysics, Corollaries* and *Morality,* predating Hegel's dialectic by 50 years. Most important, however, Edo society had already attained its own unique modernity, quite distinct from Europe. No doubt the speed with which Japan was able to assimilate Western ideas and practices in the Meiji era, like a blotter absorbing ink, related to the basically modern character of mature Edo society.

Indeed, it is in Japan's own unique and mature modern society of the Edo period that we should search for Japan's cultural roots.

An Urban Centre of Popular Culture

First, Edo Japan was a predominantly popular culture. In the eighth century, the total population of Japan was five million; a thousand years later, immediately prior to the Edo period, that figure had only just reached ten million. One hundred years into the Edo period the population had tripled, reaching 30 million by the time of shogun Tokugawa Yoshimune (1716-45). This in itself made for accelerated urbanisation.

The city of Edo, the world's largest metropolis, was home to the world's first mass popular culture. The vast shrine and temple complexes of earlier ages gave way to the popular architecture of *sukiya*-style tea rooms, Kabuki, Noh and Joruri theatres, as well as vernacular masterpieces in the forms of farmhouses and merchant townhouses.[5] As papermaking and woodblock printmaking techniques developed, a vast popular literature burst forth in the form of romances, humour, erotica and several varieties of picture books named after the colour of their covers – 'blue books', folios and 'yellow covers' for adults, and 'red books' and 'black books' for children. Bookshops sprang up all over Edo.

High Population Density and Non-verbal Communication

The second special feature of Edo was its extremely high population density, which resulted in the cultivation of subtle sensitivities. The average family had six members and lived in a home with a frontage of only two *ken* (about 3.6 metres). Under those circumstances, it was impossible for a married couple to have a private bedroom. Even in my own childhood I remember that my parents slept in the same room with one child, and my grandparents slept in an adjoining room with the other children. This was the norm in Japan.

In Tokyo today, with some 250 people per hectare, we speak of a high population density. But there were 688 people per hectare in old Edo. In a city that crowded, one loud voice can annoy scores of people. In Japanese we say

'The eyes are as eloquent as the lips', and we speak of 'probing another's stomach'. Silent communication of the eyes and the 'stomach' – which is the Chinese and Japanese metaphorical equivalent of the heart or breast in the West – was a corollary of Edo's high population density.

In such a densely populated society, the slightest change in feeling or expression, gesture or attitude, can have an impact on interpersonal relationships; consequently a subtle and refined sensitivity is fostered. It was this sensitivity that produced the subtle psychological dramas of the Kabuki theatre's *sewamono,* or domestic plays. The heightened sensitivity to materials that characterises *sukiya*-style architecture can also be traced back to these roots. From another perspective, feudal society with its rigid class distinctions, densely populated cities, and tight web of human relationships, did not permit the individual to expand his frame of reference and open his world out to broader horizons. Instead an intense in-turning was fostered, a concentration on and refinement of the internal world, which found expression in the human emotions of love, hate, duty, in an extreme sensitivity to the changes of the four seasons, and a love of plants and animals.

In modern city planning, high population density is regarded as undesirable. The ideal is thought to be single-family dwellings spread out at a very low density among spacious parks and greenery. Yet I am convinced that it is far more natural for human beings to live together in relatively dense population environments. What are the best examples of the modern ideal of low-density urban populations? Take Canberra and Los Angeles – the people of those cities are definitely not satisfied with their living environments. In Canberra, houses dot the open landscape at wide intervals. Is fruitful human interaction possible when you have to get in your car and drive to your nearest neighbour's home? And the high crime rate of Los Angeles, where there is no way of knowing what has happened at one's next-door neighbour's house, makes it difficult to claim that these low-population-density communities are good urban environments.

The Edo Rowhouse: An Urban Model

Another trait of the Edo urban environment was its mixed, hybrid, pluralistic nature. The comic monologues of this period regale us with tales of colourful characters who lived in the rowhouses, or *nagaya,* so characteristic of the city: the landlord, a wise old sort, now retired; the stranger with a mysterious background; the quiet young couple, actually the daughter of a feudal lord and the head clerk of a great merchant, who have eloped together and are in hiding; the quack doctor; the hardworking carpenter with a large brood of children; and many other interesting characters shared the same lodgings in the typical Edo *nagaya.*

The Edo period is often thought of as a time of strict social castes, with little opportunity for people to move between them. But though externally these castes may have defined people's lives, internally a completely different principle was at work. The samurai class, for example, was actually very poor. The merchants, who were officially the lowest class, were in contrast relatively well off. Many of the merchant class were also leaders of the intellectual world, particularly in the study of Western science ('Dutch Learning' or *Rangaku*). As a result, samurai had to swallow their pride and ask to be accepted as the disciples and pupils of these merchants. In other words, though an external class structure divided the populace into samurai, farmers, craftsmen and merchants, other divisions cut across these groups: an economic class system, an intellectual class system, and an artistic class system. Social position was defined by the overlapping combination of all these relationships. There was nothing strange about a samurai setting up shop as an umbrella maker next door to a carpenter's shop, for example.

In fact, the present is, if anything, more class conscious than the Edo period as far as housing is concerned. When a public housing project is designed now, care is taken that all of the units should have a nearly equal amount of living space. Rent is calculated from the price of land and building costs in the so-called cost-price system. These uniform conditions ensure that the people who move into the housing project are very similar in social class. For example, if the rent is just about right for a couple in their 30s with one child, the housing project is very likely to fill up with thousands or tens of thousands of couples in their 30s with a single child. The children that move in will all go to school at about the same time, and their fathers will all be at about the same step on the ladder of worldly success. The social environment of this housing project becomes, as a result, tremendously competitive. Which is more humane, the modern housing project or the Edo-period *nagaya,* populated by people of all ages, classes and professions?

The separation of the social classes in modern society results in the exclusion of the weak from the social situation. The modern housing project is not a suitable place for the elderly or the handicapped to live. To avoid this unfortunate situation, I have always insisted that in designing public housing it is important to begin with a breakdown of the percentages of the different types of projected inhabitants, ensuring that a wide variety of people will be able to live together in the project. We must start by determining the ideal percentages of couples in their 30s, 40s and 60s, handicapped people, and all other groups. Only on this basis can the real design and planning begin.

For over 20 years I have continued to insist that if homes for the elderly are to be built at all, they should be located next to day care centres. Then the elderly residents have a chance to play with the children, just as if they were their own grandchildren. The generations need places which enable them to come into contact with each other. Some people think that because the elderly are not very active, homes for them should be located in quiet places out in the midst of nature. This way of thinking reflects the coldness of modern society's functionalism and segregation, which regards efficiency above all else. On the outskirts of San Francisco I visited a retirement community built quite

Woodblock print by Sharaku of the actor Ichikawa Ebizoh as Takemura Sadanoshin, 1794-95. By portraying an exaggerated facial expression it introduces an element of fantasy while retaining the realism of the work.

Detail of Kohakubai screen by Ogata Korin, of the highly
stylised Rimpa school of painting.

some time ago as part of a survey I was conducting. The entire town was designed with the needs of the elderly in mind: because many older people have trouble walking, the land is flat and houses are all single-storey dwellings. And because they tend to wake early, the dining hall opens at five am for breakfast and the games room opens at six.

At first glance it really does seem to be a town designed entirely for the elderly. But after breakfast, almost the entire population of the community gathers in the games room to play cards. This is indeed a strange sight. It speaks of a society so harsh that there is no place in it for the elderly, who must be segregated from the real world. In the week I spent interviewing the people of this town, I learned that some 60 percent of the residents regarded the move there as a mistake. Living in an ordinary city has its inconveniences and can be noisy, but at least there they could see their grandchildren and other younger people. The consensus of the residents of this retirement community was that they should have stayed where they were. Unfortunately, in most cases the move had exhausted their life savings, and they were unable to return to the real world.

The segregation of modern urban planning creates inhuman living environments like this. In cities the world over, there is a conspicuous segregation by economic class. The high-density communities of Edo, in which different generations and classes lived together in symbiosis, offer us an important hint for urban planning of the future.

An Art of Symbiosis of Abstraction and Realism

The third characteristic of Edo-period culture is the importance of fantasy. The mysterious woodblock-print artist Sharaku for example, draws the features of actors in a frankly exaggerated fashion, yet his work does not lose its realism.[6] In the *shunga* pornographic prints the male organ may be depicted as almost a metre in length, yet it works in the picture because the same level of realism and stylistic technique in the rest of the print is applied to it. The works of the Rimpa school of painters – Koetsu, Sotatsu, Korin and Kenzan among others – are strongly fictitious in their structure in sharp contrast to the concrete realism of their Western contemporaries.[7]

The combination of abstract and realistic techniques, pioneered in the West by Picasso was already applied most effectively by Japanese artists some four centuries ago. Kabuki costumes and stylised *kumadori* make-up also illustrate the characteristically Japanese combination of abstract and real.[8] The transition from fantasy to abstraction can be seen in other Edo-period arts as well, such as in Kimono patterns, strikingly similar to modern aesthetic tastes in design and artistic conception.

The importance of fantasy in Edo culture can also be seen in its attitude to nature. Edo was known as the city of blossoms – in part a metaphor for the city's brilliant and flourishing culture as the capital of the realm and the seat of the shogunate; but the city was also extraordinary for the amount of greenery

Kabuki actors with Kumadori make-up. The costumes and stylised make-up show a combination of Edo abstract and realist techniques.

and flowers it cultivated. Though Edo lacked the public squares of Paris and the parks of London, the doorways and backyards of people's houses were lined with rows of potted bonsai, and in the summer, morning glory and flowering gourd vines climbed the facades of Edo's buildings. Flower markets were held most days of the week, and peddlers hawked flowers and potted plants throughout the city.

The bonsai of Japan are not natural, but in the tiny tree we read a sign of nature. When the citizens of Edo looked at a bonsai pine they saw a hoary, thousand-year-old tree and heard the salt breezes of the sea shore. I applied the symbolism of the bonsai in my design for the Prince Hotel in Roppongi, placing a camphor tree in the centre of the interior poolside area. The curved shape of the pool is a metaphor for the ocean. It is a small pool, not really large enough to be of much use, but the sides are made of acrylic so people can watch the swimmers and enjoy it as an image of the sea. The single tree set in the centre of the poolside area is like a bonsai, standing as a metaphor for the forest. With that single tree, people can feel the coolness of shade in summer, imagine the soughing of the wind through its branches, and sense the arrival of autumn seeing its fallen leaves.

The feudal lords in residence in Edo had official residences on plots near the shogun's castle assigned to them by the shogunate and they also built private residences further from the castle, incorporating large gardens. *Sukiya*-style architecture also spread among the wealthier commoners, and with this a more highly developed awareness of the garden evolved. Japanese gardens, of course, have a long history, dating from the palace-style gardens of the Heian period and including the sand and stone Zen gardens of the medieval period, but gardens first enjoyed general popularity in the Edo period. Japanese gardens exhibit a high degree of abstraction and fantasy. If you want the ocean in your garden, you dig a pond and read it as the sea; if you want islands, you place a big rock in the pond and view it as an island. Nature in this fashion is man-made and fictitious in the context of the densely populated city of Edo.

Sukiya-style architecture itself, the tea house, built of wood, paper and earth, is nothing more than a fantasy for viewing nature.

The sort of androgyny of present-day pop idols was also quite popular in Edo; this is another example of a culture of fictions. The beauties depicted by the mid-Edo-period woodblock-print artist Suzuki Harunobu are as thin as Twiggy in her heyday.[9] They are rejections of female physicality, androgynous presences which represent the exact opposite of a figure like Marilyn Monroe. In Kabuki, the convention of men playing the roles of women is exploited to present woman as fantasy. The same impulse must have lead the geisha of the Fukagawa district of old Edo to adopt men's names.[10] This type of inversion is a kind of sophistication that is part of the essence of an ambiguous culture. A culture that pursues a straightforward masculinity and femininity – where all men are John Wayne and all women are Marilyn Monroe – is based on a simplistic physicality. This is the aesthetic of the 1960s, when the goal of human

Kisho Kurokawa, Roppongi Prince Hotel, Tokyo, 1984, views of the curved pool and bonsai. Evoking an image of the ocean, the acrylic-sided pool allows a view of the swimmers. The bonsai is metaphorical of the forest and a reference to the fictional nature of Edo.

life was thought to be material welfare — the aesthetic of Western-style Modernism. In contrast, a fictitiousness that allows men and women to exist in symbiosis is what is now sought after and will continue to be pursued in the future. The feminisation of men, the masculinisation of women and gay culture, are not signs of the collapse of civilisation: they are the pulse of a new aesthetic consciousness being born.

The Intentional Artlessness of *Sukiya*-style Architecture
The fourth trait of Edo culture was its preoccupation with detail. The work of Kobayashi Rekisai, a craftsman who specialised in making tiny models of everyday objects, transmits to us today this Edo fascination with detail.[11] Kobayashi stood in a long line of superb craftsmen, stretching back to the Edo period. Among his many amazing works is a writing box only a few millimetres in size, yet painstakingly decorated with inlaid *maki-e* designs.[12]

There are many other examples at hand: the famous and finely detailed Edo *komon* kimono patterns, miniature books and Buddhist altars constructed as tiny miniatures of Buddhist temples.[13] The architecture of the Edo period is also preoccupied with detail. The carvings that decorate the Toshogu shrine are an obvious example, and Edo castles, exemplified by Himeji Castle, exhibit a far greater wealth of design detail than their Momoyama predecessors.

Sukiya-style architecture, when compared to the palatial *shoin* style that preceded it, makes greater use of natural materials and a simple, even rough design.[14] But aside from the question of sheer amount of decorative detail, *sukiya*-style architecture shows great concern for the details and the proportions of the materials it uses. A naturally bent branch used in a *sukiya*-style work may at first seem to be an artless thing that might be picked up anywhere, but in fact that single branch was painstakingly selected from hundreds of naturally twisted branches, especially chosen to appear artless and natural.

The fifth trait of Edo-period culture was its symbiosis of technology and humanity — what I call the concept of *karakuri*, or the automaton. In contrast to the West, where technology is opposed to humanity, technology in Japan has traditionally been regarded as an extension of humanity, that can exist in symbiosis with humanity. I will come back to this idea later in the book.

A Hybrid Style: Synthesis of East and West
The sixth trait of Edo culture was the development of a hybrid style of architecture. Carpenters of the Edo period freely combined the styles of all previous ages, to create a unique hybrid style. The Hiunkaku, or Flying Cloud Pavilion of the Nishi Honganji temple in Kyoto is a masterpiece of the hybrid style of the early Edo period.[15] The *sukiya*-style is a blend of the residential *shoin* style and the *soan*, or grass hut, style of tea room architecture.[16] The Joan of Oda Uraku is a masterpiece of this hybrid tea room architecture.

Another style that gained popularity in the Edo period was the so-called *gongen*, or avatar, style of architecture.[17] The Toshogu shrine is the outstanding

This woodblock print by Suzuki Harunobu (*OPPOSITE*) showing a slender, androgynous woman is akin to the image of Twiggy (*ABOVE*) but stands in sharp contrast to a figure like Marilyn Monroe, highlighting the difference between the ambiguity of Edo and the straightforward aesthetic of Western-style modern culture.

ABOVE: Marilyn Monroe. *BELOW*: John Wayne. Images of a culture pursuing simplistic physicality.

example, combining Buddhist and Shinto architectural styles (the name reflects the concept that Shinto deities were avatars of the Buddhas and Bodhisattvas). The secret carpenters' manual known as the 'transmission of Shrine Architecture' (*Jingu Soden*) handed down through the Kenninji lineage of carpenters, contains instructions for linking the main hall and the worship hall of a Shinto shrine with a stone-floored room, a combination of Buddhist and Shinto architectural styles. Relatively early works such as the tomb of Daitokuin, Sugen'in, Gen'yuin and Joken'in in Ueno, and the tomb of Bunshoin in Chiba can be regarded as precursors of the *gongen* style. By the mid-Edo period, full-blown examples abound: Yushima Tenmmangu shrine, Kanda Myojin shrine, Kamakura Hachimangu shrine, Nezu Gongen shrine, Kameido Temmangu shrine and Tomioka Hachiman shrine.

Japanese culture has always maintained a skilful synthesis of different inputs, and a hybrid style of architecture is hardly anomalous in Japanese history. But this hybridisation reached its peak in the Edo period, an era of architectural methodology, when the method of design and construction was given great importance. This tradition culminated in the hybrid Eastern-Western architecture from the late Edo through the Meiji period: the Tsukiji Hotel, the First National Bank of Tokyo, the Mitsuigumi Headquarters at Nihombashi and the foreign merchants' houses in Yokohama are all representative works of this style. Contemporary master carpenters incorporated Western styles into their work, producing buildings with a naive yet creative blending of East and West.

The arch of the gate of the Tsukiji Hotel, for example, suggests Islamic architecture. The building itself is a dramatic combination of diverse and hybrid elements: crisscross lath and plaster outer walls, bell-shaped and round windows in the tower, a hipped Western-style roof, a weathercock and the red-lacquered sash and frame construction. At the same time, it clearly surpasses any of the imitations of Western architecture produced in Japan from the mid-Meiji period on. This is because it was designed before Japan had adopted Western values as its own; the beauty of the Tsukiji Hotel is the product of the collision of two different cultures and their symbiotic synthesis.

Unfortunately, due to the Meiji government's determined policy of Westernisation, the value of this hybrid architecture was not recognised, and was destroyed. With the Meiji era, the symbiotic culture of the Edo period was rejected as backward and chaotic; the age of modernisation and the 'pure' Westernisation of Japan began.

For over 20 years I have been working to re-create these works of hybrid architecture, most of which have been lost to us. The richest source of documentation is in woodblock prints of the period, the so-called Yokohama prints and 'Civilisation' (*kaika*) prints.[18] From the last years of the Edo period on into early Meiji, prints illustrating foreigners and their customs were popular. These lively prints depicted the new 'civilisation and enlightenment' that the government aimed for, and showed such scenes as Western ships, steam locomotives, foreign dress and accessories and foreigners disporting in the

Hiunkaku, or Flying Cloud Pavilion, at Nishi Honganji temple in Kyoto, built in the early Edo period, is a masterpiece of hybrid styling, combining the residential *shoin* with the thatched hut *soan* to create the *sukiya* style.

brothels and gay quarters. The hybrid architecture of the age was also a popular subject, and many buildings are shown in prints.

Yokohama and Civilisation prints were produced for a period of about 20 years, spanning the last decade of the Edo period and the first decade of Meiji. Some 80 percent were created in the years from 1860 to 1865. In 1868, the last year of the old regime and the first year of Meiji, Tokyo's harbour was opened to foreign ships, and popular interest began to move from Yokohama to Tokyo. In general, the Yokohama prints depicted scenes in and around Yokohama, and the Civilisation prints showed scenes of Tokyo.

It is my ambition to re-create the plans for these works of East-West hybrid architecture depicted in the woodblock prints but otherwise lost to posterity. I believe we can discover the tremendous dynamism of a Japanese aesthetic of symbiosis in the process of re-creating these works, as well as the true path that Post-Modern architecture should take as it transcends the limits of Modernism.

From Centralisation and Decentralisation to Centralisation and Decentralisation

The seventh special characteristic of Edo culture was the symbiosis of part and whole under the system of the centralised shogunate and decentralised fief governments. The shogunate determined all national policy; it was a centralised administrative system with an enormous amount of power. But from the mid-Edo period on, the shogunate, in financial difficulties partly because of the enormous expense incurred in the construction of the Toshogu shrine, encouraged each of the fiefs to develop its own economy. The Satsuma fief in Kyushu developed cut glass wares, Nagasaki encouraged the manufacture of blown glass; Ako was known for its salt production and Kanazawa for its Kutani ceramics and Wajima lacquerware. Wakayama also produced lacquerware, and Ibaraki *yuki tsumugi* cloth; Oita manufactured a special kind of tatami matting and Tosa supplied camphor. All of these were fief-run local industries.

In intellectual circles too, each fief had its own educational system of village schools and fief academies. In addition, specialised private institutes were established to teach Western studies, neo-Confucianism, military strategy, the art of poetry and various practical skills. The crown of these local systems was the Shoheiko academy in Edo, the official academy of the shogunate. But since the Meiji Restoration, Japan's educational system has gradually become more and more centralised and standardised.

The re-evaluation of Japan's educational system initiated during the Naka-sone administration suggested reforms to reintroduce more freedom and individuality, but in fact we could learn much along these lines by looking back at the educational system during the Edo period.

The shogunate's policy of requiring the feudal lords to commute back and forth from their fiefs to Edo contributed greatly to the development of communication and transportation networks linking Edo to the fiefs; but still

ABOVE: Kanda Myojin shrine. *OPPOSITE ABOVE*: Nezu Gongen shrine. *OPPOSITE BELOW*: Yushima Tenmmangu shrine. These three shrines, from the mid-Edo period, were named after the *gongen* doctrine of Japanese Buddhism which taught that Shinto deities were local, Japanese manifestations of cosmic Buddhas. This style freely combined elements from Shinto and Buddhist architecture.

the fiefs were not absorbed into the central government and each retained its own independence and vitality. This precedent can guide us today: it teaches us that we are not forced to make a choice between centralisation and decentralisation; we can have both, in the ideal model offered by Edo.

The cities of the Federal Republic of Germany are a European example of the success of decentralisation. Since the capital of the republic was moved to Bonn, the cities of Germany have been decentralised to an almost ideal degree. Frankfurt, Hamburg, Düsseldorf, Cologne, Bonn, Munich and Stuttgart are all cities between one million and three million inhabitants; no huge megalopolis like Tokyo dominates. Each region has its own universities and newspapers, independent and individual in character. The country itself is a federal republic, and historically the individual states have always been strongly independent.

Yet others argue that Berlin, one of the great world cities in the 1920s, should be restored as the capital of West Germany; that without the culture of a great city, their country cannot be an international centre. In France, on the other hand, everything is concentrated in Paris, yet the French value each of the regions of their country for its unique culture and atmosphere, its local wine and its more relaxed pace of life. While all Frenchmen are proud of their great capital, the other regions of France exist in symbiosis with the centre.

In this context, the current criticism in Japan concerning the concentration of the country's energies and resources on Tokyo seems to be exaggerated. Our goal should be to ensure that the great cities and other regions of the country all develop independently, in a simultaneously centralised and decentralised fashion. That is why the model of the shogunate and the fiefs is such an apt one as we face the future.

ABOVE: Tokyo Station, 1914. *BELOW*: Kaichi Elementary School, 1876. The Meiji-period station here contrasts with the Edo-type school which shows Eastern-Western elements rather than an obvious imitation of the style in the West.

Rikyu Grey, Baroque and Camp
Ambiguity and Ambivalence

Rikyu Grey as a Symbol of Japanese Culture

There are many inexplicable feelings and sensitivities which are neither intellectual concepts nor capable of definition. Their undefinability is part of their very nature, and the more we try to explain and analyse such feelings and moods, the more we lose their true essence. To identify the outlines of such a mood, follow its history and find its point of origin, we must feel simultaneously a deep sympathy for it and the pleasant stimulus of a certain resistance to it. Rikyu grey is the name I have applied to a certain sensitivity of this type.

The words Rikyu grey appeared in the Japanese hit song *Jogashima no Ame*: 'The rain falls and falls, on the beach of Shirogashima, the Rikyu grey rain falls.' The term dates back several centuries, but according to Isamu Kurita, the author and critic, its origin is unclear. I use Rikyu grey however, as a symbol of the ambivalence and multivalence of Japanese space and culture. I have enlarged its scope to include other terms which express the same sensitivity – Mannerism, early Baroque and Camp – and finally have adapted it to describe the essential quality that all art should possess.

The feeling of Rikyu grey is similar to that which we find ambivalent or multivalent in art. I first began to be interested in this type of art 22 years ago when I was beginning to feel very dissatisfied with functionalist architecture. With a group of colleagues I formed the Metabolist movement. We found that when space was analysed and segregated according to function, the ambivalent, multivalent spaces that had existed in its peripheral and border areas in an undifferentiated, unarticulated state were sacrificed to a cold, clear rational analysis by function; in the process, space lost its essential nature. In our cities, in our buildings and even in our lives, it is the mazelike, the secret, the ambiguous area which may even seem a little sinister, that lends charm and charisma, that excites us and arouses our expectations. When I was trying to find a name for this lost essence of space I hit upon the term Rikyu grey.

The Four Primary Colours in Opposition

Masayoshi Nishida traces the origins of the Rikyu Grey concept back to *Choando Ki*, the tea writings of Kubo Gonnadaisuke Toshiyo (1571-1640), head priest of Kasuga Shrine in Nara. Toshiyo writes:

> From the time that he came to serve as tea master to Lord Hideyoshi, everyone began to study Soeki's (Sen no Rikyu, 1522-91) way of tea. Thus did Soeki's distaste for colourful show achieve a widespread following, as

ABOVE: Hishikawa Moronobu's female type – symbolic of the population and economy boom, the urbanisation and material prosperity in the Genroku era – similar to the voluptuous female beauty of Modern Western prosperity. *OPPOSITE*: *Ukiyo-e* ('pictures of the floating world') print by Suzuki Harunobu, showing spirituality and androgyny in the female form. The beauty depicted is difficult to define but it captures an essence of charisma and ambiguity; and corresponds to the sensitivity of Rikyu grey.

did his verses advocating *wabi*. [Practitioners were instructed to] change the colour of the collar of their underkimono and to wear cotton kimonos dyed with ash to a neutral hue. . . From then on, the colour grey enjoyed great popularity, and large quantities of grey cotton twill and broadcloth were imported from China.

It was this 'ash-dyed neutral hue' that Sen no Rikyu gave as an example of simple dress which came to be known as Rikyu grey. It is a shade of dark grey-green, or grey with a green tint.

Traditionally, grey was not a popular colour, associated with the Japanese words for 'ash' (*haiiro*) or 'rat' (*nezumiiro*). But from the later Edo period, when it became known as Rikyu's colour, grey was much favoured as a stylish shade along with sombre indigo blues and browns. As the art of tea spread among the populace, people showed an increasing fondness for grey and we see a proliferation of shades of the colour and names for it: Fukagawa grey, silver grey, indigo grey, scarlet-tinged grey, lavender grey, grape grey, brown grey, dove grey, maroon grey. The grey in which all other colours cancel each other out was called plain grey – the colour of no colour. In contrast to grey in the West, which is a combination of white and black, Rikyu grey was a combination of four opposing colours: red, blue, yellow and white.

The greys of the Edo period were all very subtle tones, and the minute variations and differences among them were highly appreciated. Nishida, in *Nihon no Bi* (Japanese Beauty), states: 'The non-sensual aesthetic sense finds expression in that colourless colour of numerous hues which completely cancel each other out – Rikyu grey.' These greys were the hallmark of the sophisticated aesthetic sensitivity from the Genroku era (1688-1704) to the Temmei era (1781-89).

Toru Haga, a specialist in comparative literature, has made studies on the An'ei (1772-81) and Temmei eras and states that 'women of the period favoured kimono fabrics known as *kabe shijira* and *akebono shibori*. The latter was a pale periwinkle lavender material tie-dyed in morning glory patterns, while the 'whitewashed-wall weave' of *kabe shijira* was a pure white silk of the finest texture which in certain lights revealed woven patterns. It pleased the most delicate and sophisticated of tastes.' Gen Itasaka, a scholar of Edo literature, notes an aesthetic shift in the ukiyo-e prints of two artists of the time, 'the change from the Genroku ideal of Hishikawa Moronobu (c 1618-94) to the An'ei-Temmei ideal of Suzuki Harunobu (1724-70).'[1] Whereas the beauties depicted by Moronobu were full-figured, voluptuous women, Harunobu depicted willowy courtesans with slender faces and swanlike necks who gave a general impression of spirituality and androgyny.

The contrast is most instructive: if we think of Moronobu's women as symbolic of the boom in population and the economy, urbanisation and material prosperity up through the Genroku era, we can see how they correspond in their way to the Marilyn Monroe style of female beauty popular in the 1960s, the era of material prosperity. Today, however, a different ideal is

ABOVE: Tamasaburo, an Oyama actor. *OPPOSITE*: Oyama, National Bunraku Theatre. In Kabuki theatre, male actors play female parts, lending androgynity to the female character. The actors are called Oyama, Tamasaburo being the most famous.

Katsura Detached Palace, Kyoto, aerial view showing palace and gardens. The effect of walling through the palace and grounds is theatrical – a two-dimensional experience with different vantage points on a continuous path.

appreciated, closer to Harunobu's beauty, a non-physical, extraordinary, androgynous sort of beauty, exemplified by Michael Jackson, David Bowie and Tamasaburo. This has come to be an expression of the more ambiguous and ambivalent spirit of our age.

Freezing Space and Time into a Flat World

The Rikyu grey I speak of is a sensitivity linked to this sort of highly developed aesthetic consciousness. The streets of Kyoto, indeed all traditional Japanese towns, take on a special beauty in the greying light of dusk. A fusing of perspectives occurs as the slate-coloured tiles and white plaster walls dissolve into grey, flattening all sense of distance and volume as the world of three dimensions is reduced to two. It is a truly dramatic sight. When I view this scene, I can't help but think that Rikyu himself, through the colour sensitivity of Rikyu grey, sought to temporarily freeze space and time into a flat world.

The same can be said of the layout of Katsura Detached Palace which unfolds as one wanders through its meandering gardens. There is no opportunity to take in the whole from a single vantage point. It is a two-dimensional world divided between different moving vantage points marked on a continuous path. And its theatrical effect unfolds dramatically in an atmosphere of dim grey.

This two-dimensionality is characteristic of the aesthetics of Japanese culture in general, whether in painting, music or theatre, architecture or city design. Japanese culture contains an anti-sensuality of time stopped that results from the reduction of three-dimensional to two-dimensional space; a continuity that is produced by the symbiosis of two contradictory elements. These elements produce the ambiguity of Japanese culture that dissolves the boundaries between two different dimensions and simultaneously preserves them both. The idea of Rikyu grey as I have conceived it is a paradigm of that process.

The illustrated scrolls of ancient and medieval Japan are a ready example. With disparate materials and disparate scales of measurement, they depict events in space and time on a single flat surface creating a quality very different from Western painting, based on the rules of perspective.

Japanese architecture too – in particular in the evolution of space from the *shoin* style into the *sukiya* style, as seen in Katsura Detached Palace and the tea rooms of Rikyu – differs greatly from Western architecture. Its material is wood, not the bricks and stone of the West, and it does not aim to create space as a solid physical entity. Japanese architecture is like a stage set in which various facades stand independent of each other. Each facade represents a mental image of a scene that transcends mere actuality.

In Japan, plans for buildings only came to be drawn with any precision in the 16th century. Before that, carpenters made do with a simple sketch on a board or a set of verbal instructions. While in the West, works of architecture are frequently shown from a bird's-eye perspective in an isometric, three-dimensional format, the Japanese master carpenter was satisfied with a simple

Ambiguity and androgynity in Western stars of today. Pictured here are David Bowie (*ABOVE*) and Michael Jackson (*BELOW*).

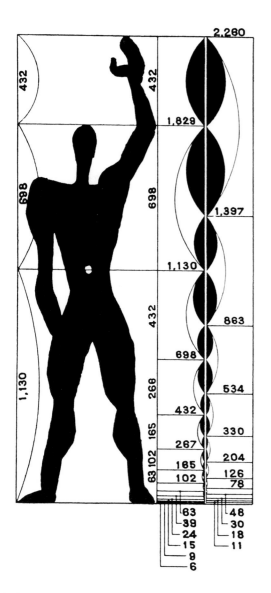

floor plan or elevation. This illustrates my suggestion that Japanese architecture is by nature an unfolding of plane surfaces and facades.

In Nambo Sokei's *Nampo Roku* we find the following remarks about Rikyu's tea rooms:

> Over and over again it must be stressed that the profound meaning of the tea ceremony is to be found in the grass hut. The proper tea ceremony of the aristocrat's mansion using the elaborate daisu utensil stand, scrupulously observing the strictures of rank and form, is the worldly law. The small grass hut and the garden path leading to it, on the other hand, are the transcendent law. Though based on the scale of the formal ceremony, they transcend it, abandon all techniques, and return to the state of no mind.

Similarly in architecture, while the *shoin* style strictly observes established measurements and proportions, the ideal of tea-room architecture is to 'transcend the scale [of established measurements], abandon all techniques, and return to the state of no mind'. There can be no greater contrast between this architectural ideal of freedom and flexibility and that of the classical West which has been firmly based on standard, even sacred, measurements and proportions from its beginnings in Greece and Rome to the modules of Modern architecture.

The claim that Japanese architecture is standardised because of the standard dimensions of the tatami mat is very much mistaken. As a rule, tatami always have been made on site and the dimensions of each mat are different. Though there are guidelines for the dimensions of tea rooms, their measurements are not standardised, and in practice they are constructed by transcending the scale and abandoning all techniques. Rikyu's ultimate tea room design far transcended the four and three-quarter mat plan, as he reduced tea room space to one and three-quarter mats. He triumphed over the physical limits of measure and scale to create an expression of spiritual space.

From the Western perspective, Rikyu's low ceilings and small windows and doors would be regarded as far too restricted and cramped. And the coexistence of so many apparently conflicting design details – round windows, the natural log tokonoma pillars, multiple ceilings of different materials, and the many different shapes and sizes of openings in the walls – is impossible to understand from the context of Western hierarchy and order.

In traditional Japanese architectural design – including that of tea rooms – ceilings, floors and walls, each with their own differing design elements and materials, are treated as independent realms. Each is an independent two-dimensional world that forms a planar surface and refuses to join in a direct three-dimensional relation with other surfaces of the same structure. The sizes and placement of windows in two adjoining walls, for example, are frequently totally unrelated to each other. This is another method of reducing space to two dimensions.

At any rate, Rikyu grey space contrasts sharply with Western space. In the

ABOVE: Le Corbusier's *Le Modulor*. Standard, strict proportions in total contrast to the ideal of Japanese architecture which attempts to abandon all techniques and return to a 'state of no mind'. *OPPOSITE*: Kisho Kurokawa, Ishikawa Cultural Centre, Kanazawa, 1977. Tiled on the exterior in Rikyu grey, providing a dramatic ambivalence transcending materiality, the building attains a state of insubstantiality and stillness.

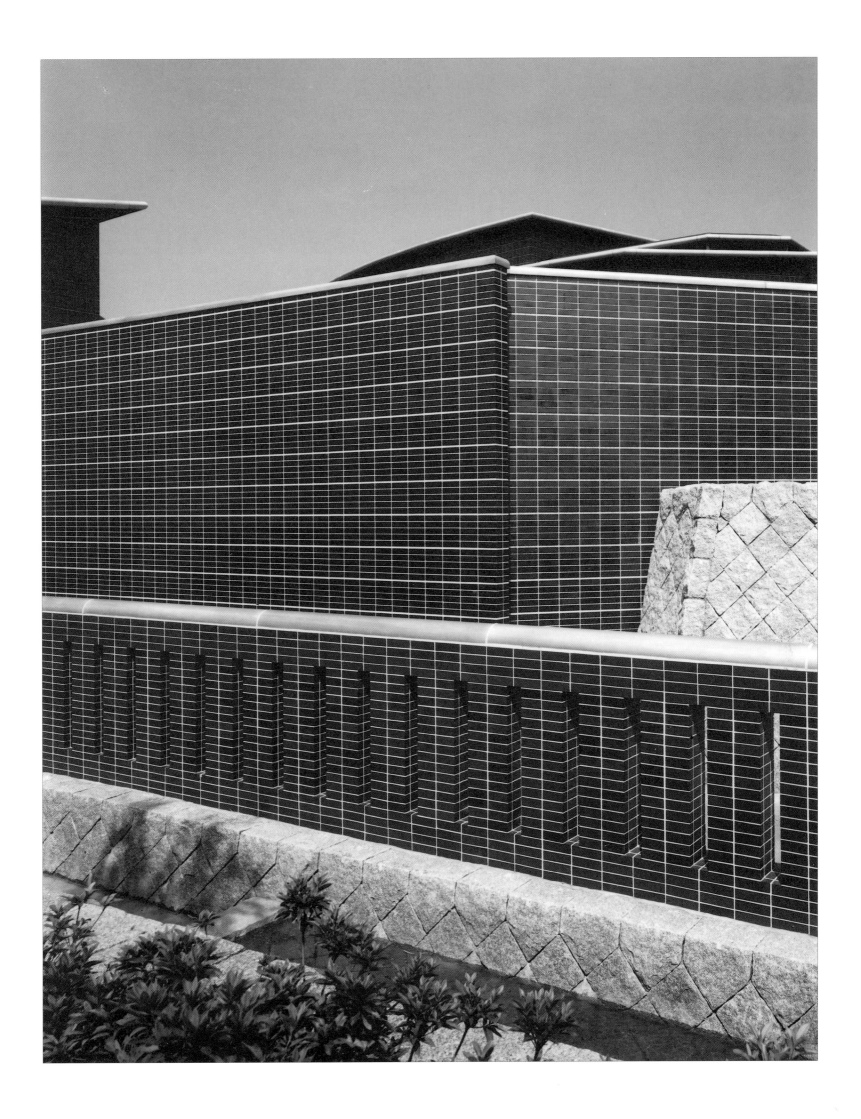

West, space is three-dimensional, sculptural, substantial and unequivocal; Rikyu grey space is planar, painterly, insubstantial and multivalent — an ambivalent, ambiguous space.

I have interpreted two of my own works in terms of Rikyu grey, the Ishikawa Cultural Centre (Kanazawa, 1977) and the Osaka National Ethnological Museum (1978). Both are tiled on the exterior in Rikyu grey, and the other materials of the buildings — the aluminium dye-cast eaves, trim, granite, Angola stone, aluminium and stainless steel — are unified in a palette of grey to charcoal. I hope no one will leap to the conclusion that what I mean by the aesthetic of Rikyu grey is that the colour grey should be used in works of architecture — though I believe it does have a unique quality. All buildings are constructed in defiance of the laws of gravity, and each expresses its own feeling of gravity. The colour grey creates an extraordinary sensation of suspension, as when the sun sets on the streets of Kyoto. Grey cancels out the physicality of the building materials; it is simply one method of making space self-sufficient and providing a dramatic theatrical ambivalence.

What these two buildings of mine have in common is a collision of two disparate structural and material elements, straight lines and curving lines, resulting in an extraordinary sensation of symbiosis. The ceilings and walls of the Ishikawa Cultural Centre are also made of aluminium plates, whose colour produces a strange stillness in the building's interior. Another feature of these works is the symbiosis of traditional and modern elements creating a state of tension between resistance to tradition and sympathy for it. At any rate, Rikyu grey is the term I have coined for the aesthetic of ambivalence and insubstantiality produced by the symbiosis of disparate elements.

Soku and *Senuhima*: **Resistance and Sympathy Combined**

The method of allowing several spaces of different dimensions to coexist can be found in many different forms within Japanese culture. Fujiwara no Teika writes of the technique of the *soku* (distantly related verses) in his *Gu Hi Sho*:

> The finest poetry is not to be found among 'closely related verses,' or only rarely at best. It is precisely because these verses are all too predictable, each phrase taking up so surely after the previous one — roots connecting to the branches, branches connecting to the leaves, and so on — that everything is so plain and ordinary with hardly anything unusual. In 'distantly related verses', however, each phrase stands apart from the next, the better for the unexpected to come about.[2]

'Closely related verses' are linked one to another directly by theme, just as leaves sprout from a branch. 'Distantly related verses' by contrast, are completely different in subject from the verses that precede and follow. From this contradiction, extremely strange and unique verses can be created, such as this example by Fujiwara no Shunzei:

As evening falls

From along the moors the autumn wind

ABOVE: Kisho Kurokawa, Ishikawa Cultural Centre, Kanazawa, 1977. *OPPOSITE:* Kisho Kurokawa, Osaka National Ethnological Museum, Osaka, 1978.

Blows chill into the heart,
And the quails raise their plaintive cry
In the deep grass of secluded Fukakusa.[3]

The poetic effect here does not come from self-explanatory links between images but rather from the way the dissimilar images are juxtaposed. As with Rikyu grey, space between the images lifts us beyond the physical plane with multivalent, ambivalent images.

This technique is similar in its operation to Zeami's 'interval of no action' (*senuhima*). In his *Kakyo* under 'Connecting all the Arts Through One Intensity of Mind', Zeami wrote:

It is often commented on by audiences that 'many times a performance is effective when the actor does nothing'. Such an accomplishment results from the actor's greatest, most secret skill. From the techniques involved in the two basic arts down to all gestures and the various kinds of role playing, all such skills are based on the abilities found in the actor's body. Thus to speak of an actor 'doing nothing' actually signifies that interval which exists between two physical actions. When one examines why this interval 'when nothing happens' may seem so fascinating, it is surely because of the fact that, at the bottom, the artist never relaxes his inner tension... during any pause or interval, the actor must never abandon his concentration but must keep his consciousness of that inner tension. It is this sense of inner concentration that manifests itself to the audience and makes the moment enjoyable.

However, it is wrong to allow an audience to observe the actor's inner state of control directly. If the spectators manage to witness this, such concentration will merely become another skill or action, and the feeling in the audience that 'nothing is happening' will disappear.

The actor must rise to a selfless level of art, imbued with a concentration that transcends his own consciousness, so that he can bind together the moments before and after that instant when 'nothing happens'. Such a process constitutes that inner force that can be termed 'connecting all the arts through one intensity of mind'.[4]

The pause and silence between one action and the next is of utmost importance to the Noh performer, because it is the moment for the expression of his inward sense of mindfulness. This same thing can also be found in the Buddhist concept of emptiness (*sunyata*) and in Rikyu grey: the gap left unfilled becomes a transitional, complex, silent, multivalent space.

The concepts emptiness, Rikyu grey and the interval of no action all have differing ranges of meaning. Linking them and probing the peripheries of these concepts is my own method for creating a context for space.

From Mannerism to the Baroque

When we look for the aesthetic of Rikyu grey in Western culture, we find it in the Baroque and in Camp. In his book *Lo Barroco*, Eugenio d'Ors writes:

Actor in Noh drama. As Zeami has written: 'The actor must rise to a selfless level of art, imbued with a concentration that transcends his own consciousness . . .' corresponding with emptiness, ambiguity and Rikyu grey.

Whenever two conflicting intentions are conveyed in one act, it belongs in the category of Baroque. Simply put, Baroque means not knowing what one wants to do: agreeing and disagreeing at the same time. It is wanting to fly while being weighed down by gravity. Here is the source of the round pillar, in which two opposing sentiments take a single, coexisting form. The spirt of Baroque tries to raise the arm while lowering the hand ... Lord, your posture in Coreggio's *Noli me tangere* in the Prado is the formula for the truly Baroque ... Mary Magdalene lies at your feet. You reject her attentions and invite them at the same time. Whilst you say to her 'Do not touch me' you hold out your hand to her.

You leave her defeated and weeping on the ground as you teach the way to Heaven. And she, too, who repents her past sins while still longing for you, is the epitome of Baroque.

Lord, while she tries to follows you, she remains stooped below you ... This is an eternal reality, the eternally feminine; and that, of course, is a particular style, the style of the Baroque.[5]

But I have not selected the Baroque to discuss formal artistic styles. I see in the Baroque a means of expressing linked opposites, or as D'Ors says, the eternally feminine that wishes to assent and oppose at the same time, a sensitivity equivalent or at least similar to Rikyu grey. In the Baroque age science and technology continued to develop, after their reawakening in the Renaissance; yet no other age has emphasised so strongly the expression of human spirituality and emotion. Perhaps this was the one point in Western history when Rationalism and non-rationalism existed in symbiosis, fostering a non-dualist spiritual climate.

The term Mannerism was used to suggest artificiality and shallow imitation by art critics of the 17th century in a derogative description of the work of artists in the second half of the previous century. In like manner, they coined the word Baroque, meaning a flawed pearl, to denigrate works that broke the strict aesthetic rules laid down in the canons of Greek and Roman antiquity. The category of Baroque art, then, is an extremely broad one, and many works included in it are not examples of the aesthetic I am describing.

For me, the works from the Mannerist period through to the early Baroque are the most relevant; towards the end of the Baroque period an excess of decoration led to a loss of tension.

The Church of Il Gesu in Rome, the facade of which was added by Giacomo della Porta around 1575, is an example of the Baroque symbiosis of rational and non-rational.[6] It is built in the shape of a crucifix, in a mix of medieval and Renaissance styles, their elements combined with great freedom and a subtle sense of balance. The Palazzo Massimo, built around 1536 by the mannerist architect Baldassare Peruzzi, displays the same sense of ambivalent balance.[7] Nicolas Poussin is, perhaps, the painter whose work best corresponds to that of Peruzzi in architecture.[8] D'Ors calls him an artist with 'a passion for rationality'. His reaction against the Baroque produced work with a balance full

ABOVE: Giacomo della Porta, Church of Il Gesu, Rome, c 1575.
BELOW: Gian Lorenzo Bernini, *Ecstasy of Saint Teresa*, S. Maria della Vittoria, Rome, 1646.

of tension between rationality and passion; Poussin's *Inspiration of the Poet* is a work of charged stillness.

Bernini's *Ecstasy of Saint Teresa*, El Greco's *Adoration of the Shepherds* and Tintoretto's *Goddess of Fortune Banishing Vices*, for example, all testify to the special ambiguity of the Baroque sensibility, a fusion of rational and emotional, the symbiosis of the desire to take wing and the quiescent, downward pull of gravity. But when the Baroque reaches the stage of Francesco Borromini's interior decoration of the church of Sant'Agnese in the Piazza Navona, it becomes too fantastic, and the aesthetic of Rikyu grey is no longer to be found.

Katsura Detached Palace and Hiunkaku as Baroque

The Toshogu shrine is usually cited as an example of the Baroque in Japan, but this does not fit my definition which equates the aesthetic of Rikyu grey with the Baroque, or Mannerism. My interpretation of Baroque is of a style in which opposing elements such as the firmly anchored and the floating, stillness and motion and straight and curving lines, exist in disjunction and symbiosis at the same time, creating a balance of quiet tension.

In that sense of the term, nothing can compare with the Yodomi tea room of Saioin as an expression of Rikyu grey and Baroque. The frame of the entrance leading from the preparation room to the host's mat is a study in the harmony of disparate elements: a curving arch, white colour and gracefully rounded edges. It is simultaneously dynamic and quiescent. The use of a curving line to demolish the classical order is a typically Baroque technique, but for me the Yodomi tea room is an even more accomplished example of the Baroque spirit than Della Porta's facade for the church of Il Gesu, the epitome of early Baroque in the West.

There are many other Japanese examples of the combination of disparate elements. The arbor seat on the grounds of Katsura Detached Palace features a post and beam construction composed of naturally bent tree trunks, each embedded in an earth-plastered wall, yet independent of the wall and unreconciled with it. These elements create a theatrical space of symbiosis, simultaneously in opposition to and in harmony with each other.

Hiunkaku, said to have been a part of the lost Juraku no Tei palace of Hideyoshi but now within the Nishi Honganji temple compound in Kyoto, is another example of my Baroque. Its three-level asymmetrical construction sustains a bewildering variety of different straight and curving lines in harmony, yet achieves an atmosphere of quiet and repose. This is the epitome of my aesthetic of Rikyu grey and the early Baroque.

Ambiguity and Ambivalence of the Boundary or Periphery

The Baroque can also be interpreted from the point of view of ambiguity. It was Herbert Read who stated that English prose incorporated ambiguity through metaphor,[9] while William Empson probed deeper into the subject in his *Seven Types of Ambiguity* (1930).[10] Quoting from Shakespeare, Chaucer, and

ABOVE: El Greco, *Adoration of the Shepherds*, c1604-14. *OPPOSITE*: The Yodomi tea room of Saioin sub-temple, Kyoto; an expression of Rikyu grey and Baroque.

Milton, he posited that poetic ambiguity – the versatility or possibility of accommodating multiple explications – depends on a choice of words or grammatical constructions capable of functioning in several different ways simultaneously depending on the context. His seven types of ambiguity are:

1) When a detail is effective in several ways at once.

2) When two or more alternative meanings are fully resolved into one.

3) When two apparently unconnected meanings are given simultaneously.

4) When alternative meanings combine to make clear a complicated state of mind in the author.

5) When the author is discovering his idea in the act of writing ... or not holding it all in mind at once.

6) When what is said is contradictory or irrelevant and the reader is forced to invent interpretations.

7) When [there is] full contradiction, marking a division in the author's mind.

Ambiguity generated in any of these ways is not limited to literature, but may characterise multiple meanings throughout the arts and culture in general.

As the Japanese anthropologist Masao Yamaguchi points out in his book *Bunka to Ryogisei* (*Culture and Ambivalence*), it is the boundary regions or peripheries which augur the ambivalence of art and culture, where images and symbols that are not given value in the course of everyday life arise continuously on a preverbal level to flourish and form new combinations and unities. Yamaguchi says this principle becomes active when 'the periphery of a culture composed of a homogeneous core reaches out to incorporate heterogeneous elements'.

Such ambiguity and ambivalence may not easily be accepted in the logical, rational climate of the Western world. From the Western perspective of logic and reason, in which culture is conceived on the model of a crystal, homogeneous in quality and of determined form, anything that appears on the periphery of culture is an enemy, a vandal, a heretic. Ambiguity and ambivalence become an issue in the West only when a heterogeneous culture begins to make incursions into the style of the dominant mode, producing a dramatic clash of rationality and emotion, or in discussing a style of literature that approaches poetry. The Baroque was an anomalous phenomenon in the history of Western culture as D'Ors implied in describing the Baroque spirit as a liberal and pluralistic attitude towards heterogeneous, external elements.

But flowing beneath all Japanese culture, as we will see later in our discussion of the logic of identity, is a stream of receptivity and aesthetic awareness which transcends the reduction of experience to logic and rationality. This is the ambivalence of the paired male and female roadside deities, the *dosojin*, harmoniously blended into a single presence; the ancient grave sites, which were treated as transitional space lying between arable farmland and wilderness; the person who lived alone on the village outskirts; the Janus-faced bridgekeeper-maiden who would take people's lives if angered or bestow rare treasures upon them if pleased – pioneering folklorist Kunio Yanagita's literature is so full of examples of cultural ambivalence that they form the rule rather than the exception.[11]

What is important now is to stop insisting on the uniqueness of the Japanese cultural tradition, and to see how Japanese culture is linked to world culture at large, articulating its values in those terms. This is another aspect of the parallel between the concept of Rikyu grey and the Baroque.

Aldo Van Eyck's Twin Phenomena and Martin Buber's I and Thou

In this context the works of Aldo van Eyck, Louis Kahn and James Stirling are of interest.[12]

The Dutch architect Aldo van Eyck's Twin Phenomena Paradigm has shattered the barriers of dualism with the two-sided declaration, 'The city is a big house and the house is a small city'. Van Eyck's most representative work, his children's home in Amsterdam (1960), is a combination of basic spatial units, but the architect has endowed his work with a theatricality that transcends its incremental structure. In some areas, the floor level changes; in others, the units are joined to produce a large open space that, in the dramatic play of light, dissolves into the whole. The children's home is a fine example of his Twin Phenomena Paradigm.

Van Eyck's theories have exerted considerable influence on architecture around the world, but what is of more interest to me is the fact that they are based on Martin Buber's philosophy of I and Thou.[13] Buber says that for human beings, the world is double in that it conforms to dual human attitudes. The basic I-Thou relation entails both being chosen and choosing; it is simultaneously active and passive. The realm of it (es) exists in a complex of time and space where the Thou does not exist. When the relationship between I and Thou is structured in such a way that it is simultaneously passive and active, both parties in the relationship are simultaneously 'I' and 'Thou'. Unless that sort of relationship is established, the 'I' is nothing more than a series of individual 'its'.

Buber's philosophy rejects the Western concept of the self, transcends the rational order of Western thought and approaches the philosophy of Buddhism: indeed, Buber frequently quotes Buddhist texts of the Pali canon. In Aldo van Eyck's Twin Phenomena Paradigm, then, Buddhist philosophy has been introduced into the thought of Modern architecture, providing it for the first time with a non-Western ambivalence.

Architects of Ambivalence

As Charles Jencks has indicated in his *Modern Movements in Architecture*, the issue of ambivalence or multiple meaning is the key to the most important current happenings in art, architecture and culture.[14]

The Leicester University Engineering Department (1963) designed by James Stirling is a dramatic sculptural form created from glass and repeated structural units. While the materials are traditional – brick and glass – the way in which

Aldo Van Eyck, Children's Home, Amsterdam, 1960.

the glass tetrahedrons of the roof project outward in angled facets and are set at a 45° angle to the facade, culminating in several towers, makes for highly dramatic architecture. The two materials are handled with commonplace techniques, yet a tense, symbiotic expression is created. The Engineering Department building also manages to unify two completely contradictory treatments of space: space compartmentalised and space as membrane.

Stirling's strategy is even clearer in his building for the Cambridge University History Faculty (1967). The glass membrane cast over the research wing, laid out in a series of stretches broken at 45° angles, creates an internalised exterior space of ambivalent nature. At the same time it stands in firm opposition to the compartmentalisation of the building's functions, producing a strong tension. The building also incorporates details ranging from traditional English town workshop architecture to echoes of the most modern communications satellites, while preserving a very restrained atmosphere. Isn't this equivalent to Poussin's 'passion for reason' in the *Inspiration of the Poet?*

The work of American architect Louis Kahn also demonstrates a coexistence of compartmentalisation and anti-compartmentalisation. He is one of the rare Modern architects who creates space that is both intellectually stimulating and aesthetically dramatic. His laboratory buildings for the Salk Institute, La Jolla, California are divided into a research facilities wing and a core, but that compartmentalisation is achieved through a balance of tensions, creating an extremely controlled and restrained state of symbiosis. It is of the same lineage as his Medical Research Center at the University of Pennsylvania (1964), which earned Kahn recognition as an architect of international standing.

Kahn's use of masonry and arches at the Institute of Management, Ahmedabad, India (1974), transcends the opposition between tradition and the present, technology and art, creating a quiet yet dramatic symbiosis between these supposed opposites. His Kimbell Museum of Fine Art (1972) achieves a unified and highly sophisticated, multivalent effect through the simple repetition of arches as a means to compartmentalise space. The concrete walls, the marble and the lead-slate roofing collide and, at the same time, achieve an ultimate repose; a feeling of movement within stillness. *Architectural Forum* (July-August 1972) lyrically describes Kahn's sensitivity:

> The mind of Louis Kahn is a cross between a gaslight and a laser beam. It is a mind full of connections, respecting the past and yet perceiving the future emerging from it. It is a mind full of compassion, having known poverty, having known the frustrations born of talents isolated from opportunities. It is a mind full of grace, of grace under pressure. It is a mind ever searching for tranquility amidst turbulence, and for continuity amidst contradiction. A mind reaching out to pull tight the final ring. To amass harmony in the service of man.

I am convinced that similar examples of the ambivalence and multivalence of space occurred in the early period of Modern architecture. In Charles Rennie Mackintosh's sketches for 'Haus eines Kunstfreundes' (1901), we discover an

LEFT: James Stirling, Leicester University Engineering Department, Leicester, 1963. *BELOW*: Louis Kahn, Institute of Management, Ahmedabad, 1974.

unsettled settledness in the tapestry of subtly curved and straight lines.[15] The Savings Bank of Otto Wagner – who declared that art is ruled by necessity alone – in Vienna gives an ambivalent feeling with its restrained combination of curving and straight lines.[16] All of these are examples of an architecture of ambivalence, and they constitute a precious resource in that they exhibit a conception of space lacking in contemporary Modern architecture.

Camp

There is another 'aesthetic' that has much in common with Rikyu grey and the Baroque, and this is Camp. Camp is an aesthetic of our present era, which coined the term; it is a type of contemporary sophistication. Camp turns its back on the customary aesthetic judgements of good and bad and offers a different way of appreciating the arts.

Camp tells us that there can be a beauty that includes ugliness, a slightly eccentric handsomeness, a charm that cannot be described as good or bad, a beauty that transcends classical harmony, a joking seriousness. This has much in common with the aesthetic of symbiosis.

According to Susan Sontag's essay, 'Notes on Camp', its origins can be found in the mannerist artists Jacopo Pontormo, Fiorentino Rosso and Caravaggio.[17] The highly theatrical paintings of Georges de la Tour are another example. In literature, the Camp sensibility begins with the euphuism of John Lyly and continues with Ruskin and Tennyson; in music, we find it in the works of Giovanni Battista Pergolesi and Mozart. It is present in the Baroquism of Art Nouveau and the disturbingly beautiful Sagrada Familia Church of Gaudí; and Joseph von Sternberg's film *The Devil is a Woman,* starring Marlene Dietrich can be seen as a Camp masterpiece. It is the Camp sensitivity that sounds a warning against modern architecture, too tightly bound to the rules of the past, and the triteness of the industrial products of good design.

The mannerist painters used shot colours to intensify the sensual effect of their subjective and capricious style; Pontormo, one of the key figures of Mannerism, in his portrait of Giuliano de Medici, creates a sense of tension of barely arrested motion. This portrait projects the same feeling as Pontormo's sculpture of the Madonna with child at the Church of San Michele in Florence.

The mannerists employed Michelangelo's *contrapposto* (tension between opposite sides of the body) and rejected the proportions of the Renaissance. Incorporating an intellectual foresight into their works, they created a new style in which feeling and intellect coexisted in a state of tension. One of their best known techniques (*maniera*) was Caravaggio's use of light, later known as *chiaroscuro.* His painting *Fortune Teller* contrasts light and dark to intensify the dramatic impact of the whole while still upholding an ambiguous balance.

Camp emphasises the complications of human nature and of space. This is Sontag's 'Urban Pastorale', the odd falsity, the androgyny, behind Greta Garbo's perfect physical beauty. In the Camp sensibility, Marilyn Monroe and Jayne Mansfield are too physically feminine; they cannot express Garbo's

ABOVE: Jayne Mansfield. *BELOW:* Marlene Dietrich. *OPPOSITE:* Greta Garbo. In a camp sensibility, a figure like Jayne Mansfield is far too physically feminine, conveying only one obvious message. In Dietrich and Garbo however, we see an indescribable charm and read a double, androgynous message.

double, androgynous message. In the same vein, we might say, 'This work of architecture is too perfect; it has no Camp'.

As Jean Genet said in his *Notre Dame des fleurs,* in order to find a sense of multiple meaning within culture, good taste requires an awareness of what is bad taste. A Camp consciousness, in other words, is a heightened sensitivity to double and triple levels of meaning where a particular phenomenon is interpreted in more than one way.

Our contemporary age has been characterised by the functionalist trend to minimise inconsistencies and increase efficiency by rational planning. This driving force behind modernisation worldwide is attested by the birth of the International Style in architecture and international standards of good design. We have achieved our initial ends; is it not time we returned to the starting point, to the actual ambivalent quality of the life we humans live? Admittedly, the acceptance of seemingly chaotic ambiguity may be difficult. I do not mean to reject the fruits of functionalism, nor the self-conscious over-achieving of 'good design'. But hasn't the time come for us to broaden our perspectives outward to the peripheries of possibility, and inward to the boundaries of the human spirit? – a spirit that in its original nature is indivisible, rich with ambiguities and harmoniously balanced; in fact, a world of Rikyu grey.

The fashion that has been created by the Japanese designers Issey Miyake and Rei Kawakubo is a true fashion of ambiguity, an androgynous fashion in which the extremes of wealth and poverty, male and female, ostentation and restraint live in symbiosis, creating a free and wide-ranging style.

LEFT: Fashion by Rei Kawakubo. *RIGHT*: Fashion by Issey Miyake.

Kisho Kurokawa, house in Al-Sarir, Libya, 1979-84.

An Experimental City
in the Desert

One of the projects I was working on in 1979 was the design of a desert city in Libya. This was an interesting case of putting the philosophy of symbiosis into practice. The town, planned for the Sarir region in southwest Libya, provided a concrete example of the symbiosis of Arab and Japanese culture and of tradition and the latest technology.

Some years earlier, I had been asked to design an international conference centre in Abu Dhabi. Although the project never materialised due to local political problems, my planning work in Abu Dhabi served as a beginning for my involvement with the Middle East. One day the leader of one of the emirates invited me to look at some housing that had recently been built. He explained that to encourage the establishment of towns in the desert they had commissioned an American architect to design housing, but it wasn't working out very well.

The population of the United Arab Emirates at that time was only about 1.3 million and its per capita income was the highest in the world. The country was trying to encourage its Bedouin population to settle down in towns and villages by providing free housing. The Bedouin were a migratory people who lived by hunting and pasturing livestock. Though they built shelters of sun-dried bricks, they frequently moved from place to place and usually lived in tents. This large migrant population made it difficult for the country to achieve the modernisation its leaders desired – providing a basic education to Bedouin children, for example, was clearly a problem – and the government wished to encourage the Bedouin to settle in towns and villages.

I went with the government leader to inspect the housing built by the American architect. When we arrived at the site, a strange scene greeted my eyes. The housing was two-storey concrete American-style residences of the kind one might encounter in California. Each unit was completely air-conditioned and had an attached garage. And there they stood in a row, in the middle of the Arabian desert.

As we approached, however, I saw that the Bedouin had set up their tents next to the houses and they had put their sheep, together with livestock feed, inside the units. I proceeded to investigate the reasons for this. The first problem, it turned out, was with the air conditioning. In the desert, the temperature rises as high as 40 degrees centigrade. Air conditioning has little effect in such temperatures, and of course it breaks down; but you can't call a local appliance repairman to come out and fix it that day – repairs take at least

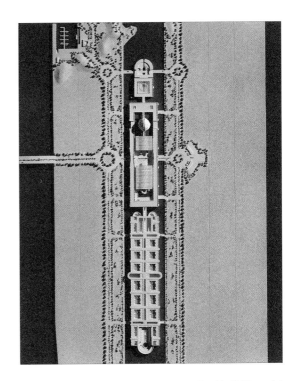

Kisho Kurokawa, Conference City in Abu Dhabi, 1985, model showing the influence of the traditional Heian grid on urban planning.

a month. All that time the concrete boxes are ovens. Not only that, but the heat that builds up in the walls throughout the day is released at night. Though it is already cool outside, the concrete is a powerful heater, roasting anyone inside the walls. Of course no-one could live in this environment. That is why the owners had set up their tents outside and put their animals inside the California-style housing instead.

When I looked at their tents, however, I was struck by how very well suited they were for life in the desert. While the surface temperature in the desert rises and falls dramatically, there is almost no temperature variance from a point three metres below ground level. When the air temperature rises to 40 degrees centigrade during the day, it is only 20 degrees at three metres underground. And when the air grows cold at night, it is still 20 degrees three meters below ground. In desert climates, the air temperature drops to as low as five degrees at night; 20 degrees is very warm in comparison.

During the day, when the Bedouin sit in the shade of their tents, a cool breeze rises from the ground. At night, they sleep on skins and rugs spread on the ground and the rising warmth from underground protects them from the cold night air. The Bedouin exploit their centuries of experience in the desert to achieve the most pleasant and comfortable life they can in their environment. To these masters of the desert, the American architect brought California-style suburban housing.

The Value of Regional Culture

When I met the American architect, I asked him why he had designed buildings that no-one could live in. He replied that he didn't expect the Bedouin to be able to live in the houses from the start, but that eventually the peoples of the developing nations, such as these Bedouin, would have to exchange their camels for cars and their tents for homes and enter modern life. Since that was the case, it was important to teach them to do so as quickly as possible, and training them to live in that kind of housing was one step toward that goal.

Here we see a typical case of the dogma of Modernism, based on the values of the West. According to this way of thinking, the functionalism and technology produced by the industrial society of Europe has raised the quality of human life and is bound, sooner or later, to spread over the entire earth. All cultures are obliged to advance under the banner of Western civilisation; their present states are merely early stages along their delayed path of development. But this way of thinking was already repudiated by Claude Lévi-Strauss, who rejected the idea of stages in cultural evolution and insisted that each culture has its own autonomous value; and that all cultures share a structure. His study of myths and family structures in cultural anthropology placed Western culture alongside others in a larger structure, as one relative member of a whole.

Of course, at certain times in history, one culture may be especially strong and can influence other cultures. At one time Egypt had such power; later, China had an equal influence. Both Rome and the British Empire had their days.

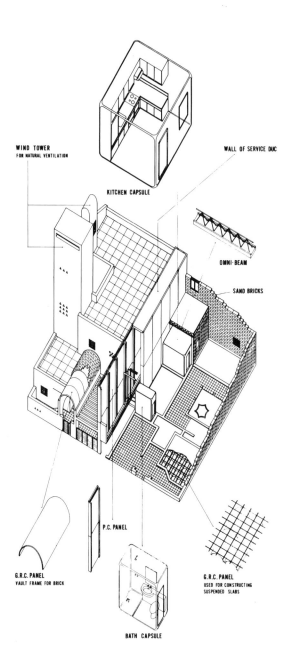

WIND TOWER
FOR NATURAL VENTILATION

WALL OF SERVICE DUC

KITCHEN CAPSULE

OMNI-BEAM

SAND BRICKS

P.C. PANEL

G.R.C. PANEL
VAULT FRAME FOR BRICK

G.R.C. PANEL
USED FOR CONSTRUCTING
SUSPENDED SLABS

BATH CAPSULE

Kisho Kurokawa, house in Al-Sarir, Libya, 1979-84, dissected axonometric.

The power of the United States after the Second World War was enormous; and in the years to come it is possible that Japan may exercise a similar degree of cultural influence: but no one culture can dominate the planet. We must recognise that human life is much richer if each region has its own identity and culture, suited to its people, its climate, geography and history.

Different countries and peoples must recognise their differences, and then look for ways to co-operate with each other. The important question is how different cultures can sustain creative relationships in symbiosis. From that perspective, we cannot but conclude that the thinking of the American architect who built California-style housing for the Bedouin had been poisoned by Modernism.

I recognise that it is easy to criticise others; and I am not just a theoretician, but an architect and urban planner who designs environments. From the time of that encounter in the United Arab Emirates, I continued to think about how I would meet the challenge of building a community in the desert.

Symbiosis of New Technology and Desert Culture

Several years later the opportunity to put those ideas into practice came to me by chance.

The Sarir region is several hundred kilometres to the south of Libya's third largest city, Benghazi. Great quantities of underground water were discovered there. These underground channels moved as much water as a river, and a plan was devised to use them to farm the desert. There were also oil fields near Sarir, which employed many workers. The government of Libya decided on a plan for a new city in the desert, to house the workers and engineers of the oil-fields, the farmers and their families, and the Bedouin of the region.

I was asked to design the project. The first thing I did was to develop a sand brick. It was my idea to use sand – an infinite resource in the desert – as a building material. The Bedouin had been making sun-dried mud bricks from antiquity, but these were extremely perishable and not suitable for housing of any permanency.

After three years of co-operative work with a British scientific research centre, we developed a process for making strong sand bricks that would last for several decades. Our idea was that the houses we designed could be built on a 'do-it-yourself' basis by the owners, using sand bricks.

The most difficult things for amateur carpenters would be the roof, the electrical wiring, and the plumbing. In particular, an arch-shaped roof of bricks would be very hard to build. So we decided to make roofs of a thin, pre-fabricated material that could simply be set and anchored on top of the house. We developed a comparatively simple method of roof production, too: a hollow dug in the sand served as a mould, into which a mixture of concrete and glass-fibre could be poured.

As far as plumbing was concerned, we decided to build a wall of service ducts – all plumbing and wiring were placed inside this double-walled unit. This

Kisho Kurokawa, housing in Al-Sarir, Libya, 1979-84, sand bricks and vault for housing.

also simplified maintenance. The builders only had to place the kitchen and bathroom next to this wall; otherwise, they were free to build whatever sort of house they liked. Unlike a public housing project, each home in this community could have the design and layout its owners wanted and could be different from all its neighbours.

To find out if amateur carpenters could actually put together our design, we conducted an experiment. Some members of my staff who had never done anything but desk-work stayed at the site for three weeks, and with the help of an English assistant, tried to assemble a house. The experiment was a success. Three weeks wasn't enough time to complete the construction, but aside from the final finishing, the houses could be built entirely by amateurs.

The houses I designed had one remarkable feature, a wind tower. This was a tower like a chimney, some 15 metres in height with open slots at the top. When the wind blew through the top of the tower, the warm air inside the house was sucked up and cool air radiating from the floor was drawn upwards to cool the interior. This design exploited the natural air movement patterns of the desert, which the Bedouins put to such excellent use in their tents.

The community in Sarir represented the encounter between the latest in technological advances from an industrial nation and the culture of the desert, the Arab culture. In it, the scientific know-how and advanced technology which allowed us to make hard bricks out of sand combined in symbiosis with the ancient wisdom of the desert.

A New Community Development

When I made the master plan for this desert community, I gave greater importance to streets than to open squares. As the illustration shows, these streets were not laid out in straight lines. I believe strongly in the superiority of streets to squares as public urban spaces. In the Japanese tradition, the street is the front. Here, the streets, gently unfolding from one house to another, are the source of the city's enjoyment. I wanted to allow that Japanese-style street as facade to exist in symbiosis with the community in Sarir. After all, the concept of the street or marketplace (in Japanese, *tsuji*) as a public space was already firmly established in Islamic cultures as the souk, or bazaar – the shopping district in Islamic cities. In old French films you often see a criminal dashing into the streets of the bazaar and disappearing in the crowd – that crowded, seemingly confused maze of streets and shops is what I am talking about. There I found a conception of public space identical to Japan's *tsuji*.

Maze-like streets in a town set in the midst of the desert have the advantage of blocking sandstorms and winds, and they also create much-needed shade. At the peak of summer's heat, you can walk comfortably through the well-ventilated, shaded streets.

In Sarir, my philosophy of symbiosis could be realised on a wide range of levels, from the conceptual to the most practical. The scale of the project was quite large: we were talking about building an entire city from scratch in the

Kisho Kurokawa, housing in Al-Sarir, Libya, 1979-84, master plan and model.

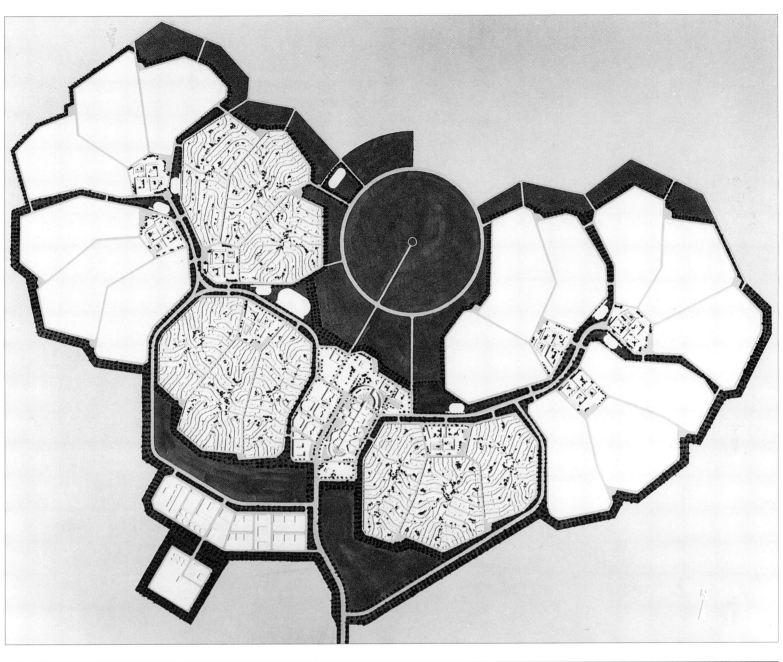

middle of the desert. It is still not finished. But this was no castle built on sand. Eventually, slowly, this sand-coloured city will rise from the desert, and then, just as inevitably, it will return to the sands from which it came.

Symbiosis of History and the Future

Shonan Life Town in the north of the city of Fujisawa in Kanagawa Prefecture is one of the town-planning projects that I have designed – this particular project some 20 years ago. It was designed for a population of 45,000. Some 35,000 are already living there, and gradually it is acquiring the lived-in feeling of a town. Before construction began, about 500 farming families lived in the area, mostly cultivating paddies. The farm houses have been preserved, together with 50 per cent of each paddy area. One of the aims of the project was to allow the symbiosis of urban dwellers and the farming community, the present and the past. This meant organising the parcels of land that became available at widely separated locations according to district, and exchanging farm plots for housing lots throughout the development.

In a farming community there is always a wooded area or a sacred mountain. To preserve the natural environment and this traditional topography, we decided against levelling all the lots and building a grid of straight roads. That would have destroyed the history and the environment of the area. Carefully choosing paths of equal elevation, we built winding, meandering roads, leaving as much greenery as possible and preserving the historical appearance of the farming village. As a result, Shonan Life Town is a great success as a symbiosis of farm and town, with roads as twisting as you could find anywhere.

At one stage, the Ministry of Construction, which was the government agency overseeing the project, objected to the meandering roads and, because they were supplying the funds for the preparation of the site, issued an order to revise our plan. But we stubbornly held to the original plan and were finally able to carry it out. 20 years later, this project is recognised as a model for the development of new communities in the future.

Publicly we emphasised that the preservation of the farming economy was important in the design of Shonan Life Town, but in fact this presupposed the preservation of the historical community – the human relationships – of the area. Brasilia and Canberra are both regarded as poor examples of new communities; in Japan, the Tsukuba Academic City is another rather unfortunate planned community. What is wrong with these new cities?

Many complaints are voiced that they are one-dimensional, dominated by the automobile, separated from other cities and isolated. They are cold, their populations lack variety, there is no community. To sum it all up, these cities all lack symbiosis. Put another way, they have no history. In 50 or 100 years, they will accumulate their own histories. But is that any reason why they must be unpleasant to live in for a century? Is there no way to allow these new towns a symbiosis with history from the start?

There is. As in Shonan New Life Town, new communities must be built as

Kisho Kurokawa, Shonan Life Town, Fujisawa, 1967.

much as possible in symbiosis with the existing historical community or town, and the entire city should not be planned in advance. One part of it must be set aside and allowed to develop in a natural way. Such development always results in a maze. New communities that possess their own mazes, that live in symbiosis with history, will be places that are attractive and enjoyable to live in.

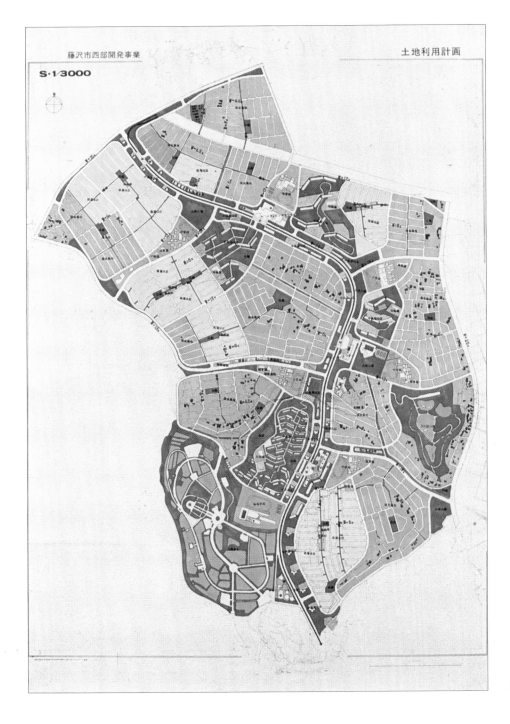

Kisho Kurokawa, Shonan Life Town, Fujisawa, 1967.

The Philosophy of the Street and Intermediary Space

***Engawa* as Symbiosis of Interior and Exterior Space**

One could say that the difference between Western and Japanese space is that Western space is discrete and space in Japan is continuous. Western architecture is created to conquer nature and the significance of the wall, dividing exterior from interior, is very great for this reason. Japanese space, by contrast, seeks to harmonise architecture and nature, to make them one, by enveloping nature in architecture and making architecture and nature equal partners. The wall as a divider between outside and inside did not evolve in Japan, partly because of a difference in the basic materials of the two cultural spheres: Japan is a culture of wood, and the West is a culture of stone or brick. But in addition, in Japan there has always been a conscious effort to integrate inside and outside.

The sense of space in traditional Japanese architecture is one in which inside and outside interpenetrate. In the country house where I spent the war years for example, we always opened the sliding exterior doors from the first light of morning, no matter how cold it was. The garden would be filled with snow; or in another season, the buds of spring would be opening and the air filled with the fragrance of flowers. In Japanese homes of the *shoin* and *sukiya* styles, there was always this kind of unobstructed interpenetration of interior and exterior; a symbiosis with the world of nature, where house and garden are one. In the West we have the picture window; the window as a frame, with nature as the painting it frames. Nature is seen as something 'out there'. An important feature of the Japanese house is the *engawa* verandah. The *engawa* runs around the house as a projecting platform under the eaves and unlike the terrace in Western architecture, serves as an exterior corridor, intermediating between inside and outside. While it protects the interior from wind, rain, and, in the summer, the strong rays of the sun, it is also a place to entertain guests and an entrance from the garden into the house. The *engawa* takes on a wide variety of functions not provided for in the conventional plan of a series of rooms linked by interior hallways.

The *engawa* is interior space, in that it is beneath the eaves; but, at the same time, it is also part of the exterior space of the garden. In our old country house, formal guests would be received in the guest room, but local merchants and neighbourhood friends would come calling to the *engawa*, to sit down and have a cup of tea and chat. Thus the way of receiving guests was distinguished spatially according to the meaning and the role of the guest.

Kisho Kurokawa, Kyoju-so villa and Ritsumei-an tea ceremony house, Hachioji, Tokyo, 1979; *engawa* space running around the house beneath the eaves.

My concepts of intermediating space or elements are linked to the idea of reintroducing a space that permits this kind of communication among people, unobstructed by any dualistic division between inside and outside, a space free from the divisions of walls. I have identified a variety of architectural details – the space beneath the eaves, or *engawa*, corridors, and lattice doors among them – as intermediating elements, and I have also studied the ambivalence and multivalence that boundaries and peripheral spaces possess.

In discussing the theories of space in Metabolism in 1960, I emphasised the importance of intermediating elements and spaces. Just as emptiness in Buddhist philosophy is a very real, if intangible entity, intermediating elements and spaces do not always necessarily take physical form. Studying the concept of the street in traditional Japanese urban space, I began to realise that an intermediary element or zone need not always be physical. And I found in the half-public, vague zone of the Japanese urban street a kind of space that was profoundly meaningful in a way which far transcended the space of the Western square.

Open Squares versus Streets

When the Japanese first travel to a Western city, what surprises them most is undoubtedly the open squares – the Piazza San Marco in Venice, the Campidoglio in Rome, any plaza in a European city is its face. We cannot conceive of a Venice without San Marco.

Public buildings such as the church and the city hall, as well as the marketplace, are grouped together around the central square. The Western city often developed with the square or plaza as its centre, from which streets projected in a radiating pattern. As the city's population expanded, other squares sprang up, and the cityscape was given a more sculptural and spatial treatment. But behind the square, away from its lively view were the backstreets – dark, dangerous, and utterly without charm. In a city structured around central authority, these backstreets were its unseen, dark face.

In the ancient Greek city of Miletus the streets were narrow pathways lined on both sides with stone-walled houses. The only openings were tiny windows, showing that the street was not considered a part of daily living space. People met and interacted on their patios and in the marketplaces, the *agora*. The streets were laid out, in fact, with a secondary function in mind: they served as sewage canals to flush away waste when it rained.

In contrast, Japanese streets were not merely transportation routes. They were part of the fabric of daily life and took the role of a space for communication. As many Japanese words testify – 'crossroad sermons', 'crossroad shrines', and 'crossroad fortunetelling' among them – the crossroads (*tsuji*), or street, was an exciting space that made a variety of encounters possible. Not only do the streets of Eastern cities perform the function of the square in the Western city, that of binding the life of the private citizen to the life of his city; but the Eastern street also possesses, at the same time, an ambiguous meaning arising from its double nature: it is simultaneously public

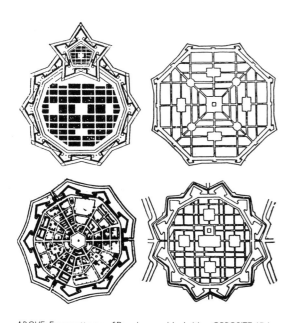

ABOVE: Four patterns of Renaissance ideal cities. *OPPOSITE*: Kisho Kurokawa, Saitama Prefectural Museum of Modern Art, Urawa, Saitama, 1982. In this detailed view of the museum we can observe the use of the lattice which acts as an intermediating element allowing an ambivalence of boundaries.

and private space, city space and residential space.

In addition, the street has no definite starting or ending point; it has a multivalence that responds to a wide variety of places and times. While the Western square has a clearly assigned function and spatial definition, the street has no single assigned spatial function. Functioning now as a space for private life and at other times as a space for public life, the Eastern city street has various complex, overlapping and profoundly multivalent roles.

Streets of the Sun and Wind

In the Vedic texts of ancient India we find the statement, 'Streets are the core of the city. Those streets are the streets of the sun and the streets of the wind.'

The Vedas offer four ideal shapes for cities: *dandaka, nandyavarta, padmaka,* and *swastika.* All of them are basically lattice or grid patterns of intersecting streets. In size, they range from 1,200 metres on a side to 7,500 metres on a side, with two-thirds of the total area reserved for farming plots. Houses in these cities ranged from 7.3 by 4.8 metres to 12 by 9.6 metres and each had a central court for domestic animals.

The cities' streets were laid out by first using a sundial to determine two axes. The *rajapata,* or king's way, ran east and west, and perpendicular to this, running north and south, was the *mahakara,* or broad avenue; together these streets formed the backbone of the city.

There were no squares in these ideal Vedic city plans. Public facilities and temples were set along the two main thoroughfares, and a bodhi tree was planted at their intersection. The bodhi tree was believed to have given birth to the sun, moon and stars. Though the tree was a spiritually powerful cosmic symbol, it was not the city's core. That social function was performed by the bright *rajapata,* on which the sun shone from morning to night, and the *mahakara,* cooled by the breezes constantly blowing down it.

The sunny *rajapata* must have been a lively place when the long rainy season finally ended, while the *mahakara* was a cool sanctuary into which people suffering during the sweltering summer nights could carry their beds and sleep under the stars. City festivals took place on these two avenues, while religious processions were held on another road, the *magaravici,* or road of blessings, that circled the city. In ancient India, the street was a multivalent space that functioned in many ways.

The Symbiosis of Activities in Street Space

This tendency can be seen in the urban space of Japan as well, based as it is on the open structure of our wooden houses. In the ancient capital of Heian (Kyoto), for example, there were no squares. Temples, shrines, and public facilities were set along the roads. Without a central plaza or core, it was a multi-coloured checkerboard of streets divided into broad avenues and narrower lanes. Citizens of relatively high social status lived along the avenues. These were the thoroughfares along which the ox-carts of the nobility were drawn, and down which the many festivals and processions paraded. The

Four patterns of Vedic ideal cities.

avenues were the framework that linked the citizens to their city both ceremonially and in terms of secular authority. In contrast, the small streets, like those that can still be seen weaving in and out among the houses of the townsmen in Kyoto's Nishijin District today, formed the actual arena of city life. The avenues divided the city into large areas and districts; the streets crisscrossed those districts.

The areas on both sides of one street would be known by a single name – for example, the smiths' district, or the armourers' district – and make up one interrelated unit. On both sides of the narrow streets, less than three metres in width, houses exploited the open construction of wooden frame design and through the device of the lattice, created a shared space with the street. On hot summer nights the streets would fill with people seeking the evening cool; through the lattice doors, people could be seen chatting and laughing. Sometimes the room facing the street was used as a shop. If the avenues were places of ceremonies, festivals, and displays of authority, the streets were an extension of residences; a place for the activities of ordinary citizens.

According to Kazuhiko Yamori, author of *Toshizu no Rekishi* (*History of City Plans*), this type of Japanese urban space developed from the latter half of the ninth century through to the tenth century. Before that time, the street was like a river, separating or encircling communities – in other words, an obstacle. In Heian in the ninth century, the square residential blocks surrounded by streets were called *machi*. These were later divided into four equal parts by drawing diagonal lines connecting the corners, and each of these parts was called a *cho*. Finally, the *cho* on opposite sides of the intersecting street were united into one unit. It was Toyotomi Hideyoshi who completed this urban structure based on the street. Hideyoshi made the streets of each *cho* the communal property of the residents of the district and exempted the street space from taxation.

This inconspicuous urban structure possesses great significance. What had previously been the basic unit of urban activity, an area bounded by streets, was transformed into a unit that incorporated streets, with its own commercial identity. Hideyoshi's policy was conceived against the historical backdrop of the disbanding of the medieval guilds (*za*), the establishment of free markets and the flourishing of a new urban culture with the rise of industry and commerce. This led to the development of the Kyoto-style urban residence (*machiya*) with the street as the core of the community – which was thus in turn a further encouragement to commerce. The *machiya* facing each other across the intersecting street evolved architectural features to exploit the common central space. In addition to lattice doors and windows, attached benches and horseguards (*kurumayose*) emphasised the continuity of the street with the open-structured wooden houses facing it.

The lattices of the *machiya*, for example, allowed an appropriate amount of openness while simultaneously guarding the privacy of residents. The people in the street outside and those inside the house could sense the others' presence as they went about their activities. The street space was neither totally public

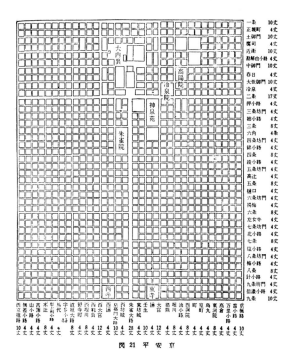

City plan of Ancient Heian (Kyoto).

nor private but an intermediary zone, performing the same function as the *engawa* between house and garden.

Thus the street has traditionally played an important, if intangible, role in Japanese society. Since the enactment of a new system of urban districts in 1962, however, Japanese cities are divided according to a system of districts and wards. In imitation of the West, areas surrounded by streets are the new units of urban space. These have been renamed for the convenience of computerised record-keeping, and the old *cho* and their names are disappearing. Wonderful old historical names such as Kajimachi (Smithies' District), Teppocho (Armourers' District), Bakurocho and Temmacho (Post-horse District) have been replaced by inoffensive, abstract, bland names such as Heiwa (Peace), Midori (Greenery), Kibo (Hope), and Hibari (Lark). I am working, as vice-president of the Zenkoku Chimei Hozon Remmei (All-Japan Place-names Preservation Society), to revise that1962 law, for I am convinced the new system of districts will doom our communities built around the streets to destruction.

An Inviting Architecture of the Street

The function of the street in the contemporary city continues to be of vital importance, and the revival of the street as it existed in Eastern cities is more appropriate than ever in city planning today. I do not of course oppose streets that are restricted to automobile traffic. Looking at the present state of our streets in which passenger cars, lorries and bicycles are crowded dangerously together, I have come to the conclusion that alternative systems of commercial intra-city transport must be developed (for example, underground tunnels) and that the urban motorway system, both intra-city motorways and bypass loops and belts, must be improved. At the same time, however, it is important to build city streets that also function as living space.

All over Japan today there is an interest in making the city a scenic place, and the preservation movement is also making gradual headway. But even in cities like Kyoto and Nanazawa, where so many historic buildings remain and we can stroll through history, there are not enough streets along which we can enjoy a pleasant and safe walk. Increasing pedestrian walkways is one answer. To allow automobiles and pedestrians to exist in symbiosis we need not restrict ourselves to a system of streets exclusively for either cars or people; experiments that allow them to share the same streets are now under way.

In mixed residential and commercial districts, for example, road humps can be installed to slow traffic and trees planted in islands in the road, and architecturally interesting, arcade-like streets can be built. All of these are methods which can be put into practice in order to restore the originally ambivalent, multivalent nature of street space.

When all urban space is divided into public and private, as it is today, restoring to the streets their nature as an extension of communal living space is a way to make our cities more habitable and interesting. I called my design for the Nishijin Labour Centre in Kyoto (1962) 'Architecture of the Street'; that

ABOVE: Road humps in a Japanese street. *BELOW AND OPPOSITE*: Lattice doors of traditional house in Kyoto, creating a shared, intermediary space with the street.

project aimed to create a new street space to make up for the streets already usurped by automobile traffic. To create a building that presents intermediary space as architectural space, on the other hand, we may employ the technique of the symbiosis of interior and exterior space. The lobby of the headquarters of the Japan Red Cross Society (1977) is an example of the interpenetration of interior and exterior space, creating an overlapping, multivalent intermediary zone. In this work, the lobby is clearly an interior space, but the ceiling is a glass arch, through which an opening to the sky is visible. The floor is water-polished red granite in the shape of a waterless pond that reflects the whole. The lobby presents a dramatic series of reversals from interior to exterior and back again.

In the design for the Main Office of the Fukuoka Bank in downtown Fukuoka City, I allowed for a large, 30-metre *engawa*-like space beneath the eaves. There are trees, sculpture, benches: it is a place to relax. Though the land is the property of the bank, people are free to use this space at any time of day or night. They can read or meet to chat; in the summer cicadas fly in and thrum from the trees: it is a simulation of nature.

The Daito Seimei Tokyo Building was designed for the space between the Nishijin Labour Centre and the Main Office of the Fukuoka Bank. Because the lot was bounded by two streets, front and back, I planned to create a new street space that permitted people to pass through the site. This space cut through the building and was a re-creation of the traditional *machi,* on both sides of the street: it had shops, trees, flowing water, streetlight-like illumination, and street furniture. Light – as well as rain to fill the man-made river – entered through an opening that divided the building in two. This space was designed to represent an opposition and symbiosis of interior and exterior.

Hasn't our urban planning since the war, based on the logic of functionalism, too strictly separated private from public space? Taking their cue from the Western doctrine of reason, our cities have been divided into cramped individual, private spaces and broad public spaces including our roads. Now that our streets, which once had many uses, are overflowing with vehicles, they have lost their image as scenes of dense urban life to become perilous rivers that separate us. This separateness can only increase the alienation of urban dwellers. Without going so far as to entirely outlaw cars from cities, there is certainly a need to restore the importance that the intermediary space of the street once played in our lives.

One of the important tasks of the philosophy of symbiosis is to offer an architecture that incorporates intermediary space, full of charm and mystery as an alternative to the rationalism and dualism of Modernism.

Creating Relations Between Opposites

The concepts of intermediary space and ambiguity are important keys to understanding the philosophy of symbiosis. In the West, dualisms are transcended through the dialectical method of resolving opposites on a higher level. The two opposites are either unified into a single entity, or one of the two is negated and rejected. Symbiosis instead creates a dynamic relationship

ABOVE: Kisho Kurokawa, Fukuoka Bank Main Office, Fukuoka, 1975; view of 30-metre *engawa*-like space beneath the eaves. *OPPOSITE*: Kisho Kurokawa, Fukuoka Bank Main Office, Fukuoka, 1975.

between the two elements while allowing them to remain in opposition. A relationship between two opposing elements can be achieved by placing spatial distance (a neutral zone) or temporal distance (a cooling-off period) between them.

In Western society, neutral zones and cooling-off periods have historically been regarded as negative and undesirable. In the contractual society of the West, all decisions are spelled out in legal agreements; ambiguity and intermediary zones are avoided. Contemporary America is a typical contractual society; perhaps mutual trust is only possible among Americans within the rules of a contract, since the nation is a conglomeration of so many different ethnic and cultural groups. It is impossible to carry on business in America without lawyers, and situations that most Japanese would regard as easily soluble with a little discussion soon evolve into legal proceedings to be argued before a court. In contrast, many projects in Japan are undertaken on the basis of verbal promises. Except in the most extreme circumstances, acquaintances or companies in a supplier-customer relationship do not carry any grievance to the courts.

Trust, in Japan, means trust without contracts. When a problem arises it is settled by making mutual adjustments. For such a procedure to work there must be room – in other words, ambiguity and intermediary space – for adjustment. The more two parties are determined to draw up a contract that provides for every future risk and contingency, the more inflexible their positions will become. Perhaps in the process their mutual peace of mind will be assured to a certain extent, but genuine understanding and the desire to deepen the relationship with the partner in the future will be much less likely.

The limits of attempting to control all human transactions by the Western contractual system are increasingly apparent, particularly in this international age, when many different nations, enterprises and individuals are living in peace although standing in opposing relationships of benefit and harm, profit and loss.

Creating a Discontinuous Continuum

Traditionally, Japanese ambiguous means of communication, such as the verbal promise and the non-verbal communication (called *haragei*), may not be completely effective as they are; but there is a crucial need to create a new system of human transactions in which some allowance for adjustments is overlaid on the present contractual system. Allowance for adjustments would derive from those keys to the philosophy of symbiosis, intermediary space and ambiguity.

In Japan, we say that we *undertake* (literally, accept and carry) an architectural project or other contractual obligation. The term implies more than the obligations specified in the contract. Whereas non-Japanese construction companies regard their relationship with the client firm as finished when the work specified in the contract has been completed, in Japan we feel a moral responsibility to look after a building we have created thoughout its life. After a typhoon, for example, the contractor will get in touch – even though the building may have been standing for decades – to enquire whether it has been

Kisho Kurokawa, Nishijin Labour Centre, Kyoto, 1962, 'Architecture on the Street'.

damaged and to enquire about any necessary repair work. This way of thinking applies not only to the construction industry but to all human relationships, and reflects a relationship of trust.

The concept of *ma* or interval is strongly rooted in Japanese life, the arts and in traditional architecture. One who hasn't grasped the concept of *ma* and is difficult to get along with, a fool; is called 'a person lacking *ma*' (*ma no nuketa hito*, or *manuke*). *Ma* is both spatial distance (a neutral zone) and temporal distance (a cooling-off period). Those who properly space (*ma*) their words are effective speakers who create a deep impression. When two sides are in fierce opposition to each other, it is often surprisingly easy to adjust their conflicting claims by inserting a *ma* - that is, a cooling-off period of waiting.

In the writing of Chinese ideographs, the space between the lines is more important than the lines themselves. This space is not nothingness; it means or speaks as much as the lines. *Ma* is also important in folk songs and Noh chants. The *engawa* is a space, a *ma*, inserted between nature and building, exterior and interior. This type of intermediate zone functions as a *ma* permitting two opposing elements to exist in symbiosis. Intermediate space makes a discontinuous continuum possible, so that a plurality of opposing elements can coexist in an ever-changing, dynamic relationship. The nature of intermediate space is its ambiguity and multivalence. It does not force opposing elements into compromise or harmony, but provides the key to their living symbiosis.

A Mandala – a schematic image with symbolic circular
figures showing the Buddhist symbol of the universe.

The Philosophy
of Consciousness Only

The *Alaya* Consciousness – neither Matter nor Spirit

I named my tea room, my place for retreat and quiet thought, Yuishikian, or the Hut of Consciousness Only, in honour of the Buddhist philosophy of Consciousness Only. For me this is the key to a philosophy of symbiosis which can help us transcend the dualism of Modernism. The philosophy of Consciousness Only is one of the major supports of Mahayana Buddhism which is deeply rooted in Japan and occupies perhaps the most important place within Buddhist religion.

The appearance of the Buddha wrought a great change on the world of Indian thought and religion. Prior to the Buddha, the concept of *samsara*, or transmigration, had been one of the central concepts of the Indian tradition: it was believed that all phenomena were bound to repeat themselves infinitely over the cyclical span of cosmic time. Another important feature of pre-Buddhist thought was the concept of the absolute self, *atman*, its identity with the ultimate truth of the cosmos, or *Brahman*.[1] The *atman* was destined to pass through life after life, its fate decided by the good and evil deeds of the self.

The Buddha, however, denied the existence of the absolute self. He taught that no self-existing, integral, unchanging, and imperishable subject existed. Instead, a series of selves was born and extinguished from moment to moment. This was the revolutionary Buddhist teaching of non-self (*anatman*), which denied the existence of *samsara* as a substantial entity.

It was the philosophy of Consciousness Only which eventually reconciled the opposing notions of *samsara* and non-self. According to the teachings of Consciousness Only, the subject that migrated was not a self but a consciousness – or, specifically, the *alaya* consciousness. The *alaya* consciousness was part of the human subconscious, a source of inexhaustible possibilities and potentialities.[2] The *alaya* consciousness contains the sources or seeds, known as *bija*, of all existence and every event.

As the seeds ripen and come into contact with causes and conditions, they appear as actual phenomena. At the same time, those phenomena produce instant feedback in the *alaya* consciousness. The *alaya* consciousness is the source both of all matter and spirit. In sharp contrast to the Cartesian declaration of existence being divided into matter and spirit, the philosophy of Consciousness Only insists that matter and spirit are both manifestations of a certain primal existence. I see the *alaya* consciousness, neither matter nor spirit, as akin to DNA – a life code, a life energy, and find it fascinating that the intuitions of religious philosophers of ancient India have reached across the boundaries of time to harmonise with the discoveries of modern science.

Good, Evil and the Intermediate, Neutral Zone

The earliest teaching of Consciousness Only can be traced back to Nagarjuna.[3] Before Nagarjuna, Buddhist thinkers centred around the numerous *Prajnaparamita,* or Perfection of Wisdom, *sutras.* They are now sometimes called the *Madhyamikas,* or Those of the Middle View and their philosophy was based on the concept of emptiness (*sunyata*) in which all phenomena were no more than conventional names. The material world was a phantasmal thing, a parade of names and concepts without true existence. Nagarjuna revised and systematised this school of thought, rescuing the concept of emptiness from falling into nihilism. In his *Mulamadhyamika Sastra,* he states, 'I am not a nihilist. By rejecting both being and non-being, I illuminate the path to nirvana.' Nagarjuna articulated his 'unobstructed middle way' in the famous Eight Negations of the Middle Way, and from his interpretation of the concept of emptiness originated a philosophy that transcended Western dualism.

Some time after his death, in about 300AD, Nagarjuna's thought took shape as the *Sandhinirmocana Sutra,* which is also regarded as the first scripture of the Consciousness Only school. In the centuries that followed, three great Buddhist thinkers appeared who fully developed and firmly established the Consciousness Only philosophy: Maitreya, Asanga and Vasubhandu.[4] The central concept of the Consciousness Only philosophy, the *alaya,* is described in the *Sandhinirmocana Sutra* as 'the undefiled and ethically indeterminate consciousness that contains all seeds.' Unlike Christianity, with its sharp distinction between good and evil, the Consciousness Only philosophy recognises three categories: good, evil and the ethically indeterminate, an intermediate zone between good and evil.

A Creative, Indeterminate State

Many creative possibilities with potential for today are concealed in the vague state of the 'ethically indeterminate'. From now on, people will constantly be forced to choose new systems of values. We will often find ourselves in an ambiguous situation where we cannot make clear choices. At least from the present perspective, action based on a simple yes-no dichotomy is no longer an adequate response to society's demands. I believe that a trichotomy, with a third, neither-yes-nor-no element, will become necessary. The state of neither yes nor no is a mode of thinking, when a conclusion may or may not be reached; compared to either yes or no, when thinking stops and becomes action, this is an extremely creative state.

The principle of majority rule, the *modus operandi* of democracy, does not value vagueness. Because of this, it encourages the suppression of thought. It forces us to choose either yes or nor, and the simple majority wins, even if the final vote is, for example, 51 in favour and 49 opposed. But if an indeterminate category were allowed, people could show that they wished to think the issue over further; and the results of their deliberations might well be the opposite of a premature yes-or-no vote. We can even conceive of cases in which the best answer to a question being voted on is, in fact, neither yes nor no. This inherent weakness in our majority rule system will become increasingly important. How we meet the risk of ignoring the category of neither yes nor no and handle it in our social policies will be a major issue from now on.

The Buddhism that has been nurtured in Japan over the centuries is mainly Mahayana Buddhism. As the core of Mahayana Buddhism, the philosophy of Consciousness Only has also made a deep impact on Japanese thought and culture. Its teachings are the key to transcending dualism.

The Symbiosis of Life and Death

I was deeply impressed by the account of Susumu Niwa, a well-known Japanese film director, of his experience of living in the African savanna and the mixture of life and death he observed there.

In a television interview the director explained that the animal realm is one of eating and being eaten. It was completely natural to see a lion, for example, kill a giraffe and eat it. The giraffe cries out when it is killed, but only for a moment. Once the lion has finished with his meal and his hunger is satisfied, quiet returns to the veldt and other giraffes nearby go on peacefully grazing.

In contrast to the intimacy of life and death in the animal world, human beings are convinced that a single human life is the most important thing on earth, a thing of the greatest value. That belief reflects a rigorously dualistic view of life and death. The human fear of death is nearly hysterical when compared to other animals. Could it be Modernism that has inflated that fear to the highest degree?

I saw in the director's remarks a parallel with the Buddhist teaching of migration in which human beings, animals, plants and even Buddhas are given life by a great spirit that transcends phenomenal life and death. The Buddhist teaching of impermanence means not only that all is vanity; it suggests that because this is so, we must live in symbiosis in the cycle of that great life. It may well be that the time is coming when we human beings must arrive at a reconciliation: a philosophy of symbiosis of life and death. The Modernism of the West has taught us that death is fearful and Hell is frightening, so we have denied death and pursued life with all our might. Death is seen as nothingness, non-being, or something even more terrifying. Perhaps it is time to take stock of our situation and look at life and death, this greatest dualism of human existence, in the face.

The Entsu-ji garden, Kyoto, aims to create a *simulacre* of nature as an abstraction. The pleasure gained from the traditional Japanese garden is not from walking around it but from entering an imaginary space while gazing at it; it is also designed with various stops along the walk for viewing the garden.

The Symbiosis
of Man and Nature

'Temporary Shelters' Blending into Nature

Buddhism teaches the impermanence of all things. People, animals, plants, the rest of nature and the Buddhas themselves are always changing, ever migrating within one great chain of life. As human beings existing within that ever-changing process of migration, we must awaken to the ephemeral nature of life. In that context our ideal should be not to conquer nature, nor to hunt our fellow animals, but to live as a part of nature, in accordance with its rules.

From ancient times the Japanese have built their homes as if they were temporary shelters, and they have adopted a lifestyle of symbiosis with nature based on the teaching of impermanence. Yoshida Kenko, the author of *Essays in Idleness* (*Tsurezuregusa*),[1] says:

A house, I know, is but a temporary abode, but how delightful it is to find one that has harmonious proportions and a pleasant atmosphere. One feels somehow that even moonlight, when it shines into the quiet domicile of a person of taste, is more affecting than elsewhere. A house, though it may not be in the current fashion or elaborately decorated, will appeal to us by its unassuming beauty — a grove of trees with an indefinably ancient look; a garden where plants, growing of their own accord, have a special charm; a verandah and an open-work wooden fence of interesting construction; and a few personal effects left carelessly lying about, giving the place an air of having been lived in. A house which multitudes of workmen have polished with every care, where strange and rare Chinese and Japanese furnishings are displayed, and even the grass and trees of the garden have been trained unnaturally, is ugly to look at and most depressing. How could anyone live for long in such a place? The most casual glance will suggest how likely such a house is to turn in a moment to smoke.

Since the home is no more than a temporary shelter, one should not take too many pains in decorating it; even when it has grown old and worn, it is better to leave it as it is and harmonise with it. In the *Nampo Roku*, Sen no Rikyu is quoted as advocating a simple, natural life: 'Lodgings that keep the rain out and enough food to keep us from starving — this is sufficiency.'

Japanese culture is a culture of wood. We have always regularly replaced wooden structural elements in our homes and buildings as they age or decay. In addition, many Japanese buildings have been destroyed by nature's violence, in typhoons, earthquakes, and floods, and we have been forced to rebuild after each natural or man-made disaster. Perhaps the perception of all buildings as no more than temporary lodgings is due to these circumstances as well.

Before modern times, water in Japan was not controlled as at present, by reinforcing all the banks and dykes in each drainage system with stones and concrete. In fact, the approach was just the opposite. A weak place was always built into a dyke or bank where an overflow or flood would do the least damage. This is a natural principle akin to that of the collarbone which acts as a defence of the neck and back bones, by breaking in their place.

We recently dismantled the house that my grandfather and father had lived in for many years, in the countryside of Aichi Prefecture. It was a rush-thatched house thought to date from the mid-Edo period. It had survived the Nobi earthquake in 1891, but had suffered damage on several occasions, and each time it was repaired it was added to and partly refurbished. Even so, our investigation showed that some of the timbers were from the Edo period and had been planed with the characteristic Edo-period tool, the *chona,* instead of an ordinary plane. The reed roof thatching, too, had been changed on alternating sides, once every two to four years.

All of this shows how much work is involved in the upkeep of a wooden house. But the visual appeal of such natural materials as wood, tatami mats and Japanese paper, and even their pleasant smells, are valued by the Japanese who are accustomed to living in an environment intimately linked to nature. Japanese houses exhibit a stronger tendency to merge with nature than to stand in opposition to it. Perhaps we can accept the eventual degeneration and collapse of buildings and dykes more easily because we see this as a part of the rhythm of nature.

Insect Sounds – Midway Between Noise and Music

Another important feature of the Japanese house is its openness. The characteristic post-and-beam construction produces a building with no need for walls. If the sliding paper doors and outer rain doors are opened, the house has a complete openness, with the *engawa* providing an intermediate space between interior and garden. Japanese architecture even incorporates surrounding scenery and nearby mountains into its gardens, through the technique known as 'borrowed landscapes', or *shakkei.* Living hedges, for example, are often used to encircle a home. Unlike a solid wall, a hedge or *ikegaki* doesn't completely block out the outside. While it protects the residents' privacy, it is also continuous with the surrounding natural environment, offering a Japanese type of semi-seclusion.

The word *ne* (roughly translated as sound, but slightly different in meaning, as we shall see below) is another key to explaining the continuity that the Japanese feel with nature. *Ne,* however, describes aural rather than visual continuity. The word for music in Japanese, *ongaku,* means to enjoy sound (*on* is another way to pronounce *ne,* and *gaku* means to enjoy). *Neiro,* or sound colour, means the nature or quality of sound. When things don't work out well

Garden at the Palace of Versailles. The Western garden can be seen as a highly idealised version of nature, with geometric artificial lawns, perfect in depicting man's victory and domestication of nature.

and we are reduced to desperate straits, we 'raise a cry' (*ne o ageru*).

In Japanese homes and restaurants, we have maintained the custom of keeping insects in cages so that guests can listen to their sounds and be reminded of the season. To the Japanese, insect sounds are not mere noise; they are the *ne* of the insects, a natural music. The single word *ne* comprises the music created by human beings and the music of nature, insect sounds, an intermediate zone between simple sound and music – further evidence that the Japanese prefer to live in friendship with nature, linked intimately to it.

The West, Conqueror and Domesticator of Nature

In contrast to Japanese architecture in which there exists a merging with nature, European architecture stands in opposition to it and emphasises its own independence and separateness.

European cities separated themselves from nature by building fortified walls. The stone walls of houses separate the inside from the outside, with their solidity often emphasised by small windows and doors. At the heart of this thorough-going division of space into interior and exterior is the European philosophy of the opposition between humanity and nature. In the European view, human beings conquer, tame and utilise nature. Renaissance and Baroque gardens, for example, are extremely artificial and geometric, mostly comprised of lawns like huge green carpets. We can perceive them as highly idealised versions of nature; to walk through them is an expression of man's victory over nature, his domestication of nature.

What a contrast this presents to the traditional Japanese garden, which attempts to create a *simulacre* of nature as an abstraction. The main pleasure to be had comes not from walking around in the garden but from entering an imaginary world while quietly gazing at it. Of course, many famous Japanese gardens also allow one to stroll through them but the path is usually limited to a sharply circumscribed area; even those built specifically for strolling through, are designed with various stops along the walk for viewing the garden.

From Selling Forests to Sharing Forests

In their relationship with their forests, Japanese and Europeans also show striking differences. Many European forests are crisscrossed by public paths and have man-made clearings and facilities for rambles, in other words, they are a tamed version of nature. They are largely a mixture of broadleaf deciduous and evergreen trees, undergrowth is not a barrier to access and they are quite bright. Woodlands may even be incorporated into city life as a man-made green space. Many European children's tales, such as the stories of William Tell and Robin Hood, reflect life in the forest as a friendly place.

In Japan, on the other hand, forests consist mostly of evergreen conifers. The ground is very damp; thickly covered with brush and there are many snakes, centipedes, and other insects. Most Japanese forests are in the mountains and therefore inaccessible. As a result, from ancient times there has been a strong

Japanese garden. In contrast to the Western garden, this garden allows the viewer to stroll through it, but with the path limited to a circumscribed area.

tendency in Japan to worship the mountains themselves, in an animist sense. They were regarded as sacred places, the dwelling place of the spirits; or a gravesite, the dens of great serpents. The only human being who would live there was a hermit or a defeated warrior in hiding. Forests were not a part of life's daily activities; but for looking at from afar: this was nature as a spiritual support. This Japanese relationship with nature has remained fundamentally unchanged to the present day. The mountains ringing Japanese cities are not incorporated into urban living space; they exist in symbiosis with the city as 'borrowed landscape'. Japanese do not enter the forest of their own volition as Europeans do. In fact, this is a major problem where the preservation of nature in Japan is concerned. Since the Japanese have no direct relationship with nature in their daily lives, they have no awareness of the need to protect the natural environment. The traditional Japanese attitude of symbiosis with nature stands in direct contradiction to our current relationship with our natural environment; the truth is that the natural environment in Japan is very much under threat.

In the international market, Japanese timber forests are no longer successful commercial ventures. This has resulted in a severe shortage of forestry products in Japan, and pushed Japanese forests to the brink of financial disaster. At the same time, many cities are undergoing the same sudden expansion that Tokyo has experienced. Large residential suburbs are growing up around these cities, created by a wide-scale conversion of farm and forest land into housing developments.

We no longer see such phenomena in Europe, because Europeans are accustomed to the appropriate use of the natural environment. Since Europeans know nature more directly, they feel more strongly about defending it. In the future, the Japanese will have to move beyond their abstract spiritual feeling for wilderness and link their forests with urban space, so that they can be properly utilised. To do that, the Japanese will have to change their thinking about re-forestation and the timber industry. Up to now, woods that grow quickly and sell at a high price – ie, evergreens such as cedar, cypress and pine – have been given the highest priority in Japan's forestry industry. Now we must designate zones for planting deciduous trees and create sunnier forests that can also serve as leisure areas. We must restore the symbiosis of humanity and nature in daily life by changing our strategy from one of forests for sale to forests for sharing on a national scale.

The parks of Frankfurt and Düsseldorf are filled with birds, squirrels and all kinds of insects. The symbiosis of the people of these cities with nature – all within a stone's throw of underground stations and motorways – is an impressive sight. Places such as these must be built in Japan.

The Urban Pastorale, A Garden City of Helicopter Commuters

The symbiosis of man and nature involves not only trees, birds, small animals and insects: the things manufactured by human beings also become, as time passes, part of nature. We must recognise not only man-made lakes, canals and forests, but even our cities and our technology as a part of nature. The binomial dualism that insists what God made is nature, and what human beings have made is artificial and therefore opposed to nature, no longer holds.

In the last generation, the majority of Japanese city dwellers were people who had been born in the country and migrated to the city. Their memories of the countryside were still strong and dear to them; it was only natural that they viewed the city as something in opposition to nature. But today some 80 per cent of all Japanese are born in cities. Just as naturally, today most children born and raised in the city, have neither memories nor experience of nature. Ask some children where dragonflies and beetles and other insects come from and they're likely to answer 'the pet shop in the department store.' It is hardly surprising that we have raised a generation which experiences the city as a part of nature and concrete as a kind of earth. The time may well come when the city and its technology are indeed a part of nature.

I have a feeling that the 21st century will see a dynamic symbiosis of the city and nature such as that hinted at by Sontag in her 'urban pastorale' or by Frank Lloyd Wright's futuristic vision of a 'garden city' crisscrossed by commuters' helicopters. In both we see a move away from city or nature, to city and nature in coexistence. Edo, for example, was in fact a completely artificial city. Noboru Kawazoe, in his book *Tokyo no Genfukei* (*Original Tokyo*),[2] relates that though Edo was a city without public greenery, it was dotted with plant markets; its citizens cultivated their own bonsai trees; and the streets and alleys were filled with the blooms of morning glories and flowering gourds. The citizens of Edo were able to nurture a rich imaginative conception of nature through their artificially grown bonsai and potted plants.

The city of the future where people will live in symbiosis with technology, animals, birds and insects, together with potted plants, bonsai and man-made forests, is not far away.

The Communal Space for the Creation of Nature

Environmental protection must go beyond the preservation of Japan's existing forests to include the creation of new forests in great cities like Tokyo. As in the environmental protection and cultural preservation movements of Europe and the United States, action should begin with the contributions of individuals dedicated to protecting our natural and cultural environments. Whether it be to preserve certain cityscapes, cultural treasures or historic buildings; any such movement must start with committed people's contributions, however small, and from there develop into a national cause.

In Japan, however, such action tends to start from the top down, with a group of 'experts' calling for the preservation of nature or cultural monuments and making a loud protest against 'development'. But those same experts either make no effort to raise the funds needed for preservation or they demand the protection of the farm and forest land surrounding the cities. But farms are places for growing rice and vegetables; and forests are the sources of timber and wood products. At a time when these very industries are in trouble and losing money, it is irresponsible to insist that farms and forests be preserved without some form of economic assistance to make them commercially viable for their owners.

We cannot simply rely on the natural environment left to us by our ancestors. In exchange for developing valuable existing sites, we must also work to create new, man-made nature to leave to our descendants. In Tokyo, the huge tract of forest land attached to Meiji Shrine is a good example. This apparently primeval forest was created only 75 years ago. Here we have a vision of the forest not as a holy site or a dwelling place of the spirits, but as nature and as a part of the living space of the city.

In the plan for the development of Tokyo that I will describe in detail in Chapter XII, I have proposed the creation of three forests, each of ten thousand hectares. These are reminiscent of the Musashino forest, which once existed in the Kanto region. They would be mixed woodlands of deciduous trees that would combine in function and feeling two traditional types of wood in Japan: the sacred grove, which surrounded the Shinto shrine of each village in old Japan, and the village wood, planted around the homes in farm communities to protect them from the ravages of typhoons.

This way of thinking is also relevant to the symbiosis of private and communal space in the urban environment. The city today is divided between private property, owned by individuals or commercial enterprises, and public property such as roads and parks, built and maintained with public funds. But there was originally in Japan also an intermediate zone between public and private – communal space. In agricultural communities, water rights and common rights were a sort of communal property shared equally by all villagers. And as we have seen, in Kyoto the street was a kind of communal property, administered by the chogumi, or district organisation. In an Edo urban district, houses were packed together with narrow frontages on the streets of a four-sided block. This district layout left an open space behind the houses, in the centre, which was called the *kaisho*, or meeting place, and this, too, was a type of communal property.

The city of Nagoya was given a unique layout during the Edo period. Each district was, like the city of Edo, divided into long narrow lots facing the main streets. In the narrow, empty space behind the houses a temple or a graveyard was built, with a single narrow path leading from it out to the street. This path was called the *kansho*, or idle place, and was also a communal space.

Nowadays, when we take one step off our own property, we are on land administered by the city or prefecture: so we have no incentive to maintain it. If it is dirty we might call the local authority and complain; but we're not likely to clean it up ourselves. In the days of communal space, however, everyone co-operated to keep the shared area tidy, and it was also a place where children could play without parents worrying about their safety. This communal space

ABOVE: Back alley in Tokyo. Houses packed together with narrow paths between them allow for the crossing over of public and private. *OPPOSITE*: Forest surrounding Meiji shrine, Tokyo. This particular forest, although seemingly primeval, was actually created 75 years ago. The forest forms part of nature, part of the living space of Tokyo.

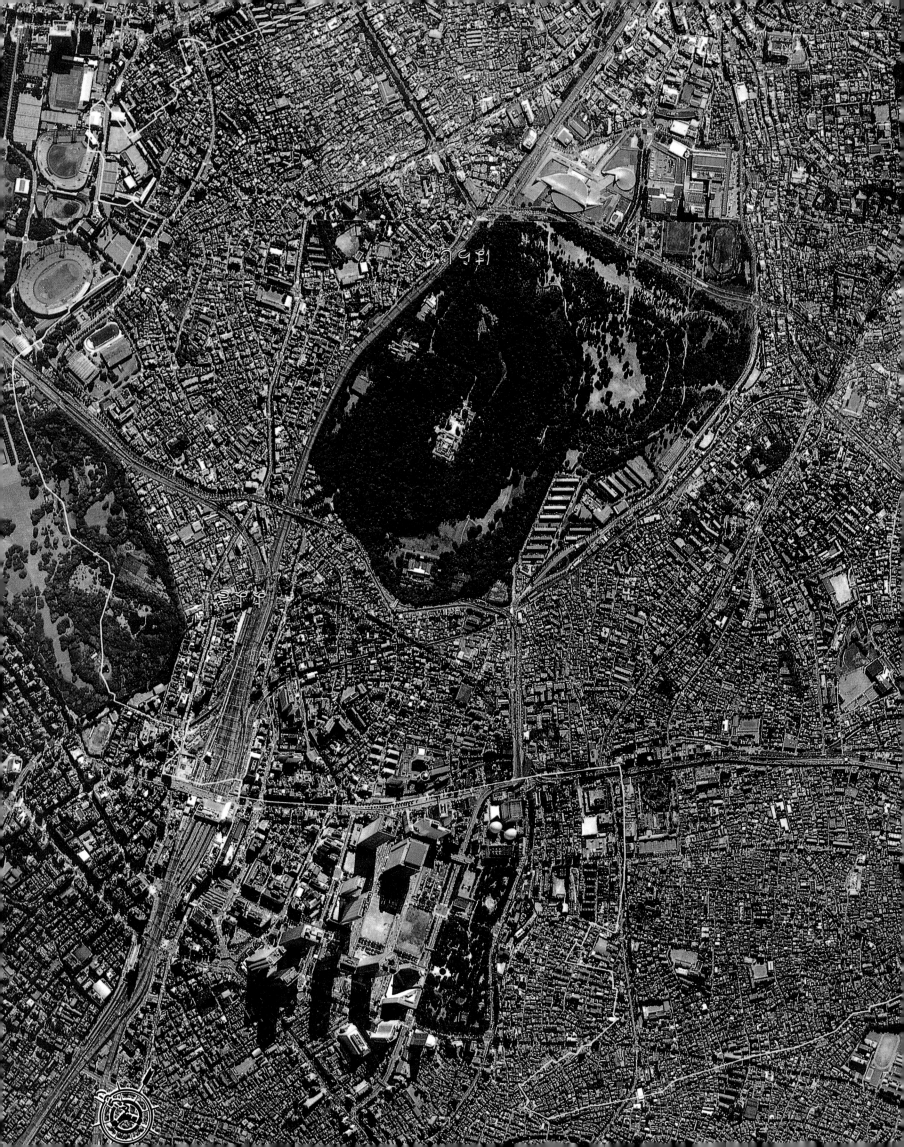

was an intermediate zone between private and public property.

The activities of the National Trust of Great Britain in preserving the environment and purchasing cultural treasures can also be interpreted as defending communal property. In Japan, too, recent interest has been shown in a Japanese version of The National Trust and the grassroots movement to preserve the primeval forest at Shiretoko in Hokkaido is also encouraging.

In the renovation and redevelopment of our cities in the 21st century, we will have to revive communal property; intermediate between private and public, in many different forms. This will be linked to the creation of natural environments within the city which might be little pockets of nature, or even spaces under the eaves of a building. Or, as I created in the Head Offices of the Fukuoka Bank, they might be private property that is open to the public: we must employ a variety of means to assure this.

In Japan, in the past, borrowing landscapes was a way of achieving symbiosis with nature. The Shugakuin Detached Palace is a famous example of this technique of incorporating surrounding nature and natural views into one's own life. This was effective when the population density was low and a rich natural landscape had survived near urban areas. But today, we cannot all borrow nature. In resort areas, many people enjoy nature's beauty but forget what an ugly sight their own vacation home is. The true technique of borrowing landscapes keeps in mind the fact that we are part of the landscape and that someone is looking at us. We must be as concerned with the landscape we lend as the one we borrow.

Kisho Kurokawa, Fukuoka Bank Main Office, Fukuoka, 1975; intermediation between public and private space.

123

The Philosophy of the Karakuri

A Tea Room in the Space Shuttle

In the Western world, technology and humanity have come to be thought of as in opposition to each other. We find the view of human beings as alienated and estranged from nature by technology in Jean-Jacques Rousseau's criticism of civilisation and his call for a 'return to nature'. But no one who objectively considers the contribution of technological progress to our daily lives would reject modern scientific technology.

Ours is not a binomial, dualistic choice between technology and humanity. The challenge that faces us today is how to develop a philosophy that humanises technology. In Tokyo, for example, my study with its IBM computer opens into my tea room, Yuishikian. Here I have created a space in which the latest technology exists in symbiosis with the traditional, natural art of the tea room without the least dissonance. 'A Tea Room in the Space Shuttle' is the slogan I have invented to express the symbiosis of humanity and technology. The space shuttle flying through the heavens does not by itself represent mature technology. Only when a space shuttle is launched that includes a human space such as is represented by the tea room will this technology contribute a new enjoyment and pleasure to human life.

For the Japanese, technology is seen as an extension of humanity. The concept of the symbiosis of mankind and technology goes back to Edo, in the form of a fascination with automata, or *karakuri*. Hosokawa Yorinao's *Illustrated Miscellany of Automata* (*Karakuri zui*) was published in 1798, followed in 1815 by Tagaya Kanchuzen's *Instructional Illustrated Catalogue of Automata* (*Karakuri kummo kagamigusa*). In the same period, Takeda Ominoshojo's automated-puppet plays became popular in Osaka, and the master carpenter Hasegawa Kambei invented various mechanical stage devices for the Kabuki theatre and introduced a new level of spectacle and excitement to the popular stage.

Hosokawa's *Automata* includes a diagram of a prototype of today's robot: the tea-carrying doll (*chahakobi ningyo*). This works in the following way. When the host, seated opposite his guest, places a cup of tea in the doll's hands, it carries the cup of tea to the guest. The guest takes the cup from the doll, and it stops. After drinking the tea, the guest sets the cup back in the doll's hands. It turns around and returns to the host with the empty cup. The mechanism of the tea-carrying doll consists of a spring made from baleen and a complicated system of interlocking gears. The doll is modelled on the form of an adorable child, rather than a machine-like robot. In the Edo period, the technology of a

Sazaedo pagoda at Seishuji, Aizu Wakamatsu, 1796, exterior view and interior view of stairs. The pagoda is an example of *karakuri* architecture, displaying a symbiosis of man and technology. Technology, regarded as an extension of mankind rather than as existing in opposition to it, is here put to aesthetically pleasing purposes in the helix structure of this snailshell (sazaedo) tower.

device was not displayed on its exterior but incorporated invisibly inside it, giving people a sense of wonder and mystery. Machines did not express their own independent identities but mirrored human beings.

Examples of *karakuri* architecture include the suspended central pillar of several pagodas and the helix structures of 'snailshell' towers, or *sazaedo*. The five-storeyed pagodas at the Yanaka Kannoji, built in 1627, and Nikko, built in 1818, both have suspended central pillars that hang from above without actually touching the ground, supporting nothing. The purpose of these central pillars is to lower the centre of gravity of the entire structure, thus stabilising it. Such 'Snailshell' towers can be found in the Sansodo at Rakanji, built in 1779, and the Sazaedo at Seishuji in Aizu Wakamatsu, built in 1796. The outer walls of these halls rise and fall in a helix structure, suggesting the Buddhist idea of migration through one birth after another, making a continuous journey up and down the tower possible.

Technology in Japan has thus been made infinitely attractive through humanisation, in contrast to the unadorned, exposed mechanisms of the West.

Biomation: What Are the Limits of Medical Technology?

Dr Kazuhiko Atsumi, who attracted attention worldwide by transplanting a mechanical heart into a goat and keeping the animal alive for 344 days, has coined the word 'biomation' to mean the application of technology to biology. Dr Atsumi has this to say about biomation in the 21st century:

> The development of technology has led to the replacement of human labour by that of the machine, in other words, automation. The labour accomplished by machines has gradually evolved from physical labour – as in the steam engine, the automobile, the conveyor belt, the telegraph, telephone, typewriter and copy machine – to mental labour, accomplished by computers and the other apparati of 'artificial intelligence'. The end result has been the widespread dissemination of information technology, which has in turn contributed to the evolution of an information society. At the same time, however, this information society has resulted in problems such as standardisation, homogenisation and alienation. To solve these problems, we must learn a lesson from the subtle behaviour of living organisms and from software. In other words, the mating of the automation of man-made technology and the *bio* of living things will give birth to the technology of a new human society. I call this hybrid product *biomation*. The age of biomation will be an age of humanity, of freedom, of multiplicity, of individuality, of art, of leisure and of health and medicine ...[1]

Since John von Neumann's work on automata, thinking machines have greatly increased in speed until they have approached the processes of human thought. In the post-machine age, human beings and machines will grow even closer, and in certain areas, the borders between the two will be crossed, creating a symbiosis between man and machine.

Agriculturalised Society	Instrument	1700
Industrialised Society	Mechanise Motorise Electronise Photonise	1800
Informationalised Society	Informationalise	1900
Biomation	Biolise	2000

ABOVE: Dr Kazuhiko Atsumi's chart showing the relationship between society and technology. *BELOW AND OPPOSITE*: Kisho Kurokawa, Karuizawa Capsule House, Tokyo, 1972, exterior and interior views.

For example, even today some people live with a pacemaker implanted in their heart. Artificial limbs have advanced so greatly that they approach human limbs in complexity. Implants of machines to supplement or replace human biological functions are bound to increase.

The reverse possibility also exists: that human beings could make up one part of a machine. A recent film, for example, portrayed a plasma production plant in which thousands of bodies of human beings in permanent comas were used to produce blood that was then trucked away for use by living human beings. This could be described as a blood factory that incorporated human beings as one part of its production machinery.

Of course most of us feel a strong revulsion at the idea of using coma patients to produce blood. But this will be technologically feasible in the near future. If it should happen, or even before it happens, a tremendous debate could arise: should we permit this? And if we do, are we to think of these coma patients as human beings or as machines?

With the progress of medicine and bio-technology, new and complicated issues of bio-ethics will present themselves. Dr Atsumi has said: 'new medical technology such as heart transplants, in vitro fertilisation, genetic medicine and the synthesis of living tissue is bound to change society's ways of thinking in fundamental ways, and agreement on the values of a new ethics will be required.' One approach to this problem is to distinguish between parts of the body that may be replaced and those that may not. Human hair, for example, is used in thermometers. Hair is undeniably a part of the human body, but since it grows back its use is regarded as acceptable. Blood too is replaceable and there will be no influence on a person's individuality or character even if all of his blood is replaced in transfusion. To a certain extent, skin and organs are also renewable, and in fact they are already being transplanted from one person to another.

If we pursue this line of reasoning, we finally come to the brain, which controls the mental and spiritual activity that is at the core of human personality. As long as the brain is healthy, an individual is himself; all other parts of the body are expendable. The brain does not function in terminal coma patients; on the other hand, they have no will, no thoughts, no feelings. We can regard their state as the extreme in which only the portions of the body that are replaceable continue to live. Of course we should respect the dignity of death, but if there is no chance that brain functions can be restored and the person has previously expressed his agreement, it might well be acceptable to allow that person's body to produce blood for others. It becomes, in the end, a matter of choice for each individual.

The Boundaries Between Life and Death, Man and Machine
I once visited a German hospital where about 20 children suffering from hydrocephalus were being cared for. Hydrocephalus can enlarge the skull to nearly a meter in circumference. These children were all suspended from the

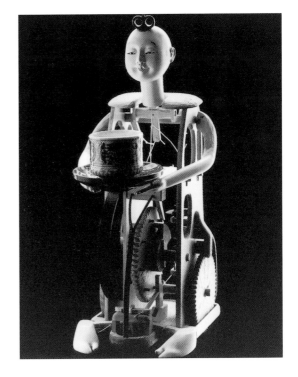

Japanese automatic tea-carrying dolls. The dolls' features are modelled on a human rather than a robot. We can see both the mechanism exposed and incorporated invisibly inside the costume.

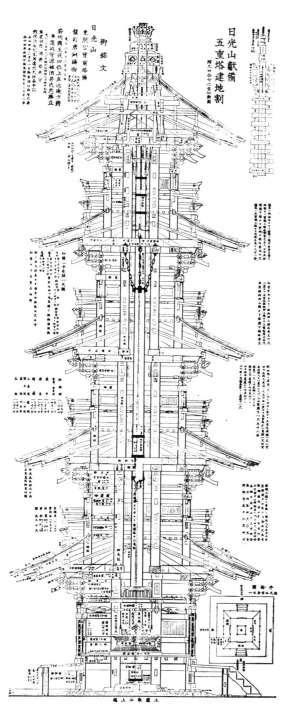

Cross sections of Sazaedo pagodas showing suspended central pillars which lower the centre of gravity of the structure in order to stabilise it.

ceiling, head down. They could not survive in any other position; if they tried to stand, the weight of their heads would break their necks, and lying down their head might be shaken by some vibration, again causing death. But the patients can survive for some time if they are hung upside down. The hospital was making every effort to keep them alive, in the hope that a miraculous treatment would soon be discovered that could cure them. The children smiled at me on my visit. Though their skulls were enormously enlarged, their features were normal in size and seemed to be pulled together in the middle of their faces. But in spite of their smiles I asked myself if these children who, even hanging upside down, would only survive a few years, could be called full human beings, and whether they were happy. Yet clearly the humanist position is to recognise that every person, no matter how weak, has a right to live and must have our assistance. The opposite belief, that the weak and malformed should be killed, is nothing other than Hitler's élitism, the Nazi philosophy of the Master Race.

In practice, most people find themselves somewhere between these two extremes. For example, millions die of starvation in Africa every year. If every Japanese were to donate ten per cent of his annual income to relieving starvation in Africa, all of those victims could be saved. But no one goes that far. Saving the lives of others is a fine thing, as long as it doesn't inconvenience you. AIDS provides another example. Some people insist on AIDS patients' human rights and say we mustn't discriminate against them, while others say they should be quarantined and not allowed to come into contact with the healthy. By defending the rights of the AIDS patient we incur the risk that his fatal disease will be spread to others, as the price of the belief that human life has no meaning unless it is guaranteed to all. As a result, we must reconcile ourselves to the fact that AIDS will spread to a certain extent. Compassion is an extremely expensive proposition, and in a sense it is very inefficient. Nevertheless, we cannot adopt the Nazi philosophy that the weak and 'inferior' should die. Whatever the cost, humanity as a whole must create a structure in which the weak can live with the strong, the sick with the healthy. If the consensus of humanity is that the human race as a whole should be 'improved' and its survival take priority over individual lives, then élitism is of course one way to achieve that goal; but no doubt we will choose instead the way of living in symbiosis with the weak and ill, even if it is inefficient and curtails the survival of the human race.

The advances of science and technology have blurred the previously clear-cut boundaries between life and death, man and machine, and humanity awaits a new ethical agenda. The issue of a symbiosis of mankind and technology, including the complex problems discussed here, becomes ever more pressing as we approach the 21st century.

An End to Hierarchy and Anthropocentrism

Another issue the next century must face is the development of a new way of

谷中感応寺五重塔図

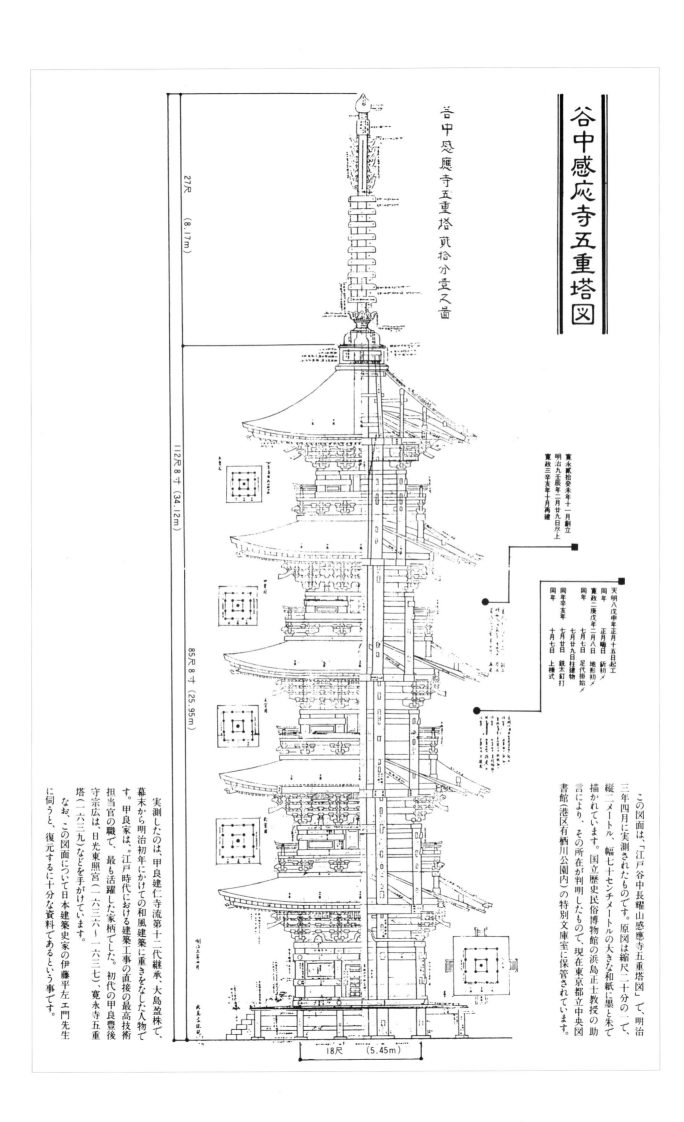

谷中感應寺五重塔 貳拾分壹之圖

寛永貳拾参未年十一月創立
明治九壬辰年二月廿九日尽上
寛政三辛未年十月再建

天明八戊申年正月十五日起工
同年　正月晦日　斫初〆
同年　寛政二庚戌年二月八日　地形初〆
同年　七月七日　足代掛始
同年　七月廿九日柱建物
同年辛亥年　七月廿日　鋲太釘打
同年　十月七日　上棟式

この図面は、「江戸谷中長耀山感應寺五重塔図」で、明治三年四月に実測されたものです。原図は縮尺二十分の一で、縦二メートル、幅七十センチメートルの大きな和紙に墨と朱で描かれています。国立歴史民俗博物館の浜島正士教授の助言により、その所在が判明したもので、現在東京都立中央図書館(港区有栖川公園内)の特別文庫室に保管されています。

実測したのは、甲良建仁寺流第十二代継承、大島盈株で、幕末から明治初年にかけての和風建築に重きをなした人物です。甲良家は、〃江戸時代における建築工事の直接の最高技術担当官の職で、最も活躍した家柄でした。初代の甲良豊後守宗広は、日光東照宮(一六三六～一六三七)、寛永寺五重塔(一六三九)などを手がけています。

なお、この図面について日本建築史家の伊藤平左エ門先生に伺うと、復元するに十分な資料であるという事です。

thinking about life and death, and a corresponding way of living. Society governed by Modernism – that is, industrial society – has placed a higher value on life than ever before in human history. This excessive evaluation of human life is greatly mistaken on two counts.

First, it assigns special value to human life at the expense of all other life. Just as God was once absolute existence, now humankind is, on earth, the absolute form of existence. This anthropocentric hierarchy places human life at the centre and all other life on the periphery. As such, it is natural that this attitude should come under attack from the science of ecology.

But we cannot return the earth to the time when life first appeared on the planet. In the ecology of nature, natural selection operates, and the weak are eaten by the strong. The population explosion of one species drives another to extinction. If our criticism of anthropocentrism is nothing more than an excessive faith in ecology, we fall into the trap of a typical binomial opposition or dualism.

Humankind cannot live without eating other living things. My teacher Shiio Benkyo, in his Buddhist teachings of symbiosis, has described the human condition, the fact that we must eat other organisms to live, as a relationship of mutual living things and life. The Buddha, human beings, animals, plants and the stone by the side of the road all exist symbiotically in an enormous life cycle, living and giving each other life in symbiosis. Human beings consume other life forms as vegetables and meat, fish and rice; and when humans die they return to earth and in turn become food for plants and animals.

The minerals and inorganic materials of the stone by the roadside are necessary to preserve human life. We should neither regard human life as more important than any other form, nor suggest a return to an ecology of a 'pre-human' age. Life and death should only be viewed from the standpoint of a recognition of other life forms. A lifestyle based on an awareness that we are kept alive by other forms of life is the philosophy of symbiosis, not simply to regard other life forms as sources of food and raw materials.

Human Existence in the Intermediate Zone

The second error is to regard man as a single organism separate from all other organisms. Careful thought shows that human beings are not made up of two opposing elements, matter and spirit. Our bodies are populated by a variety of organisms, including different viruses and bacteria and all sorts of inorganic substances, some of which are necessary for life. Most of us also harbour disease organisms and disease-causing viruses. A human being is actually a symbiotic complex made up of a plurality of living things in dynamic relationship with each other.

In contrast, the modernist view of humanity is that we are an unadulterated organism composed of matter and spirit. This abstract model of a human being has come to be accepted, along with a concept of health as progress, or the unending approach to a purer human state. The invasion of any other form of life is called disease and that form is repelled as an enemy or an attacker by classic Western medicine. To kill this invader, a typical Western treatment is surgery – the cutting away of the disease producer and even the 'invaded' tissue with it.

Recently, other methods of treatment are gaining attention, including holistic medicine, which seeks to encourage the body's natural defences and to enlist mental and spiritual energies to assist the body. The techniques of traditional Chinese medicine are also being studied, but the belief that a healthy organism is one from which all foreign bodies and other life forms have been eliminated is a strong one.

An excessive affirmation of life may reflect an absolute terror of death. In the present age there is greater fear of sickness and death than of war. As Susan Sontag has said, sickness, especially such incurable sicknesses as cancer and AIDS, has become an unnecessarily prevalent metaphor for death, for fear, and has thrown society into anxiety.

In their fear of death, people try to avoid the thought of it. To enjoy life, they banish death from their awareness, denying its reality. But from birth we are half-healthy, half-sick. There is no absolutely perfect human, who from birth is completely pure, without any other form of life, who never experiences physical breakdowns. All human beings have some physical imperfection, large or small, and live in symbiosis with other organisms.

Sickness is none other than the collapse of that symbiotic balance, a change leading to death. All humans live in the intermediate zone between total life and total death. The future science of medicine will no doubt learn to preserve that intermediate state of symbiotic balance with disease organisms. The philosophy of symbiosis offers us the prospect of enjoying a coexistence of life and death.

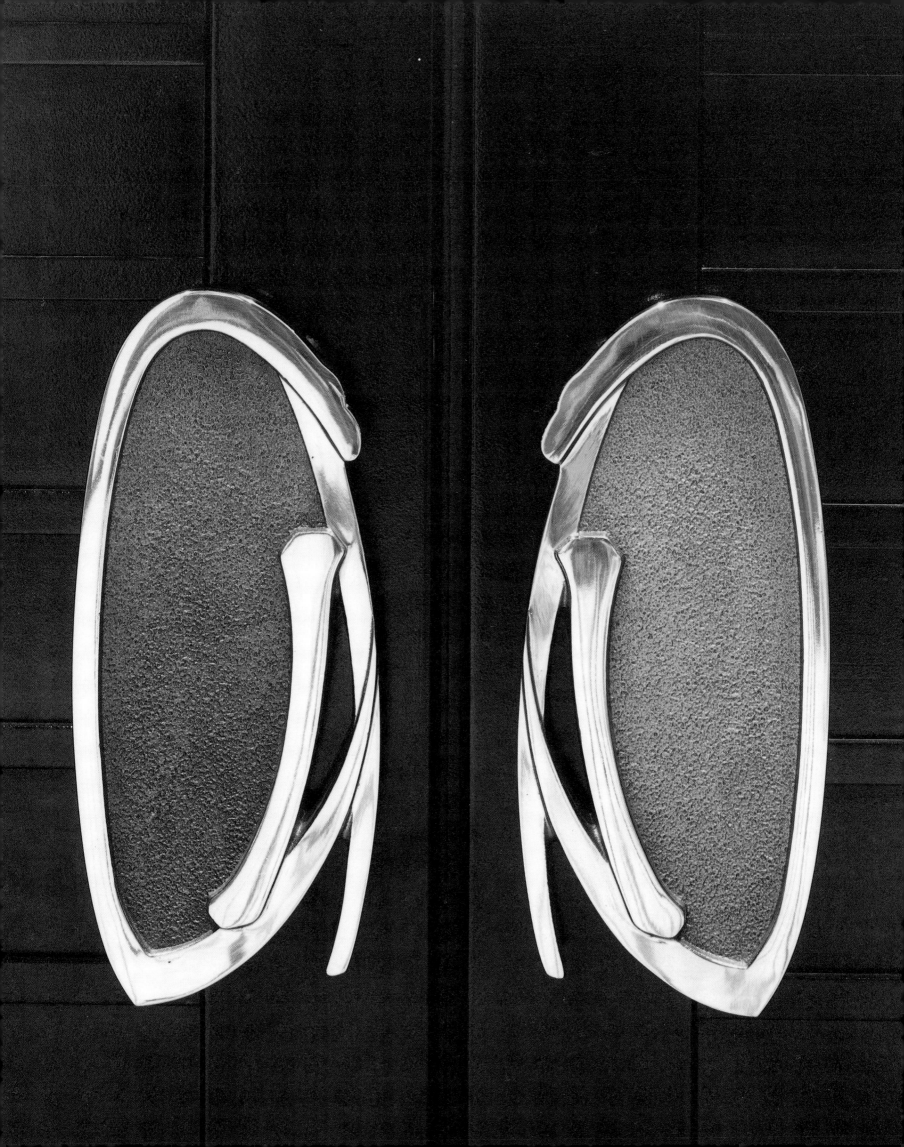

From Post-Modernism to Symbiosis

Single-coded Modernism

As I have shown in Chapter II and elsewhere, the use of Modernism in our daily lives has reached its end. Modernism is based on the pursuit of desires fostered by a material civilisation, and the technology that has made such advances to fulfil those desires has begun to turn against humanity. Environmental pollution, for example, shows us the unfriendly face of technology and we see that even should the human race find a way to survive the practical results of the Modernist creed, it would not be a very desirable survival.

This has led to a reconsideration of the modern period, industrial society, material civilisation and Modernism as a whole, and a search for a new philosophy to replace it in harmony with the present Post-Modern issues. The search for a new culture, art, society and a new state of knowledge has become more and more active. The French philosopher Jean-François Lyotard, in *The Post-Modern Condition: A Report on Knowledge (La condition postmoderne)*, 1979, explains the term Post-Modernism: 'We call the present state of knowledge of our highly advanced society "Post-Modern". This term is widely used by American sociologists and critics at present ... for the state of a culture that has undergone a transformation brought about by the sweeping revision of the rules of the game, beginning in the late 19th century, in the fields of science, literature and art.'[1]

For the world of architecture, Charles Jencks suggested six defining principles of Post-Modernism in *The Language of Post-Modern Architecture* (1977). The first is an architecture that speaks to people on at least two levels simultaneously. A sign on the motorway, for example, 'Exit 5km', has only one reading; it would no longer function if it could be read in different ways. Unless legal codes and government documents have only one clear reading, they cannot serve their respective purposes. They are designed to have, as far as possible, only one reading, clear to all.

Documents of that sort, not surprisingly, do not make for interesting reading. This is the nature of what is called a single code. Novels, however, can be read in many different ways, though they are written with words from the same language as single-code documents. The reader uses his imagination to find meanings beyond the literal, enriching the story with his own experience – that is one of the pleasures of fiction. The more room there is for the reader to participate imaginatively, the richer is the literary quality of the work. In semantics, language that can be read in two or more ways is called a double

Kisho Kurokawa, National Bunraku Theatre, Osaka, 1983, detail of door handle.

code. Or, to borrow Charles Jencks' term, we could call such forms of expression 'multivalent'.

To give another example, an artist who paints with great realism but whose work does not move its viewers is called an uninspired sign painter. However, even among realists and super realists, there are those, such as Andrew Wyeth, who are respected as artists – and those who are not. This is the difference between one who can, and another who cannot, successfully incorporate a capacity for a multivalent reading of his work.

Inarticulate Architecture Transcended

Modern society was above all a single-code society, and Modern architecture was an unreadable architecture, an architecture of steel, glass and concrete that valued convenience and functionality only, from which no narrative could be read. The most representative work of this school is the Lake Shore Drive apartments by Ludwig Mies van der Rohe, completed in 1951. Widely regarded as a masterpiece of Modern architecture, these high-rise luxury apartment towers are extremely abstract in design, a silent architecture that has abjured all historical symbols and narrative quality. The only way in which it can be read as an icon of Modern architecture.

When the Modern Movement was founded by Le Corbusier, Mies van der Rohe and their contemporaries, it was important as a rebellion against the status quo. The French *Académie des Beaux-Arts*, for example, concentrated entirely on the teaching of historical styles and completely dominated the world of architecture. No architect who dared to stray from its historicism, much less challenge it, could hope to find employment. The founders of the movement declared their secession from the *Académie* and their opposition to it, as to all historical styles and decoration.

But the avant-garde role of Modern architecture has now come to an end. The *Académie* long ago lost its authority to the orthodoxy of Modern architecture. At Sydney University in the summer of 1984, I was warned that Post-Modernism was a taboo subject in the department of Architecture – the faculty regarded it as a blight. That is when I realised how Modern architecture had begun to exercise the same unbending, rigid authority as that of the old *Académie*.

I do not totally reject the Modern by any means. My own work always makes use of what I regard as the positive aspects of Modern architecture. But when I see how rigid it has become, how it has lost all flexibility, I am forced to ally myself with those who attack the weaknesses of the Modernist doctrine both of architecture and society.

Modern architecture appeared at a time when abstract art was believed to be more advanced and avant-garde than representative art. Modern architecture was appreciated for its abstraction just as were the painting and sculpture of the age. There is something to be said for the superiority of abstract art over concrete representation. After all, while other animals can only respond to direct, concrete stimuli, humanity can respond to abstractions through intellectual processes. But the abstraction of Modernism is a by-product obtained as a result of industrialisation; it is only accidental. That is why it has ended up as a single-coded – or a completely silent – architecture, lacking, as Louis Althusser put it, an epistemology.

When we walk through the streets of an Italian Renaissance city – Florence, for example – the experience of just strolling along is highly enjoyable. Each building speaks to us, each sculpture engages us in conversation. We can read the streets, just as we read a novel. The city as a whole is a work of literature, and we can browse through it as we walk.

Unfortunately, cities built since the advent of Modernism are quite the opposite: they disturb and exhaust us. No tourists flock to Brasilia or Canberra, and young couples don't stroll hand in hand through the bleak banking and business area around the Kasumigaseki Building in central Tokyo. It is in this sense that Jencks has offered his first definition of the Post-Modern as architecture that speaks to us on at least two levels.

His second definition of Post-Modernism is hybrid architecture, mixing and hybridising opposing elements such as historical styles with contemporary life, and high art with popular culture. One example of this process is the use of elements of the popular cultures of Las Vegas or Hollywood which have fascinated the masses to enliven contemporary architecture. To discover the essence of charm and interest even in such paradigms of 'bad taste' is one of the strategies of Post-Modern architecture.

Modern architecture scorned Las Vegas as vulgar and, like modern literature and abstract art, made no attempt to hide its élite consciousness. Post-Modern architecture, however, has set itself the task of destroying the boundary separating high art from popular art.

Jencks also sees Post-Modern architecture as being intentionally schizophrenic. The term schizophrenia, of course, describes the mental illness in which a person is possessed of two conflicting mental states at the same time, but Post-Modernism uses it to refer to a healthy person who intentionally behaves that way. Here we see an impulse similar to that of the second definition, the hybrid nature of Post-Modern architecture.

The fourth definition of the Post-Modern is an architecture with a language. In other words, to be read in a multivalent fashion, it must have an architectural language, while the fifth definition proposes that it is also an architecture 'rich in metaphor, new and embracing rather than exclusive'.

Finally, Post-Modern architecture is 'an architecture that responds to the multiplicity of the city'. It must be created based on a reading of the plurality of the city's values and its complex context.

The Value-Added Nature of the Information Society

I would like to continue by taking these definitions and re-working them into my own argument, point by point, in the context of contemporary culture.

1) The economies of the developed countries have already moved from heavy industry to research and development, education, publishing and broadcasting – the industries of an information society – together with the service industries and the banking and financial sector. This is a major transformation of society from an industrial to a non-industrial base.

In industrial society, the production of things is paramount; quantity is preferable to quality, and the important thing is to produce goods of standard quality in great quantity at the lowest price possible. But in an information society, the added value attached to goods plays a major role. We see a shift from the goal to produce inexpensive goods, to producing goods that are also well designed. Even the old 'star' products – automobiles and electrical appliances – must take note of the value-added factor of design, which now accounts for a fair proportion of the cost of the finished product.

Japan was once an important silk-producing centre, specialising in the spinning of silk thread and exporting large quantities of raw silk. Yet it is inconceivable that Japan should be a silk exporter now. Japanese wages have risen to the highest in the world and it is impossible to make a profit by producing raw materials. Now Korea, China and Taiwan are the raw-silk producers, while Japan designs silk fabrics and sells them to foreign markets. The products of designers such as Issey Miyake and Rei Kawakubo, with the value of their designs added, are sent out into the world. This is how roles have evolved in the international division of labour.

The cost of the raw materials of a garment designed by Issey Miyake makes up less than ten per cent of its retail price. With Miyake's value-added design, however, it becomes a high-priced product. The fields of education, publishing and broadcasting are based, too, not on hard costs but on 'soft' costs. The hotel industry is another example: four-star and five-star ratings are determined by such value-added features as the quality of the service, the restaurants and the décor of the rooms.

In this evolution of an information society, we look to city planning and architecture for more than mere convenience, function and pleasantness. It is not enough to regard Post-Modernism as a movement of art and literature that has influenced architecture and urban planning. The production base of our society itself is changing profoundly, and as we evolve from an industrial to an information society, the defining traits of Post-Modernism are converging as an accompaniment to this great transformation of the values of society as a whole.

City Space Becomes Novelistic and Private

2) In the age of Modernism, much was made of 'humanism'; we could even call this the slogan of industrial society. Humanism was the dispensation that permitted the unchecked development of technology. But in the post-modern age, this concept of an idealised, abstracted humanity must be cast away.

What, for example, does it mean to design with such a notion of humanism in mind? There are no abstract human beings but men and women, old people, middle-aged people, young people, children – individuals of both sexes and different ages. There are Japanese, Americans, the British – individuals of different countries; and if we pursue this line of reasoning to its end, there is person A and there is person B.

You can search the world in vain for the abstracted, average human being, the 'humanity' that has served so long as the slogan of Modernism, for it is no more than an icon labelled as human. In this age however, we must build cities and design buildings and homes for the actual, concrete person A; for a man, for a woman, for an elderly person – for real individuals, with their own identities and personalities. This is the task of bringing human beings down from their pedestal of ideal abstraction and returning them to the milieu of private life.

Let us enter a Gothic cathedral: this cathedral is a work of architecture inspired by devotion to God. When we lift our eyes, light pouring through the stained-glass windows falls on our heads. The music of the organ also cascades down on us from above. In that imposing space we fall to the earth in submission, we repent, and we pray that we may come nearer to God. This is the Medieval cathedral.

Following the Renaissance, the achievement of Modern architecture has been to create a humanist architecture that replaces God with man, and is offered to a mighty, faceless, ideal image of humanity. Since that architecture is offered to an abstraction of humanity, and to human society, the individual person not only finds no peace or comfort in its superhuman scale but also feels a crushing alienation.

As the role of government has grown with the rise of a modern industrial society, public spaces in cities have been enlarged in the name of the public welfare. The lobbies and halls of public buildings are enormous spaces with no place for a person to make himself comfortable. To return to a normal living environment, where they can laugh and cry, people have to rush back to their own homes. In other words, the city denies the possibility of private life. But in the post-modern age, architecture and the city will restore private life to its rightful place, in many different forms. For example: narrow streets that one can walk along alone; pocket parks just the right size for a couple to squeeze into, hand in hand; a bench set under a single tree; space with the excitement of a maze; special places, restaurants, shops that suggest you are the only one who knows where they are; places that are so frightening that you never dare to return; places that come alive at night; a little hidden corner where you can lose yourself in your own thoughts. By incorporating such core images of private life into the city and into its public spaces, we will make our cities more complex and interesting.

The reason that the old Shitamachi area around Asakusa is so interesting; and the crowded, twisted, up-and-down, ever-changing back streets of Harajuku and Akasaka are so much fun, is that they have achieved a good combination of public and private living space. In the cities and buildings before

OVERLEAF: Shitamachi area around Asakusa showing crowded space. This area achieves the combination of public and private living space in which there pervades a feeling of interest, surprise and stimulation.

Modernism, we find a mixing of the frightening, the fascinating and the reassuring. In old Edo, there were 'haunted houses' (*obakeyashiki*) where you could go for a good scare, there were frightening old streets that people used for tests of courage; and the night was different from the day: a dark, mysterious time when spirits reigned. But modern city planning tears down haunted houses, destroys the mazes, and banishes a city of night that might satisfy our curiosity. Now night is inferior to day, little more than a diluted version of it. We need to recapture the symbiosis of the cities of day and night.

Making space novelistic and private again is just this: restoring interest, surprise and stimulation to our curiosity in our monotonous cities, so that the people who pass through them can weave their own stories from the environment. Much is made of the present as the age of private enterprise. But 'private enterprise' has a greater purpose than simply to reduce the role of government by placing a greater part of the financial burden on the private sector. Private enterprise can do much to re-create the city of night, the city of private, novelistic space in contrast to the public centres of the daylight city.

Ruled by an Invisible Icon

3) The pre-modern age was the age of the central authority. The king or ruler – or, in his place, a vast government – was always in the centre from which all rules, all lines of sight, radiated out.

In the urban planning and architecture of the pre-modern age, and that of the Renaissance in particular, a square or plaza occupied the centre and the streets radiated out from it. Standing in a square in Rome or Paris and looking down one of those streets, we see buildings of equal height neatly lining both sides and extending off into the distance in a dramatic demonstration of the law of perspective. Our lines of sight extend into infinity from the central square, symbol of authority.

If the pre-modern age was an age of a transcendent code, then the modern is an age that has liberated itself from codes. Michel Foucault has offered Jeremy Bentham's Panopticon as a model for the pre-modern age.[2] The Panopticon was a prison design with radiating wings made up of blocks of cells. Between every two wings was a tower from which the prisoners could be observed. The design ensures that the prisoners feel the eyes of their guards on them at all times, even if there are actually no guards in the towers.

Similarly, in the pre-modern age the 'king' of the lectern, the teacher, stood at the front of the class, and all his pupils faced him. In the modern age, the authority figure of the teacher no longer exists, but the pupils still feel his gaze on their backs. The modern reality is that though the authority figure is gone, we are each ruled by his icon inside ourselves. For example, when we drive a car we observe the rules of the road. We may say that we do so because the rules exist; but this can also be an example of rule by an invisible authority.

The rule of the icon manifests itself in a variety of fields – education, industry and all other aspects of life – as self-control and self-discipline. The

International Style of Modern architecture is an icon of this sort; although an architect who refuses to design according to its laws will not be punished by society, architects have been possessed by an internal fear of liberating themselves from the Modern; an obsession that they must design in the International Style.

In the post-modern age the spell of the teacher's gaze on our backs will be broken: I call this the age of the third classroom. In the first classroom, the teacher stands in front. In the second classroom, we feel the teacher looking at us from behind. In the third classroom, there is no teacher, either real or perceived, in the front or at the back of the classroom.

At first glance it may seem a confused age, and there will be those who will seek to restore hierarchy and order. But a new age cannot be forced to bloom through political or moral coercion. In the end, no one will want to return to an order of the past.

Introducing Diachronicity and Synchronicity

We can compare the absence of the king, or central authority, to the movements of a school of fish. When a school of minnows changes direction, the action is not initiated by any established leader. An individual within the group volunteers to lead by making the first move, and the rest of the fish follow as if they shared a single mind. The school has no king or authority. Each individual member can act as leader at any moment, yet the group as a whole does not lose its dynamism.

The concepts of diachronicity and synchronicity will become important. In time, Modern architecture cuts itself off from the past and places the future far ahead; in space, it regards the West as the leader and all other places as inferior and less advanced. But my philosophy of architecture is to introduce diachronicity and synchronicity into urban space, thus relativising space and time.

How are we to consider the past, the present and the future with regard to architecture? In Giambattista Piranesi's *Imaginary Prisons* (*Carceri d'Invenzione*, c1743), there is neither present nor future;[3] in the *New City* (*Città Nuova*, 1914) drawings by Italian Futurist Antonio Sant'Elia there is no past or present.[4] Modern society is a society of the present, with no interest in past or future. That is why Modern architecture rejected the history and tradition of the past, along with its symbols and decorative language. At the same time, it rejected the future as unfathomable: Modernism could only conceive of the future as an extension of present trends.

All that was required of Modern architecture was that it rationally serve its present functions and meet the demands of present-day people and society. Le Corbusier's Unité d'Habitation apartment complex outside Marseilles (1945-52) and Mies van der Rohe's Lake Shore Drive apartments are both examples of contemporary architecture as offerings to the frozen icon of an ideal image of society.[5] Modern architecture conceives of time as a pyramid of three layers:

the past is a base on which the present stratum rests, and on top of the present sits the future stratum. In this model, past and future are only articulated in terms of the present, which forms the central layer of the pyramid. For me, on the contrary, architecture is an evolution from the past to the present and on into the future, a maturing and metabolising process.

Time is not a linear series, nor does it have the hierarchical structure of a pyramid or a tree. It is an interwoven network, a rhizome. The term 'rhizome' as used by Deleuze and Guattari, represents a model in which there is no clear hierarchy, unlike the pyramid, or the tree with its trunk and branches. It is like a spider's web, with neither core nor periphery; neither beginning nor end. A rhizome never ossifies – it is a series of relationships that are always dynamically re-forming and regrouping.

If the past, present and future are conceived of after the model of a rhizome, we can consider ourselves at an equal distance from all times and freely engage in relationships with any. No longer do we feel close only to the present, while past and future are distant. This relativity of time is what is meant by diachronicity.

Synchronicity, on the other hand, is the relativity of space. Lévi-Strauss linked all cultures on earth and thereby relativised Western culture, which had been accorded absolute superiority until then. Structuralism gave the cultures of Western Europe, America, Africa, the Islamic countries and Asia all equal status, with each placed at an equal distance from the others.

In the age of the 'third classroom', time and space are made relative in this way. As a result, we are able to weave different times and histories – past, present and future – and different cultural values – those of Western Europe, Japan and Islam – into a single work of architecture where they can exist in symbiosis.

Sacred, Profane and Pleasure in the City

4) A major feature of the post-modern era is the elimination of dualism and binomial opposition. The boundaries between such apparent opposites as flesh and spirit, religion and science, artifice and nature, technology and humanity, pure literature and popular literature, seriousness and irony, work and play, and life and death will gradually become hazy, and from the intermediary space between these pairs of opposing poles many creative possibilities will well up. The post-modern sensitivity will be one in which we straddle the spiritual and the material, the sacred and the profane. Things that seem contradictory at first glance will turn out to be compatible, even all of a piece, like the Klein bottle. And from this situation a new set of values will arise.

Roger Caillois, in *Man and the Sacred* (*L'Homme et le sacré*),[6] proposes adding a third element to the traditional dualism of sacred and profane: pleasure. The sacred corresponds to the 'first classroom' where the king, or authority, claiming to be sacred, looks down over the people. The profane corresponds to the 'second classroom' and Modernism, the age of the masses, of mass

Back alleys in Harajuku. Here again the twisted, up-and-down and ever-changing back streets have an element of both the frightening and the reassuring, but are always fascinating, constantly arousing our curiosity.

production, of an Esperanto-like universality, of Heidegger's *das Mann* – man as an ordinary person. To be ordinary is the value that Modernism has lauded; it rejects variety and difference; its paradigm is ordinary domesticity.

Pleasure is the 'third classroom', the post-modern age, which rejects the division of sacred from profane. In architecture, for example, the neighbourhood police boxes of Japan are designed in a multiplicity of shapes and styles: in brick, with onion domes, or other curious shapes; and the thought of the familiar policemen glaring out of them is a delightful image. This will transform the city into a blend of the sacred and the profane.

In the world of thought, the New Academism discusses difficult concepts with the flippancy of the comic strip in a blending of sacred and profane. Deleuze and Guattari write: 'Be the Pink Panther and your loves will be like the wasp and the orchid, the cat and the baboon.'[7] In the past, philosophy restricted itself to a rigorous, self-enclosed language of its own, but here we see a mix of philosophical investigation and everyday words and images that will appeal directly to the mass sensibility, while the authors place themselves at an equal distance from both languages. This, too, is an example of the rhizome.

The age when philosophy is restricted to philosophical terms has come to an end; the rule of dualism and binomial opposition is already starting to crumble.

From Association to Bisociation

5) The post-modern age will have conviviality which is another way of expressing Zeami's *hana*, or pleasure, novelty and enjoyment.

Modernism allied itself with a type of purism, and made the functional the highest good while rejecting play, ease, interest and pleasure as extraneous elements. In the Baroque, Renaissance and earlier architecture, decoration was regarded as an important element. The rejection of decoration began with Modernism, and this is one reason why the Modern is an architecture that cannot be read.

6) Post-Modernism recognises the value of the world's variety and the worth of hybrid styles, acknowledging that Western values are not the only legitimate ones and that a near infinite variety of cultures exists around the globe.

As Western culture, hitherto regarded as totally superior to all others, is recognised as just another local culture, English and French, for example, will be seen as no more than local languages, and the world will be enormously transformed. In the post-modern age, we will be forced to recognise the divergence among cultures world-wide and allow different cultural identities to live in symbiosis.

In architecture, this will lead to the reappraisal of combinations of elements from different cultures and a new hybrid style. This will no longer be criticised as the product of compromise, 'neither bird nor beast', but seen as a positive expression of a multivalent energy. My high regard for the architecture of the late Edo and early Meiji periods – the Tsukiji Hotel, the Mitsuigumi House – is because they are fine examples of this creative hybrid style.

7) The concept of the whole will crumble and part and whole will exist in symbiosis in the post-modern age. The modern age was an age of Hegel, an industrial age, in which the concept of the whole – the nation, massive industrial and scientific complexes – was formulated. The post-modern age instead will be a utopia after the fashion of Charles Fourier's phalanxes, or co-operative communities.[8] It will be a world in which small groups take the initiative to form co-operative federations. Arthur Koestler calls this a change from 'association', with the nuance of free and friendly co-operative relations among groups that recognise their mutual differences, to 'bisociation', a more delicately balanced relationship that even includes a certain degree of mutual opposition.

Koestler remarks: 'The essence of creativity is to be found in the integration on a new plane of two previously unrelated structures of consciousness.' Association is a relation between two parties with some connection to each other, but bisociation is the collision of two completely unconnected parties. Naturally, a tremendous tension, resistance, and stimulus results, in which Koestler finds the essence of creativity. Koestler described the Janus-like relationship between part and whole with the acronym SOHO, meaning 'self-regulating open hierarchic order'. The atomism of the 19th century was akin to Koestler's thought in its concern with the part. But the 'self-regulating' part is quite distinct from that earlier line of thought. The shared observation and management of the 'third classroom' can be identified in this self-regulation which has led me to call my own concept of a society based on shared management a SOHO society.

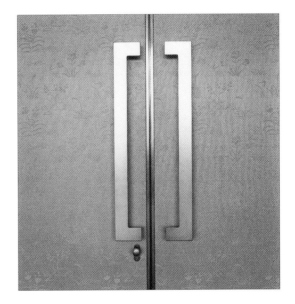

In short, the post-modern world will be one where equal value is accorded to the whole and to the individual; industry and the individual; and society and the individual. It will be a society of a type rejected by Modernism, to some extent inefficient. According to the logic of Modernism, to maximise its efficiency society must be unified and highly organised. Whatever ideals may be professed in our age, and however much capitalist societies claim to value the individual, in reality the trend has been to cede priority to the whole. The great challenge of Post-Modernism will be whether it can achieve a society of symbiosis in which the part, or the individual, is valued as much as the whole.

My own approach to the actual work of architecture is to design, for example, door handles and carpet patterns at the same time as I am making sketches for the whole building. I thus design from both the part and the whole simultaneously. Most architects first settle on the shape of the work overall and then proceed to think about the shape of the rooms inside it while the door handles are the last of the last. That is the way we are trained, to always move from the whole to the part.

In urban planning, too, it is the roads, the parks, the large spaces and facilities that are decided on first, and last of all the houses that will line the roads are considered. That, however, is wrong. We cannot create new cities unless we consider the city and its houses at the same time and give them equal value.

Kisho Kurokawa, Japan Red Cross Society, Tokyo, 1977. Carpet patterns and detail of door handle.

True creativity emerges from the process of conceiving the part and the whole together.

A complete deconstruction of the social status quo took place between about 1900 and 1930, three decades which perhaps best represent the special character of the 20th century. Planck's theory of quantum mechanics, Heisenberg's Uncertainty Principle, Bergson's creative evolution and Einstein's theory of relativity were all articulated at that time. Then, as we entered the 1930s, a transcendence of that deconstruction was explored on various fronts. These years saw the appearance of Ortega y Gasett's *The Rebellion of the Masses*, Benjamin Cremieux's *Inquiétude et la réconstruction,* and Freud's *Civilisation and its Discontents.* The Western concepts of individualism and the self had reached maturity before the 20th century began, and now a community based on those concepts was created on the basic model of part and whole, individual and society. In reaction to emphasis on the whole, the individual is given more importance, or theories for the deconstruction of society become popular. When deconstruction proceeds too far, the reconstruction of society is called for. This pendulum swing has repeated itself again and again in Western society.

The Arts and Crafts Movement in England was a reaction against industrialisation that called for a renewed recognition of the value of the craftsman's hand labour. In Europe, ages that emphasise the whole have alternated with ages that emphasise the part, the individual. Periods when technology is encouraged alternate with movements to preserve nature in oscillation – a reflection of the dualism of Western civilisation. In the post-modern age we must transcend dualism, and the part and the whole come to live in symbiosis.

From the Economy to an Exchange of Symbols

8) The materialism of the modern age has valued things in terms of their function and utility; parts of things that have no apparent function are rejected as frivolous. But in the post-modern age, spiritual elements will become important.

I do not reject the principle of functionalism *per se,* nor will it be rejected in the post-modern era, because functionalism is not really a product of Modernism. It can be traced back to ancient Greece and Rome. Edward Robert de Zurko, in his book *Origins of Functionalist Theory,* traces functionalism back to Aristotle and the Roman architect and engineer Vitruvius, on through Saint Augustine in the fourth century, Saint Thomas Aquinas in the medieval period, and the Renaissance architects Leon Battista Alberti, Leonardo da Vinci and Andrea Palladio.[9] Functionalism has been advocated by such 18th-century figures as Claude-Nicolas Ledoux, Lessing, Goethe, and Schinkel, and, in the 19th century, Horatio Greenough and Louis Sullivan.[10] From there the baton was picked up by Modern architecture, and it will just as surely be passed to the post-modern era.

The essence of the problem is not functionalism but the one-sided over-

ABOVE: Kisho Kurokawa, Fukuoka Seaside Momochi, Sawara, Fukuoka, 1989, floor patterns. *OPPOSITE:* Kisho Kurokawa, door at the National Bunraku Theatre, Osaka, 1983.

dependence on the intellect and rationalism that is the basis of Western culture. Intellect is more highly valued than emotion; rationality is seen as the essence and true form of humanity, the ultimate and unadulterated good. Industrial society developed from scientific thought and experimental and analytic methods that are based on such a thorough-going rationalism.

Rationalism has played an important role in industrial society, but it has also led us to disdain and devalue philosophies emphasising the role of consciousness, spiritual phenomena and emotions. In the post-modern age, the material and the mental, the functional and the emotional, the beautiful and the terrifying, analytic and synthetic thought will have to exist in symbiosis.

We might say: 'The ability to look at a thing and discover its function is due to our analytical capacities, but the ability to discover its aura is due to our perceptive capacities.' The non-functional aspects of things – their design, their aura, intangible context, their spiritual nature – will become increasingly important in an information society. The ability, the sensitivity, the perception to see what is not visible to the eye will be much sought after. Jean Baudrillard has used the bold term: 'the death of the economy' to describe the new age,[11] which will be one of the exchange of symbols. In the age of a mass consumer society great quantities of goods and currency are exchanged: manufactured products are bought and discarded again and again, in a repeating cycle. But in an information society it is not goods but symbols, information and signs which are consumed. The frequent redecoration of shops and restaurants that has become popular can be regarded as a sign of the tendency to discard things. When café bars are popular, suddenly there are scores of them, all with the same white walls, revolving overhead fans, and generic high-tech atmosphere. But this style is soon finished and shops made from renovated warehouses are the next rage. Fads and fashions change at an amazing pace, and premises are constantly being redone to keep up with those changes.

They redecorate not because the shop no longer functions well, or because the heating no longer works, but because the symbols and signs their store presents have grown old. What is being so avidly consumed here is not goods but symbols, information, the value-added part of the store. Baudrillard, in his *L'échange symbolique et la mort,* offers a radical criticism of the ideology of production. In modern society, production and economics have, through long association, merged together. He suggests that we are moving away from an age of the accumulation of value and meaning to an age of *la poétique,* in which all excess value and meaning is pared away in what he calls the 'exchange of symbols'. Poetry can be thought of as the creation of atmosphere, but the contemporary age is one in which an aura, the likeness of a thing, is created from signs that possess no particular meaning. A piano that has never been used, a clock that does not tell the time, a chair that can't be sat on, weapons that cannot be fired – our lives are filled with evidence of an age of the exchange of symbols, which Baudrillard calls *simulacres.*

The *Simulacre* as Symbiosis of Sanity and Madness

This age of the exchange of symbols will effect great changes in human relationships. Even among friends, information that you don't have but your friend does, which may not be available through the mass media, will be extremely valuable. The value of information will link people in relationships.

In search of new information, people will come together and separate, or join special groups. A person who told you a wonderful story yesterday will be dismissed out of hand if he tries it on you again today: his information has already been consumed and no longer has any value. In turn, people will look for friends and join groups as a way of gaining access to information of rare value.

This represents a great change from modern society. The age has come when we find our purpose and interest, and our difference from others, in the information we have that is different from what others have. Compared to the lukewarm relationships in the modern age, the pleasures, stimulation, and joys of life will be intense. But on the other hand, each of us will need his own gyroscope to seek an independent lifestyle, different from that of others. In that sense, it will also be an extremely challenging time. Because each of us will have to select information for ourselves, we will need heightened sensitivity and mental powers.

The times are changing from an easy-going, hedonistic mass society to one society that will make great demands on our intelligence. On television, news shows, debates, and other 'hard' programming will be popular. The appearance of the New Academism in philosophy is a sign of the same trend, which will only increase in intensity from now on.

The key word in the age of the exchange of symbols will be *simulacre*. Baudrillard says, 'A *simulacre* is the structure of atmosphere, or a system constructed of the extraordinary.' The film director Yoshimitsu Morita has made a film titled *Something Like It* (*No Yo na Mono*) – which is precisely the definition of a *simulacre*.[12]

There are nearly five million pianos in Japan today, of which a fair proportion are little more than a silent piece of living room furniture, never played. These pianos cannot function in their original role. These are not musical instruments; instead, they help to create an atmosphere of wealth and culture. In Morita's film *Kazoku Geemu* (*The Family Game*), an automobile acts as a *simulacre*. Whenever a problem arises, the hero, with a wink, calls his wife or the son's tutor out to the car in its parking place to have a talk. His car is not something to drive; he uses it as a private room – a reflection of Japan's housing situation. The hero also uses it as a space that he controls, a metaphor for a space where he can regain intimacy and take the initiative in his life. Here the car has already been transformed from a vehicle into 'something like a car'.

Consider the sale at a tremendously high price of the Rolls Royce that once belonged to the Beatles. It was precisely because it carried the cultural cachet of having been their possession, not because of its functional value, that it sold for an enormous figure.

In the future we will live in a world surrounded by *simulacres:* 'things like' other things. The Japanese have a long tradition of appreciating objects for their background and context as well as their function. This is their sensitivity to *ki,* or aura, energy. The element *ki* (also pronounced *ke*) appears in words such as *kehai* (presence or seeming), *fun'iki* (aura), and *kibun* (feeling or mood). It has the sense of a symbol or spirituality, a cultural value attached to, arising from or surrounding an object. *Ki* is also used to point to the irrational, the religious, the transcendent. Through the concept of *ki,* a corridor is opened linking the symbiosis of function and aura, material and spiritual elements with the symbiosis of sanity and madness, science and religion.

La Poétique: Deconstruction Beyond Meaning

The theory of the exchange of symbols is linked with the linguist Ferdinand de Saussure's theory of *la poétique,*[13] the symbolic function of language which he uncovered using anagrams to decipher poetry.

According to Baudrillard, '*la poétique* is an exchange of symbols from which, ultimately, nothing remains, a reverberating interplay of structural elements.' Language reverberates within the bounds of the poem and then perishes of its own accord. Whereas the role of literature and philosophy is to point to a subject, such as a transcendent God, and make 'meaningful' statements about it, in poetry, that meaning is completely extinguished.

Let us apply this concept to architecture. The creation of meaning is the task of a certain type of architecture, one with a strong, clear narrative quality. Examples of this are frequently encountered in socialist countries in the one-dimensional, aggressive attempts to create a city district devoted to a mythologised Lenin, with symbolic statues of Lenin and streets named after him. But this monumentality is a thing of the past.

Though I have said that our living environments, our cities and our architecture should be novelistic, with many different readings, I also believe that this 'novel', when finally deconstructed, should be akin to a poem that expresses, finally, nothing. As Baudrillard has written, '*La poétique* as the exchange of symbols brings into play a strictly limited and determined group of words. Its purpose is to totally exhaust those words.'

The Science of Ambiguity or Fuzzy Logic

9) In the modern age, vagueness and the 'irrational', were rejected or forced into a dualistic mould. We were faced with a choice between exterior and interior, public and private, eternity and the moment, good and evil. But at last, I think, the truly ambiguous nature of human existence is being rediscovered.

We have learned that the human brain, especially the frontal lobe, is more creative than analytical, and has a high tolerance of ambiguity. The more we learn about ourselves the more we discover that human beings are an ambiguous form of existence that, in many respects, confound analysis.

Modernism makes a great mistake in assuming that this ambiguity remains simply because science has not yet advanced far enough to solve all these mysteries. Human beings are not made up exclusively of parts that can be clearly distinguished and analysed. Ambiguity is also essential in the human make-up. Shuhei Aida, a professor at Denki Tsushin College, comments from the perspective of engineering in his book *Aimai kara no Hasso* (*Thinking from Ambiguity*): 'The dictum "I think, therefore I am" is famous as a philosophical expression of the essence of humanity. The wellspring of the 'ambiguity' of human beings is thought, which depends upon the activity of the brain. The brain is a miracle of nature, made up of a tremendous number of groups of cells that form a mass of matter which can perform an infinite variety of functions.'

The brain processes not only physical stimuli such as sound, light and heat but human feelings as well. It exercises a subtle control over our emotions and each part of the body, and to preserve both our biological balance and our emotional balance, initiates many different activities. The brain's information processing and transmission of instructions are carried out by electric impulses. Thus, when 'I think', impulses within the brain flash in many different patterns, are unified according to a certain order, and take shape as thoughts and mental images.

In each person's brain there is an independent environment, a world, a language, props and a stage, and every day a grand drama unfolds there, directed by thought and intellect. The body is not only a tool or prop for implementing one's thoughts and will, but it is also the very thing that makes the self possible. Here lies the special character of the human being as a form of coexistence of brain and body. Ambiguous engineering starts here, and from this perspective reaches out to include many other phenomena. This multivalent system is based on the recognition that the coexistence of brain and body is the essential nature of the human being.

Nowhere are life and matter more intimately intertwined than in our brains. The broad, dark valley that lies between the worlds of thought and matter is where ambiguous engineering arises. By building bridges across that valley it seeks to gradually discover methods for grasping ambiguity, and eventually construct a system to bring the machine and contemporary civilisation closer to mankind.

Lotti Asker Zadeh, of the Department of Electrical Engineering at the University of California has advocated what he calls 'fuzzy logic'. If we think about it, the language, colours, forms and sounds that surround us are all ambiguous information. There is room for judging, interpreting and under-standing all of these data, and in that margin of ambiguity we come to a mutual agreement. This is precisely why words can mislead and different colours and shapes convey different images to different people.

Traditionally, engineering has tried to eliminate the naturally existing margin of ambiguity. Fuzzy logic, however, attempts to put ambiguous information to use in engineering. Its advocates seek to build a fuzzy computer and software that can steer an automobile by remote control.

This ambiguity, the intermediary zone that cannot be explained by dualistic logic, is an important element in the post-modern age of symbiosis. We find a new image of humanity in the 'moratorium human being', a concept articulated by Keigo Okonogi in his *Moratortiamu Ningen no Jidai* (*The Age of the Moratorium Man*). The 'moratorium person' is one who remains uncommitted, unfinished, with no rigid self-definition or social role. This is a human being as potential, a human being in waiting – a very similar concept to the idea of mankind as an ambiguous existence.

The Non-linear, the Fractal and Implicate Order

Ambiguity has become a major theme in science and philosophy as well. In his book *The New Scientific Spirit*, Gaston Bachelard describes this new age:

> If the modern age sought an all-encompassing truth, the new age will seek relative truths. If the modern age was the age of Euclid, the new age will be one that combines the Euclidian realm with a non-Euclidian realm. If the modern age was one of rejection or contradiction, the new age will be a combination of rejection and contradiction. In mathematics, the modern Euclidian realm will be pushed into a non-Euclidian realm by the new age. In physics, if the modern age is one of a Newtonian realm, the new age will be moved into a non-Newtonian realm. In science, if the modern age is that of Lavoisier, the new age will be a move into a non-Lavoisieran science. In logic, if the modern age is one of Aristotle through Kant, the new age will be non-Aristotelian and non-Kantian. And, in contrast to the age of Modernism, the age that waits for us will be one in which all of those negations of their predecessors will encompass and embrace their opposites, in other words, the ideas and beliefs that existed before.[14]

Up to now, progress and revolution in Europe have occurred through a complete rejection of the status quo, an about-face reversal; but Bachelard tells us that the new age will be one in which the status quo will be at once rejected and embraced, a time of symbiosis of old and new. This Bachelard calls the new science of negation.

From this perspective, Japan's Meiji Restoration may come in for a re-evaluation. It was pronounced ambiguous and incomplete in comparison with Western-style revolutions as it did not reject all tradition, but sought to carry tradition into a new realm. This Japanese characteristic of continual revision and reform is well adapted to Bachelard's new age.

In mathematics, Benoit Mandelbrot's fractal geometry and non-linear analytic geometry have replaced Nicolas Bourbaki's systematic, axiomatic mathematics and the Newtonian world view. Non-linear analytic geometry analyses phenomena such as wind currents and tornadoes, previously regarded as non-mathematical phenomena without structure or order. Fractal geometry, too, treats the 'nested structures' found in nature, revealing chaos within order and order within chaos. Ilya Prigogine's dispersal theory and Hermann Haken's synergetics also describe the state of chaos, where order and anti-order exist together.

Traditional science is limited to simple phenomena possessing a clear order, ignoring the disordered and chaotic. Post-modern science will study both order and disorder and pursue the relations between them. Returning to a Leibnizian view of the world, the previously ignored realm of disorder will live in symbiosis with order in each branch of learning, and a theory of chaos will be born. Leibniz declared that the whole exists in the part, a view that has much in common with Koestler's *holon*.

As post-modern science and the science of ambiguity develop, Christian civilisation will receive a great shock. Christianity teaches that nature and man are both the creations of God, but for post-modern science, each of us possesses within ourselves the power to create nature. This would appear to mean the irrevocable death of God. Post-modern science is approaching the Buddhist teaching, that all existence – animals, plants and minerals – is inhabited by Buddha nature.

Since his encounter with the Indian philosopher Krishnamurti, David Bohm, the logician and physicist, has begun to develop a unique new physics. For Bohm every part of the natural world contains an 'implicate order' that embraces the rest of existence. He quotes Spinoza's remark that 'Mind is incorporated in matter, and in that sense matter is all-embracing. Matter is an extension of God.' Bohm goes on to say that 'In classical physics, matter is regarded as exclusively material, a mechanical form of existence. There was no room for mind, feeling or soul in this model. But in the new physics, there can be no true separation between inhabitants of the same zone. The mind is born from matter.'

From this revolutionary new position, Bohm advocates holistic medicine. Conventional medicine has treated the body as if it were only matter, but our spiritual and physical functions are interrelated. In Japan, the word for sickness is 'afflicted energy' (*byoki*); traditional Oriental medicine has long regarded mind and body as a unit in a way very similar to holistic medicine.

We have examined several defining characteristics of Post-Modernism as a new current transcending Modernism. To sum them up, we can regard Post-Modernism as the philosophy of symbiosis.

In architecture there is a post-modernist group represented in America by Robert Venturi and Michael Graves, and in Japan Arata Isozaki is often called a post-modern architect. But in my opinion, they are post-modern only in the narrowest sense of the term. Their method is to incorporate the architectural styles of the past – predominantly the European past – into contemporary architecture. They do not subscribe to the broader Post-Modernism I speak of, which seeks to eliminate the domination of the West and transcend Modernism.

Towards the Evocation of Meaning

The Name of the Rose

The title of Umberto Eco's powerful novel is taken from a hexameter composed in Latin by a 12th-century Benedictine scholar-monk, quoted at the end of the book: '*Stat rosa pristina nomine / Nomina nuda terminus*' ('The name of the rose is given by God; our roses are roses without names'). This is Eco's contemporary, semiological challenge to the great philosophical controversy of the Middle Ages, the debate concerning the existence of universal natures.

The novel is set in a northern Italian monastery in the 14th century. A Franciscan monk, William of Baskerville, arrives at the monastery with his pupil, Adso, to investigate a strange series of murders that has occurred there. As they make their inquiries, they learn that hidden in the monastery library there is a labyrinth, where the second, lost half of Aristotle's *Poetics* is kept. Aristotle's work is said to teach that laughter is the remedy that prevents us from becoming the slaves of truth (universal being). This is a powerful rebuttal of the doctrine that universal natures actually exist, of Plato's doctrine of ideas, and of the Scholastic philosophy that was the servant of theology in medieval Europe.

The meaning of 'catholic' is, of course, universal. The Catholic Church is not simply a congregation of believers but a universal, and therefore sovereign institution that exists prior to and beyond its members. And without the abstract notion of humanity as a universal, the concepts of original sin and salvation through Christ are also inconceivable.

The English Scholastic philosopher William of Ockham, on the other hand, proposed that universals exist only as terms, signs that stand for and refer to individual existences. Eco's name for his leading character William of Baskerville is a pastiche of William of Ockham and the 'Baskervilles' of the famous Sherlock Holmes story. Here we can decipher the intent of Eco the semiologist, with his belief that meaning is invoked as words (or signs) to produce more words (more signs), and interpretations create interpretations. In addition, Eco sprinkles his novel with references to Thomas Aquinas, Roger Bacon, Meister Eckhart, and Arthur Conan Doyle, and quotations from and references to church architecture, philosophy, politics, pharmaceutics, and many other fields of art and learning.

A look at the layout of the monastery depicted in the novel reveals that the church, which is set in the centre of the complex, is not the centre of the novel's action. The main events take place in the aedificium, a large castle-like structure located at the edge, the periphery of the complex. The scriptorium,

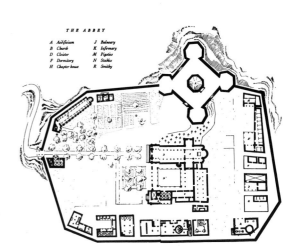

ABOVE: Plan of the monastery in Umberto Eco's *The Name of the Rose*. *OPPOSITE*: Four bamboo poles at a Shinto groundbreaking ceremony. The ceremony takes place before a construction is to begin and has a fictional connotation. The physical nature of the bamboo poles disappears giving way to a symbolic aura of the place for the descent of the gods.

where the story reaches its climax, is also located here at the monastery's periphery.

In the centre of the library that houses the second volume of Aristotle's *Poetics* is an octagonal, 12-storey scriptorium and a stairway with 60 steps connected in labyrinthine fashion. The steps lead to a wall with a hidden door in it, disguised as a distorted, fair-ground type mirror and moved by secret springs. The number eight of the octagonal labyrinth that represents the universe is a multivalent symbol: it refers to the eighth day, when the universe had been completed; to the last day of our universe; and also to the sequential steps in the sequence of the development of Eco's novel.

I begin this chapter by introducing Eco's *The Name of the Rose* because I believe it is a masterful presentation of the most pressing contemporary issues not only in literature but also common to philosophy, architecture, art and technology. The world depicted in this novel is the new world – whether we call it Post-Modern, Next-Modern, or whatever – to come.

From Epistemology to Ontology

From Greek and Roman times to the modern period, architects have tried to answer the question 'What is architecture?' The epistemological question of what being is, and the nature of the existence of the world, has been the central issue of Western metaphysics from the time of Aristotle, through Plato, Descartes, Hegel, and the thinkers of the modern age. This presupposes a single, true notion of existence that can be fully described in terms of logos, or reason. The epistemology of architecture has been that there is one universal, true phenomenon 'architecture', which can be comprehended logically by people of every nationality and culture. This is the epistemology of Modern architecture, whose ideal image, the International Style, was conceived as a universal creation that transcended all differences of culture and applied the world over.

What system of values produced this universalised icon? Clearly, the answer is the values of industrial society, based on the pursuit of material comfort; or in other words, the values of Western society. Here we have a phenomenon that is similar to the creation of Esperanto. However, don't we enjoy a more richly creative world when Arthur Miller writes in English, Dostoyevsky in Russian, and Yukio Mishima in Japanese? Then, through the media of translation and interpretation, we can be moved by our readings of different cultures and participate in mutual communication.

Yet the notion of the universal persists. The Cartesian linguist Noam Chomsky postulates an infra-structure, a universal grammar, beneath the surface of the various languages of the world. Some, encouraged by such theories, go so far as to suggest a meta-level hierarchical structure common to all humanity within the heterogeneous cultures of the world, and from which a single and unified notion of existence can be extracted. But this meta-linguistic theory of existence is an issue restricted to the context of Modernism, and has been fiercely attacked by the forces of Post-Modernism.

For example, J M Benoist, in *La révolution structurale,* criticises Chomsky's universal grammar: '... the concept of a universal grammar is nothing but the extreme generalisation of a particular notion that is specific to Western culture. This concept can be easily challenged by the theory of the relativity of all cultures.' The Cartesian definition of substance demands a reduction of reality to an unchanging unit, which is why Chomsky, with his theory of deep structure as universal grammar, calls himself a Cartesian linguist.

The application of transcendent meta-statements to the exterior of individual works and the meta-theory of a universal image of existence (architecture with a capital A) has been the target of criticism from the Post-Modern movement. Lyotard, in his *La condition postmoderne,* has remarked:

> As long as science refuses to limit itself to expressing a simple functional regularity and aims to pursue the truth, it must legitimise its own rules of operation. In other words, a statement that legitimises the status of science is required, and that statement goes by the name of philosophy. When that meta-statement is based in a clear manner on some grand scheme – the dialectic of the mind; the study of the deciphering of meaning, rational man, or the liberation of the proletariat and the creation of wealth – in order to legitimise itself, we call the science based on those schemes or stories, 'modern'. At the risk of greatly oversimplifying the matter, Post-Modernism is, first and foremost, a suspicion of these meta-schema.[16]

If we can say that Modern architecture created a universal icon based on Western culture, we can see that this was very much a meta-statement (architecture with a capital A).

Culture and tradition are not limited to the tangible. Styles of life, customs, aesthetic sensibilities and ideas are intangible, indivisible aspects of culture and tradition. Japanese culture, in particular, transmits its traditions with greater emphasis on its mental and spiritual aspects, aesthetic sensibilities and ideas, than on physical objects and forms.

While Modern architecture in Japan is extremely contemporary in its forms, it also manages to incorporate the cultural tradition. In the same fashion, the city of Tokyo seems at first to be a modern metropolis of no nationality; but actually Tokyo contains extremely Japanese characteristics and elements.

For me, architecture based on the philosophy of symbiosis is created by being deeply rooted in one's own history and culture and at the same time making positive efforts to incorporate into the work elements from other cultures. Since no single, universal ideal architectural iconography exists, architects must first express their own culture. At the same time, they must collide with other cultures, engage in dialogue with them, and, through symbiosis, create a new architecture that is both local and global.

The history of Modernism in the West reflects the control and suppression of nature by logos. The city is created by controlling nature, and modernisation

ABOVE: Traditional Japanese warehouse or 'Kura'. *BELOW*: Kisho Kurokawa, Hiroshima City Museum of Contemporary Art, Hiroshima, 1988. An example of how the modern can borrow from the traditional.

has meant that cities that had grown and evolved naturally had to be efficiently reconstituted on a geometric plan. Architecture was seen as a means of controlling space and demonstrating the rational capacities of human beings. Reason was the means of controlling and subjugating nature which was exterior to human existence. Modern man is a person whose interior nature – his spontaneity and sensitivity – is controlled and subjugated by his reason. Reason, science, technology and economics take precedence over culture, art, literature and thought. To challenge Modernism and Modern architecture is to challenge Western Rationalism. Contemporary Post-Modern architecture has not yet achieved the essential conquest of Western dominance and Rationalism. Lévi-Strauss' structuralism, which relativised Western culture, is being further developed by the post-structuralists who deconstruct metaphysics (philosophy based on logos) and Western dominance.

The essential transformation of the Post-Modern age can be described as a change from epistemology to ontology. In his *Sein und Zeit*, Martin Heidegger writes, 'The epistemological question has been whether we can properly describe being. In contrast, ontology asks what the nature of existence is.' While the question 'What is architecture?' is an epistemological one, in seeking the right order of architectural being (its single, universal, ideal image), ontology asks the question 'What is the meaning of architecture?'. Ontology is linked to semantics; both disciplines seek not a single, true order (a notion of architecture) in the form of the universally applicable International Style, but rather the evocation of meaning in architecture.

They do not assume a single, ideal image of architecture that exists as a truth transcending time, history and the differences among cultures. Rather, it is the very differences that arise in the unfolding of time and history that produce meaning. From the epistemological standpoint of Modernism, which asked 'What is architecture?' the truth was given *a priori*, and the problem was how to attain that truth through the power of reason.

It is easy to see that Post-Modern architecture will evolve as an architecture of minor, heterogeneous cultures, an architecture of deconstruction that seeks to reintroduce 'noise', and that sets itself off-centre. In this sense, the Post-Modern is often an architecture of *mélange*, with tendencies toward hybridisation – but a hybridisation fundamentally different from a style that simply mixes together historical architectural styles. Since there is no single ideal architecture and no one correct order, architecture does not express a single system of values. It is a conglomeration of many different value systems, or an order that embraces many heterogeneous elements. As the ontological question suggests, architecture will be the stage for the evocation of a variety of meanings. The collision of different cultures and their introduction as 'noise', creates a new culture. This is the discovery of meaning by means of our sensitivity to differences. In architecture, the conscious manipulation of elements from different cultures evokes meaning through difference and disjunction, and this distinguishes it fundamentally from a simple hybridisation.

Eco's *The Name of the Rose* is rich with quotations, metaphors and signs. But who would say of this bestselling novel that it is nothing more than a hybrid pastiche, lacking in creativity? For Eco, medieval Europe served as a *prétexte* to transcend Modernism. All of the quotations, metaphors and signs of his novel are extracted from the culture, religion and philosophy of the Middle Ages. His method is similar to my own, as I have chosen Japan's Edo period (the 17th through to the 19th century) as my own *prétexte* from which I have extracted my own quotations, metaphors, and signs.

A hybrid style, produced by the aesthetic combination of different historical styles, is a clever technique that produces beautiful proportions on a surface level. In this formal manipulation we cannot expect to find the intellectual operation of creating new interpretations of historical periods and cultures and pointing to the future. The indefinite, merely aesthetic quotation of architectural styles of the past clearly results in a contemporary hybrid style of architecture, and because of that I am opposed to this sort of historicism in Post-Modern architecture.

We must ask why a particular period is chosen as a *prétexte* from which we extract quotations. For Eco, the Middle Ages in Europe served as the *prétexte* for his thought. The same phenomenon can be observed in many others: for Schinkel, the classical architecture of Greece had a special import as a *prétexte*; for Le Corbusier, the architecture of the Mediterranean had special significance; and for Picasso, the primitive art of Africa had special meaning.

My reason for focusing especially on the culture of Edo-period Japan is that Edo at that time was the largest city in the world, and it produced a unique popular culture. Another reason is that the unique character of that culture resembles my own philosophy of symbiosis. At any rate, for the artist the decision of which historical signs to extract and how to incorporate them in his work is an extremely creative process. There is a fundamental difference between imitation and hybridisation.

Modern architecture has regarded the abstract forms of steel, glass, and concrete in the form of the International Style as its universal. The quotation of historical signs and the symbiosis of heterogeneous elements has been regarded as impure, and rejected. But I believe that the presence of historical signs and the symbiosis of heterogeneous elements lend a richer significance to works of architecture. Very few today would argue that a city in which historical buildings are preserved and exist alongside contemporary works of architecture in symbiosis is not preferable to the purely abstract ideal city of Le Corbusier or Oscar Niemeyer. Nor is it appropriate to dismiss this city in which history and the future exist in symbiosis as hybrid.

Of course, we cannot assume that the ten million readers of Eco's *The Name of the Rose* all grasped each of the author's quotations, references and signs. As can be seen from the many different essays of criticism and interpretation on the novel that have appeared since its publication, there are many different ways of understanding it. This multivalence and ambiguity will take the place of the universal, and they are precisely the essence of the new age, in which we will transcend the logocentrism of Modernism.

Will = Text

I have noted how Modern architecture, as a modern epistemology, is deeply rooted in Western dominance and 'logos'. If we are to move on to Post-Modern architecture, which asks ontological and semantic questions in its attempt to create an evocation of meaning, how must we transform the design methods of Modern architecture?

The basis for Modern design methods has been an ideal image of architecture (an order) which is single and universal, known as the International Style, articulated by means of reason. The design processes of analysis, structuring, and organisation were stressed, always pursued according to principles of reason and logic. The final result of the design process was expressed as a synthesis with universal application.

Heterogeneous elements were excluded from this design process, and everywhere the operations of introduction, connection, clarification, denotation, and co-ordination were given greatest importance. Reason and logos were always called upon to control and subjugate intuition.

We have seen how dualism and binomial opposition are inherent in Western metaphysics and logos: the dualisms of reason and sensitivity, body and spirit, necessity and freedom. In the history of architecture as well, the binomial opposition of reason and sensitivity has always manifested itself in a pendulum phenomenon. The industrial revolution was followed by the Arts and Crafts Movement, which was followed by Art Nouveau and Jugendstil. They in turn were followed by the Rationalism of Peter Behrens and Tony Garnier; and after the expressionist and futurist movements, Modern architecture emerged, waving its banner of functionalism. This dualistic process of action and reaction has had an unfortunate effect on Modernism.

In Modern architecture, dominated by reason, the wild revolts of sensitivity by such architects as Alvar Aalto, Frank Lloyd Wright, Hans Scharoun, Paolo Soleri, and Bruce Goff have always been regarded as exceptions. These men have been declared geniuses, and have thus been excluded from the mainstream of Modern architecture; but their revolt of spontaneity and sensitivity against the rule of reason is also a product of the age of Modernism. With the advent of a new age, the advocates of sensitivity and spontaneity are not likely to play any role in the defeat of Modernism. If we have no need for one true image of architecture (order) provided *a priori*, where should we direct our search for architecture? When there is a universal order, it is sufficient for architects to be led by it, to try to approach as near to it as possible. The architect's talent is to successfully ride the current or flow of that order and express his personality in the appropriate manner within the confines of that rational order.

We live in an age of the transformation of the paradigm of Modernism. Post-

Modern architecture must begin from the expression of the will towards the changes of the new age. The will or philosophy that tells us what we should transform and how, will become the driving force that motivates the creativity of architects the world over. The ontology suggested by the question 'What is the meaning of architecture?' will be established through the expressions of the wills of this wide variety of people.

The expression of my own will is, as I said earlier, the transformation of Western domination and logos. My will is linked with the expressions of will that are taking the form of battle lines unfolding on a variety of fronts – in literature, philosophy, art, and many other areas. The philosophy of symbiosis is the present expression of my will, previously articulated as Metabolism and metamorphosis, and it enables me to search in my architecture for an evocation of meaning. The philosophy of symbiosis is not another metaphysics; I believe it is more accurate to call it the text of a movement.

An architect's text or philosophy is rooted in that person's history and culture. The architects of the modern age sought an internationalism, a universalism that transcended their own personalities and regional characteristics. Post-modern architects, on the other hand, must set out from the expression of their own will, deriving from their own history and culture. A keen sensitivity to the differences in history, time, and culture will enable them to evoke the meaning of architecture.

Whereas the ultimate goal of Modern architecture was to achieve synthesis, the ultimate goal of Post-Modern architecture will manifest itself as evocation. As far as the methodology of design is concerned, symbolisation will replace analysis, deconstruction will replace structuring, relation will replace organisation, quotation will replace introduction; intermediation, synthesis; transformation, adaptation; sophistication, clarification; and connotation, denotation. These design methods will have an important and conclusive role in the evocation of meaning.

These methods will not necessarily be carried out more under the direction of intuition than of reason or logos. Rather, we can expect the simultaneous operation of reason and intuition. The processes of symbolisation, deconstruction, relation, quotation, intermediation, transformation, sophistication, and connotation, however, depend greatly on a keen sensitivity to differences among times, cultures, and among elements.

The philosophy of symbiosis is a text for the deconstruction of metaphysics, logos and Western domination. This philosophy encompasses the symbiosis of heterogeneous cultures, of human beings and technology, the interior and the exterior, the part and the whole, history and the future, reason and intuition, religion and science, human beings (their architecture) and nature.

This philosophy of symbiosis finds its sources in the Indian Buddhist philosophy of Consciousness Only and Japanese Mahayana Buddhism. In other words, this expression of my will is rooted both in my own identity and in Japanese culture. I do not regard tradition as being restricted to the transmission of tangible forms but as including such intangibles as styles of life, customs, thoughts, aesthetic sensibilities and sensitivities.

In the transmission of Japanese culture in particular these intangibles are paramount. While we can transmit Japanese culture by injecting it into contemporary architectural expression employing the latest high-technology materials, it is also possible to represent very traditional forms within the Japanese aesthetic sensitivity, including the absence of a centre, open-endedness, asymmetry, the expression of detail, and disjunction (deconstruction).

These elements of the Japanese aesthetic appear as a sense of balance, not in the form of a system but when they are disposed as separate elements. We might also say that their special character is that they possess form as aura, mood, feeling. The essence of Japanese sensitivity can be described with the philosophy of symbiosis, which is a text both for the special nature of Japanese culture and for the transformation of the modern paradigm.

Mood, feeling and atmosphere can each be described as a symbolic order without an established structure. It is through a variety of dynamic, intersecting relationships and juxtapositions – the relationship between one sign and other symbolic elements with which it stands; the way the content of the sign changes when it is quoted; the existence of a medium, an intermediating space introduced between different elements; the relation of the parts to the whole – that mood, feeling and atmosphere are created.

In architecture, the meaning produced by the individual elements placed here and there, and by their relationships and disjunctions, is multivalent and ambiguous. When this meaning creates a feeling and an atmosphere, architecture can approach poetic creation.

To regard architecture as no more than actual space, a stacking of bricks on top of each other, is to accept the models of the pyramid and the tree. But the alternative is to consider all elements of architecture as words (signs), between which new meanings and atmospheres can be created. Since all elements of the work of architecture – the pillars, ceilings, walls, stairways, windows, skylights, rooms enclosed by walls, entranceways, open spaces, furniture, lighting, door handles, the treatment of the walls – exist as quotations, transformations, sophistications, connotations, symbolisations and intermediations, the solid, substantial architecture, the stack of bricks is already deconstructed.

Another way of describing the discovery of meaning in the intermediary (vacant) space between elements is to say that we are evoking meaning by setting elements in relation to each other. Pillars and walls, which have only had meaning as structural elements in architecture up until now, can be deconstructed from the hierarchy of structure and given independent symbolic existence.

The four bamboo poles that are set up at the Shinto-style ground-breaking ceremony which is observed before commencing each construction have a fictional connotation. Their physical nature as bamboo poles disappears and they connote the symbolic aura of the place for the descent of the gods. In his work *Le système des objets*, Baudrillard wrote of space enclosed by elements he calls things: 'Space, too, has a fictional connotation. All forms are relativised as they pass through space. A spacious room has a natural effect. It breathes. When there is a lack of space, the atmosphere is destroyed because our breath is robbed by the things crowded into it. Perhaps we should read a reflection of the moral principles of separation and division in this distribution of space. If that is so, it is a reversal of the traditional connotation of space as a full, existing substance.' The space he refers to is the vacant space between objects, called in Japanese *ma,* or 'in-between space'. It is natural in the sense that it is outside existing, wild and breathing. Unlike a pile of bricks, it does not have the connotation of solidity, of actuality, but of emptiness, of nothingness.

Atmosphere is evoked along the ties of relation that link thing to thing. Baudrillard's theory of architecture brilliantly reverses the epistemology of Modern architecture, transforming it into an ontology.

If the pyramid and the tree are models of modernist hierarchy, the models of post-modern order are the semi-lattice structure and the rhizome of Deleuze and Guattari. The rhizome represents the principle of union and difference, a multiplicity in which relations are possible at any number of points. It is completely different from the tree, which is a model of a unilateral, frozen hierarchy. The concept of the semi-lattice resembles the rhizome's multiplicity. It, too, is an open-ended order in which different points are continually evoking meaning in their relations. Julia Kristeva describes this type of ontological relationship as a 'polylogue', the condition in which 'many different logics, many different selves, exist in different places and at different times.' It is 'an active, parallel order of things that arise in the process of the evocation of meaning.'

In any case, the evocation of meaning is not realised through some established hierarchy, but is an active state evoked in the process of relation.

Architecture for the Information Society

Just as Modern architecture and the International Style belong to the industrial society, Post-Modern architecture will be the architecture of the information society. The present collapse of Modernism and repudiation of Modern architecture can be attributed to the transformation of the paradigm of industrial society. The most advanced nations are rapidly shifting from industrial production to the production of information. And, while industrialisation has followed the stages of evolution described by the American economist Walt William Rostow, handed down from developed to developing nations, the information society transcends economic and technological evolutionary stages and differences of ideology, enabling the entire world to progress at the same time.

Specifically, the information and related industries include: broadcasting, publishing, finance, research, education, tourism, design, fashion, trade, transportation, and the food, leisure and service sectors. What all these industries have in common is that they do not depend mainly on the production or assembly of things; instead, their products are information, added value and culture itself.

In the fashion industry, the added value of design is worth many times the cost of the materials themselves. In restaurants, the skill of the chef, the quality of the service, and the décor are worth far more than the cost of the ingredients that make up the food served. Even in industrial products, there is a shift from mass production to limited production of a greater variety of goods giving added value through variety, and the added value of design is receiving increased attention.

While the industrial society aimed for universality and homogeneity, the information society will aim for multiplicity. Universal, homogenised information is of reduced value; in order to establish their own identities, people try to distinguish themselves from others. In this manner, things, people, and society will grow infinitely various, and architecture is no exception. The differentiation of architecture will be achieved in the evocation of new meanings, bringing differences and variety into new work.

It is mistaken to regard the Post-Modern as a chaotic transitional period. The appearance of a highly differentiated architecture, the eruption of the evocation of new meanings is the manifestation of the architecture of the information age. Differences are created by giving consideration to relations, or by Heidegger's 'care' (*Sorge*). The evocation of meaning through difference requires a keen sensitivity as an essential prerequisite.

The information society will create trans-global relationships in real time through travel and communication. Different languages, ways of life, and different cultures come directly into our homes via television and other media. This allows for a depth of multivalent meaning unthinkable in the age of Western dominance. The transformation of the paradigm of an industrial society to one of an information society is playing a large role in shifting the world from the dominance of the West and logos.

Roland Barthes, in his *Mythologies,* calls this the 'age of the power of meaning'. Since the age of an information society is a time when meaning will be evoked through differences, we will see a shift from the 'syndigmatic' linear, explicit thought patterns of Modernism and denotation to 'paradigmatic', non-linear, latent thought patterns and connotation.

Barthes refers to transformations or expansion of meaning achieved through connotation as a mythological function. Theodor Adorno, the German philosopher, also speaks of the importance of the mythological function (mimensis) in contemporary society. In his *Aesthetische Theorie,* he describes mimensis as the 'reason of harmony', and predicts that the unfortunate dualism and binomial opposition of reason and intuition in Western metaphysics will be harmoniously resolved through mimensis.

Modernism and modern rational thinking were given their basic nature through the objective rationalism of Galileo, Newton and Descartes. The principle of identity, in which there is an objective and universally applicable

Kisho Kurokawa, Hiroshima City Museum of Contemporary Art, Hiroshima, 1988.

view of the world common to all, is epitomised by the perspective drawing, used in architecture and the visual arts. Perspective, which depicts the entire world from a single, visible point, is like the head of Medusa, turning all who look on it to stone. In perspective, not only is the viewer himself eliminated from the picture, but all that is beyond his line of vision is rejected.

We must abandon single-point perspective and move the point of vision so that it reveals the relationships among all things. A point of view in which the world and people are seen from the perspective of things is probably also necessary. This would imply a point of view of the infinitely varied whole. Modern man, who has depended too much on his eyes to view the world, cannot understand why a person from a 'primitive' tribe doesn't wear clothes. The 'primitive' man answers: 'My entire body is my face.'

Recently, the theory of measurement in quantum physics has revealed that even the one true measurement made through scientific processes is actually nothing more than a state which has been accidentally selected, whereas that selection itself causes the instantaneous collapse of the quantum wave function, rendering the state perceptible – that is, measurable – to us. In fact, all possible states exist at the same time, overlapping each other. This is called the Copenhagen Interpretation.

The image of architecture revealed through reason alone, a whole established solely from the point of view of the visible, the single, correct measurement made by science, is actually no more than a partial glimpse of a rhizome-like multiplicity.

Without a doubt, the architecture of the information society will shift from a paradigm of symmetry to one of asymmetry, from being self-enclosed to being open-ended, from the whole to the part, from structuring to deconstruction and from centrality to non-centrality. It will aim for the freedom and uniqueness of all human beings, for the symbiosis of different cultures, and for a spiritually rich pluralistic society.

The Realisation of Architectural Works

The Symbiosis of History and Nature

The hill of Hijiyama now stands in the centre of Hiroshima City, but it is said to have once been an island in Hiroshima Bay. Hijiyama was chosen as the site for the construction of a new symbol of contemporary Hiroshima City, as distinct from the Hiroshima Peace centre built after World War II as a symbol of 'No more Hiroshimas'. After the completion of the master plan for the layout of the facilities and the general design of the Hijiyama complex eight years ago, work proceeded in stages, as roads, the observatory, the park area, and the Aozora Library were completed.

The Hiroshima City Museum of Contemporary Art is situated on the ridge of the hill, just off the axis of the Aozora Library. With the eventual completion of a natural history museum and a museum of local history, the Hijiyama complex will become a cultural centre – a new symbol of the city of Hiroshima.

Kisho Kurokawa, Hiroshima City Museum of Contemporary Art, Hiroshima, 1988.

ABOVE AND BELOW: Kisho Kurokawa, Honjin Memorial Museum of Art, Ishikawa, 1990. *OPPOSITE*: Kisho Kurokawa, Melbourne Central, Melbourne, 1990, view of model.

The design of the Hiroshima City Museum of Contemporary Art is based on the philosophy of symbiosis. The reappraisal of Modernism and Modern architecture means the reappraisal of the dominance of the West and the logos which are part and parcel of Modernism. The cultural references of Post-Modern architecture in Europe and the United States are also based on the West, and in that respect Post-Modern architecture does not differ from Modern architecture. The doctrine of rationalism and logos meant that humanity (and architecture) were called on to control and restrain the nature that lay outside. In addition, human reason was to control and restrain the nature that lay inside: the 'wildness' or sensitivity. The concept of the symbiosis of humanity (architecture) and nature is a transformation of that paradigm of the dominance of logos.

Modernism was also a doctrine of the present, and the quotation of historical signs and symbols was deprecated as 'hybridisation'. Instead, pure, abstract geometric figures were regarded as the triumph of reason.

This obsession with the present must also be reconsidered, yet the method of quoting historical symbols and styles directly, is especially likely to degenerate into mere hybridisation. In order to evoke a more creative and multivalent meaning, a symbiosis of history and the future, the historical signs and symbols must be subjected to transformation, articulation, sophistication and intermediation.

The Hiroshima City Museum of Contemporary Art was carefully situated on the ridge of the hill to give priority to the preservation of as much of the wooded areas on the slopes of the hill as possible. In order to keep the height of the building from exceeding that of the surrounding trees, part of the exhibition space was set underground, so that some 60 per cent of the total floor space is below ground. Many intermediary zones between the work of architecture and its natural setting have been incorporated into the building's exterior – a central approach plaza with a colonnade, a patio, a corridor, a stone garden, a stairway sculpted from stone – facilitating the symbiosis of architecture and nature, interior and exterior. The materials used on the building exterior also evolve gradually, from the natural stone foundation upward to roughly finished stone, polished stone, tile and aluminium; from earth to sky, from ground to the universe, from the past to the future – all are in symbiosis. I have been using this method for nearly a decade, for example at the Melbourne Central and the Okinawa Prefectural Government Headquarters, now under construction.

The overall shape of the museum is a linked series of gable roofs. It is segmented, a work of architecture that is a village, a group of dwellings: we might call this the symbiosis of part and whole. This has permitted the museum to achieve a scale that does not dominate its natural setting.

The gable roofs are a quotation of Edo-period earthen storehouses, but the use of the contemporary material aluminium transforms that historical sign and imbues it with ambiguity. This is the efficacy of connotation. The central

approach plaza is a quotation of a Western city, yet there is no fountain or work of sculpture in its centre, indicating an empty centre, or the absence of a centre. The roof of the colonnade that rings the central plaza is cut away at the front, in the direction that faces the city centre, connoting the site of the atomic bombing, and the pillars of the colonnade rise from stones exposed by the blast. Like the *roji* entrance-way garden leading to a tea room, this approach plaza has no particular function, yet it is an important area in the evocation of the meanings of the symbiosis of history and the present, and of heterogeneous cultures.

A Henry Moore arch is set in the outdoor sculpture garden opposite the approach plaza, and from the cut-away section of the plaza, it suggests a gun sight that automatically leads the eye to the site of the atomic blast. The approach plaza also acts as an intermediary zone between the permanent exhibition space on the right and the galleries for special exhibitions on the left. The circular corridor that links these is a dynamic intermediate area. The stairway that connects the permanent exhibition space with the first floor and the underground level is a sculpture created by Inoue Bukichi, a new experiment in the symbiosis of architecture and sculpture. The Hiroshima City Museum of Contemporary Art is the first museum in Japan to include works of contemporary architecture, industrial and graphic design in its collection: in 1988 it exhibited the architectural models and plans of Le Corbusier in its possession. It continues to pursue a unique collection, including works which it has commissioned from some 80 Japanese and foreign artists on the theme of Hiroshima, and I believe it will prove itself a museum of international calibre and interest in the years to come.

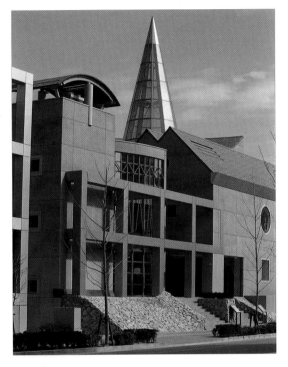

The Symbiosis of History and the Present

The theme of the design for the Honjin Memorial Museum of Art is the symbiosis of history and the present. As in the Hiroshima City Museum of Contemporary Art, I have quoted the Edo-period storehouse as a metaphor. The pure geometric form of the circle is displaced, and a complex, fissured space has been created for the façade.

The square moat and lattice-style fence that surrounds the perimeter of the building is a modern manifestation of the ancient Chinese theory that the Heavens are round and the Earth is square. The moat surrounding the building is a sign that this lot was once the site of a moat-surrounded castle. The centre space of the interior has a simple two-storey open space, but even this is unfinished, and with its wedge-shaped skylight it expresses the absence of a centre and a rejection of the universality of pure geometry. By emphasising asymmetrical forms, the work challenges the centrality of logos and the West.

The basic theme for my prize-winning plan for the New Osaka Prefectural Headquarters Complex is the symbiosis of past and future. Since the historical monument Osaka Castle is located on the same site, its moat, its stone walls and the castle itself have been quoted as historical allusions. While other

Kisho Kurokawa, Fukuoka Seaside Momochi, Sawara, Fukuoka, 1989.

designs submitted included twin high-rise towers, one for the administrative headquarters and the other for the police headquarters, my plan has only one, for the administrative headquarters. The rest of the structure is of medium or low height, in an attempt to attain a symmetry with Osaka Castle. Administrative, police and prefectural assembly blocks, the governor's mansion, a family court, lodging for assembly representatives, a separate administrative block and a cultural hall are all planned for the ten-hectare site. Geometrical forms such as domes, vaults, four-sided pyramids, triangular roofs and patios have been employed symbolically to distinguish the different architectural forms. The high-rise administrative block is a three-tier superstructure, which, aside from its own intrinsic meaning, is an allusion to the form of Osaka Castle.

The Symbiosis of Heterogeneous Elements

Fukuoka Seaside Momochi is presently serving as an exhibition for the work of eight architects, but eventually it will be a multipurpose structure housing a branch of the Fukuoka Bank, a bookstore, and an information centre. This is an attempt to allow these various works of architecture to function individually and, while permitting each of them to express itself in the signs of it own unique form, to forge them into a fluid and yet composite whole.

The exterior walls are made from water-polished stone mixed with natural stone; the trusses are made of wood, and natural light enters from the skylights; all of these are metaphors for nature. Signs of traditional Japanese architecture are quoted in the designs of the windows and the lattices. The light tower and the curving walls are connotations of European culture. The exterior space is designed to be complex and to create an intermediary space that leads people into the interior, so that they may experience the symbiosis of interior and exterior that characterises traditional Japanese architecture.

The Shibuya Higashi T Building is a small office building in the middle of Tokyo. The narrow approach hall of this building is filled with many different signs: a metal folding screen, a polyurethane screen alluding to lacquerware, an unfinished concrete wall and a granite wall all exist in synthesis. Here is the symbiosis of past and future, the West and East. Though the work is a simple square form, several wedge-shaped aluminium exterior curtain walls serve to reject the universal, the pure, and to cast the building off-centre. The roof, suggesting a cross-section of an aircraft wing, alludes to flight, defying the building's gravity.

The methodology that all these designs have in common is that the philosophy of symbiosis – the expression of my will – is at their base, and they present a challenge to the dominance of the West, of logos, of dualism, and of the universal. In contrast to the methodology of Modern architecture – analysis, structuring, organisation, introduction, synthesis, adaptation, clarification, denotation – the processes adopted in the plans I have introduced above are symbolisation, deconstruction, relation, quotation, intermediation, transformation, sophistication and connotation.

Kisho Kurokawa, Shibuya Higashi T Building, Tokyo, 1989.

Following each respective method, the signs that are quoted in these designs are situated as free elements, and each person who reads them is free to adopt his own method of interpretation. There is no one accurate reading of each sign; the objective of this method is to permit the various signs to operate in free combination and to contribute to the evocation of meaning, create *la poétique* and produce an atmosphere of its own narratives in symbiosis.

Kisho Kurokawa, Shibuya Higashi T Building, Tokyo, 1989, entrance and elevator hall on the third floor.

Kisho Kurokawa, Tokyo Bay design depicting the forest, the
Loop City and the Loop Canals.

The Symbiosis of Redevelopment and Restoration

Non-economic 'Life Factors' in Regional Planning

The towns of Vasto and San Salvo in southern Italy, along the Adriatic coast, are beautiful cities that still look as they did in Roman times. Agriculture is their main industry, and since they have not succeeded in introducing any secondary industries, per capita income is low compared to the industrialised cities and towns of northern Italy.

At a public meeting on regional planning in the provincial assembly, people from the region declared that their aim was not the high per capita income of northern Italy. They didn't want to bring all sorts of factories into the area and make it like the north, but wanted to preserve their beautiful coastline, their lovely cities, their delicious seafood and their lifestyle. They sought, accordingly, a plan for their region based on a true understanding of these wishes.

I was deeply impressed by this declaration of the people of Vasto and San Salvo. When the day arrives that we hear the same sentiments expressed by the people of various regions in Japan, we too can have regional cities that preserve the unique character of each area. As long as every city aims to match and mimic Tokyo, we are bound to see thousands of mini-Tokyos sprout across Japan; but how much more attractive is the image of regional cities, each distinct and rich in local character.

If the increase of per capita income is the guiding economic principle of regional development, distinct local character and lifestyle, in contrast, are decidedly non-economic principles. 'Character' and 'lifestyle' are instead life principles which guarantee that the local residents will be able to live a human life with pride in their surroundings and their history. We cannot afford to ignore these life principles: today we need a plan for regional development that balances the economic and non-economic factors.

From the 1960s, Japan's national planning has consistently been linked with the economic policy of achieving a standard per capita income throughout the country. The Ikeda cabinet (1960-64) was the first to make this a national goal. Its 'Plan for Doubling Per Capita Income' (1961-70) spurred the Japanese on to greater productivity, towards a goal that could be clearly grasped by anyone. That government constructed what is now known as the Pacific coast industrial belt. The region was chosen for development because of its excellent harbours, ready supply of labour, and proximity to a large consumer market. It was very well suited for the development of the secondary industries of processing raw materials, which made up Japan's leading industrial sector at the

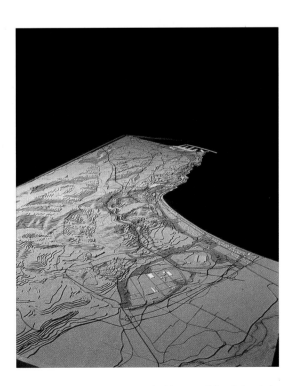

Kisho Kurokawa, regional plan for Vasto and San Salvo, Italy, 1975.

time. The intensive development of this region so rich in potential led, in the end, to a concentration of the nation's capital, industrial power, and population in the Pacific coast industrial belt. In response, there arose a cry from other regions of Japan, particularly those along the Japan Sea coast, for a fairer share of the national productivity and a rectification of the gap between per capita income on the Pacific coast and the rest of Japan.

The slogan of the succeeding Sato cabinet (1964-72) was 'Social Development'. This government sought to decentralise industry, which had become too concentrated, planning and building new industrial cities throughout Japan. These cities were supposed to stop the flow of labour, especially of young workers, from local areas to Tokyo and the Pacific belt. If that exodus could be stopped, local economies would revive, tax revenues increase, and public works projects could be undertaken and the local environment improved.

This was the rationale for the new industrial cities and the start of decentralisation. This strategy appeared to be an ideal plan for the improvement of local life throughout Japan, highly advantageous to the residents of those regions; and, in fact, within certain limits, the 'decentralisation = standardisation of per capita income' equation was effective. The gap between earnings in Tokyo and other regions shrank.

But the complete decentralisation of Japan proved to have some major disadvantages for local areas, too. First, it was extremely wasteful in terms of the investment required in public works and facilities. The old ideal of a regional city was of a self-sufficient unit that could meet all the needs of its residents, from cradle to grave. People were born, educated, married, raised families and died in their city. A very strong community spirit, almost a family feeling, is promoted in such a city.

However, isolated and static communities of this sort need all the goods and services of modern life brought to them, which thus have to be supplied to a very limited market. In its most extreme form, this policy would mean that all the facilities of contemporary life, from cinemas and department stores to universities and research centres, Kabuki theatres and opera houses, would have to be constructed and supported in each region, for a limited local population. But every city does not need its own Kabuki theatre or opera house; several cities can share one. The market or audience for these arts is then greatly increased. We must conclude that entirely self-supporting small and medium-sized regional cities are economically unfeasible.

Network Cities for the Age of *Homo Movens*

The second disadvantage of complete decentralisation is that it makes it difficult for people to move between regions. The title of my book *Homo Movens*, (meaning of course, man on the move, after the models *Homo sapiens*, man as thinker, and *Homo faber*, man as maker), expresses the importance of mobility as the special characteristic of contemporary humankind. Just as the concept of *Homo faber* is linked to principles on which industrial society is based, *Homo movens* is linked to the principle of industrial society.

The mobility that characterises modern society cannot be explained simply in terms of the development of transportation. The fact is that in our information society, mobility has begun to possess considerable value for its own sake. It is choice that makes movement possible. According to your own inclinations and values, you can now choose things that are not found in the place you were born. People today look on the availability of choices as one of the riches of life – 'a wealth of choices.' The city of the future, as we continue to evolve into an information society, should be a city that guarantees freedom of choice and makes positive provisions for movement.

The third disadvantage of decentralisation is that, economically speaking, a small city simply cannot compete with a big one. There is no way that a small city can match a large one in the amount of available capital, population, or consumer activity. Simple decentralisation only leads smaller cities to make fruitless efforts to achieve that which they never can.

All in all, a policy of total decentralisation has many disadvantages and is no better than the opposite policy of total concentration in a single region. A truly ideal plan can never be achieved as long as the dualistic choice is either decentralisation or centralisation. National planning in Japan has been grappling with this problem, and at last has produced a New National General Development Plan. A completely new policy of regional development, neither centralisation nor decentralisation but a network city is at last taking shape.

The concept of the local city as an independent and self-sufficient unit will be abandoned in an age of *Homo movens*, with people always on the move from city to city. Cities will be connected by transportation and information networks that will weave a spider's web of linked cities, in a symbiosis of centralisation and decentralisation.

The network theory of cities is based on two major assumptions. One is that an information society will supersede our industrial society. The second is that each city in the network will establish its own cultural identity and pursue its own development based on that culture. If the kind of network we are talking about is formed in an industrial society, there is great danger of a 'siphon phenomenon' occurring between large and small cities: the economies of the smaller cities, which have less accumulated capital and labour, might be siphoned off by the larger cities with densely concentrated resources. This has actually happened along the bullet train lines, where economies of the smaller cities have been siphoned off by the larger cities. The leading sector of industrial society, manufacturing finished products from raw materials, depends to a great extent on concentrated capital, productivity and consumption, so the 'siphon phenomenon' is very likely to occur.

By contrast, in an information society, the leading sector of the economy is made up of such tertiary industries as broadcasting, publishing, education and the service industries. These depend mostly on accumulated culture, and so the economies of small cities do not fall victim to the 'siphon phenomenon'; they may even take an enormous lead over large cities.

Kyoto, for example, cannot be compared economically with Tokyo or

Osaka, but its accumulated cultural wealth is one of the highest in the world. In the 21st century, the information value of cultural treasures, skills and scholarship will continue to increase. As a source of information, Kyoto is far superior to Tokyo, and this will be a powerful weapon for Kyoto, and cities like it, in the information age.

An 'Event Economy' for the Regions

In the information age, the character of each regional city, no matter how small, will be a source of economic strength. At the same time, the evolution from an industrial to an information society will be a move from an age of economic priority to one of the priority of knowledge and expertise. Already it is becoming possible to enlarge regional economies, which have been strictly limited up to now, through the power of knowledge.

The 'event economy' that I propose is an example. A calender of local events can generate enormous income by attracting visitors from outside the region. The economic scope of tourism and resort industries is completely unrelated to the size of the local population.

Another example is the sweet-potato liquor 'Downtown Napoleon', which has expanded its market to the entire nation. The governor of Oita Prefecture, Morihiko Hiramatsu, has led a successful 'village product' campaign, in which many events have been held. When local groups hold exhibitions and fairs, promote international conferences and cinema festivals and encourage local festivals, they can sell their agricultural and other products on a nationwide scale. Regional efforts to expand local markets now achieve success through these kinds of events.

Local tax revenues have until now been determined by certain set, inflexible figures: the taxes on forestry, farming and the local population. In the future, however, local governments will start offering financial support for ideas. The conduct of regional government itself will change as it turns to supporting ideas for events that will get the region's economy moving.

In an information age, an age of ideas, networks between big and small cities will avoid a one-way siphon phenomenon, promoting the symbiosis of cities. As this continues to develop, small cities will increase their own information-generating capacity and exploit the markets of large cities. This is one reason why regional planning should adopt the concept of the network.

Cities with High Information-generating Capacities

The Japanese Fourth National Development Plan (1983-2000) focuses mainly on the Tokyo metropolitan zone, and many have criticised the plan as another attempt to centralise Japan around the capital. Let us look at a portion of the plan's intermediary report that has stirred considerable controversy, under the heading 'Tokyo as an International Centre':

Tokyo is not only the capital of our country but, in such respects as international finance, for example, an international centre. It also provides information of international scope to other cities of Japan, and with

'Downtown Napoleon' (*Iichiko*).

its highly developed capacities contributes to the development of the economies of Japan and the world. To ensure that the entire Tokyo area can function as an international centre, we recommend the general development of the Tokyo Bay area, for which high-use demand continues to increase, and the adjacent coastal areas, while encouraging at the same time the selective decentralisation of various functions to other business centres and the reform of regional structures. We also recommend the development of access by regional cities to Tokyo, so that Tokyo's highly developed capacities may eventually be carried out across the nation. We especially recommend the creation of a data base of high-priority government and business information, now concentrated in Tokyo, together with a lowering of communication costs, so that other regions will have easy access to this information.

This section of the report caused a great stir among regional governments, as these newspaper headlines show: 'The Flames of Discontent Spread: Fourth National Plan Favours Tokyo'; 'Many Problems Remain with the Fourth National Plan'; 'The Regional Argument Against the Fourth National Plan: Mere Terminals of the Main Computer?'; and 'An Outdated National Plan – Concentration on Tokyo, an End to Regional Development and Support'.[1]

Of course, we cannot fail to recognise various problems with the present implementation of the plan. My own suggestion for the plan is that, since it has spotlighted Tokyo as an international centre, it must also offer the other regions methods for resisting Tokyo's dominance. Concretely speaking, it is time to rethink the traditional system of allocating public works projects uniformly across the country. Instead, the national government should make more investment in regional cities that have already achieved a certain degree of concentration and accumulation of resources, capital and population: Osaka, Nagoya, and Kyoto, as well as Sapporo, Sendai, Kanazawa, Hiroshima, Takamatsu, Oita and Kumamoto. These cities must be allowed to develop an appeal as living and working environments that can rival Tokyo.

An attractive city, in other words a city with a strong information-generating capacity, contributes enormously to establishing a regional identity and is linked also to the economic development of the region. One of the reasons regional cities are not as attractive as Tokyo is their relative poverty of choices: they simply offer far too little to choose from. People are drawn to a city that has more than one department store, or more than one university.

The relocation of the universities from Tokyo is a good idea. It would be confusing for various reasons to move universities with place names, such as Tokyo and Kyoto, positive steps should therefore be taken to get around this, such as renaming the universities with numbers, as was the practice in the previous century: First University, Second University, etc. When these major regional cities attain the functions of information centres they will lead the development of the entire region in an information society.

My second suggestion to the Fourth National Plan is to look for large-scale projects to undertake in other regions.

A Tunnel Connecting Shikoku and Kyushu

In 1988, the bridge connecting Honshu and Shikoku was completed, and right now the New Osaka International Airport project is under way. We need to continue to look for this type of project as we approach the 21st century.

Those projects, in addition, must be linked to the creation of a network of regional cities. Unless they link regional cities into a federation that can rival Tokyo or contribute to the further development of major regional cities which will then provide leverage to the surrounding towns, the investment will be of little meaning. One of the first projects that comes to mind is the expansion of the bullet train lines, indispensable for the creation of a network linking regional cities. Another project that I have been promoting for years is a tunnel linking Kyushu and Shikoku. This would play a major part in forming the network of regional cities.

Today all of Japan, with the exception of Okinawa, is linked. Hokkaido and Honshu are joined by the undersea tunnel from Aomori to Hakodate. The Seikan undersea tunnel connects Honshu to Kyushu, and three bridges span the sea between Honshu and Shikoku. Yet there are no plans to join Kyushu and Shikoku. If those islands were linked by a tunnel, a network comprising Kyushu, Shikoku, and the Chubu region of Japan would be created. This would be an enormous economic zone and an important urban federation.

The privatised Shikoku Railway Company is not doing well because at present Shikoku is a dead end. Yet one of the bridges joining it to Honshu is constructed so that a bullet train line can travel over it. If that bullet train line passed through Shikoku to Kyushu, the fortunes of the railway company would be revived in a single stroke. If the highway under construction in Shikoku now – also said to be very uneconomical – were linked to a Honshu-Shikoku bridge on one end and to Kyushu on the other, it would become a major national artery, and an economically justifiable one at that.

These projects would not only increase Shikoku's economic performance but would have a major economic impact on the Chugoku region of Honshu, on Kyushu, and even on the Kinki area of Honshu, contributing to the formation of a regional urban federation.

Encouraging more investment in the major regional cities and undertaking projects outside Tokyo will establish and enrich the regional network needed in an information society, and these are highly effective strategies for fostering the ability of other regions to rival Tokyo in activity and drawing power. Only when regional cities have acquired this power can there be a symbiosis of centralisation and decentralisation.

The Symbiosis of Three Networks

A third network is formed by international capitals of finance, which has now arrived on the Japanese archipelago.

With the deregulation of finance, Japan's short-term money market is growing at a rapid pace. When the total from trade in foreign currencies and interbank transactions, excluding reciprocal trading, is added to that of the open market, Japan's short-term money market reaches 627 billion dollars. This is the figure for 1989, converted to dollars at the 1989 rate. The Japanese market has already surpassed that of West Germany and Great Britain and is second only to the United States.

The Japanese money market will continue to grow. As the financial sector is completely deregulated, companies that have been investing overseas because they were unhappy with Japan's regulations are likely to return to domestic bonds. Japan's low interest rates make Japan's money market extremely attractive to international investors. The low interest rates are a result of Japan's huge economic surplus. The surplus for 1989 was 77 billion dollars. This enormous amount of money sits in the Japanese financial market, and of course, interest rates are low.

With its excess of money, Japan is investing in bonds and real estate in other countries, and buying up companies as well. Today, Japan's purely foreign investment capital totals more than 266 billion dollars, and it is predicted that within a few years it will reach 500 billion dollars. This is the enormous amount of capital that Japan is investing overseas. The more extensive this relationship with other countries becomes, the more important Japan's money market becomes. Whether we like it or not, we are a part of the network of the international financial markets.

The major American commercial bank, Banker's Trust, moved the general manager of capital markets division from New York to Tokyo in 1985. When IBM transferred the headquarters of its Pacific Group from New York to Tokyo, it made quite a splash in the weekly news magazines. Dupont Japan and Japan Texas Instruments have established research facilities in Japan. All of these are further demonstrations of Tokyo's importance in the eyes of the international financial market.

Another reason that Tokyo finds itself in the centre of the international financial network is geographical. The world of finance is in the age of 24-hour dealing. Making use of the time differences among different markets across the globe, 24-hour trading has become possible by moving on to Tokyo after New York closes, and then to London after Tokyo. Lights may remain on all night in the offices of major trading companies and banks. To keep up with 24-hour dealing, they have to watch the yen and the dollar and the international markets around the clock, in shifts.

The international money market needed an opening in time somewhere between New York and London – somewhere in Asia. Hong Kong and Singapore have been regarded as promising, but Tokyo, with its far superior investment capability, has taken the lead. Tokyo now exists in symbiosis with three networks – a federation of Japanese regional cities; the three major urban centres: Nagoya, Osaka and Tokyo; and an international money market network of an entirely different dimension.

This multilayered network has resulted in the following conditions in the city. According to the estimates of the Fourth Plan, by 2025 the number of non-Japanese residing in Japan will have reached 2.3 million. This is a conservative estimate, and I believe that 2.5 million is closer to the mark. This is equivalent to a city the size of Osaka and it will have a great influence on the country. The 'internationalisation' that had been little more than a vague slogan will take concrete form before our eyes.

The majority of those non-Japanese residents will be living in the international financial capital, Tokyo. Just as today New York has become a thoroughly international, global city, Tokyo will support its end of the international network. As a city, it will no longer belong completely to Japan.

While some will insist that the other regions of Japan should also internationalise to counterbalance the concentration of human and economic resources in Tokyo, Tokyo's development is linked with the development of the regions just as the development of another prefecture only occurs when it has a major city – an Osaka, a Nagoya or a Hiroshima – with its own concentration of people and information. We need simultaneous decentralisation and centralisation; we need, in other words, more urban centres.

France, for example, is now following a decentralisation policy, in a way which offers an interesting contrast with the Japanese. A communications and liaison committee of all government departments for the 'grands projets' under President Mitterrand has been at work on the redevelopment of Paris. The new Bastille opera house has been completed; the largest museum of science in the world and a unique music centre have been constructed in Parc de La Villette; the Musée d'Orsay has opened in the restored Orsay station; the Institute of the Arab World has been built on the Seine; an international competition (of which I was one of the judges) was held for the design of an international communications centre (La Tête Défense) to be built in the newly developed Défense area. Major additions are being made to the Louvre, after the move of the Ministry of the Treasury, which had occupied part of the Louvre's space. These new cultural facilities commemorate the second centennial of the French Revolution, just as the Eiffel Tower commemorated the first anniversary in 1889.

What is interesting is that there has been no resistance from other parts of the country to the further concentration of cultural facilities in Paris, already so richly blessed with them. As long as Paris continues as one of the leaders in the international network of global cities, the rest of France will have access to the same level of information through its domestic networks. Other regions of France are confident that they will prosper, their unique local cultures intact, by remaining linked with Paris.

In the 1920s, Berlin created a unique cultural environment, often labelled 'cabaret culture', as a world capital of cinema, theatre and architecture. In 1987, the 750th anniversary of the founding of the city was marked by an international architectural exhibition: the IBA. Some 50 architects from around the world were invited to participate in this ambitious project, including myself representing Japan. Each was given a site and asked to design a plan for its redevelopment, which should be left as architectural exhibits for the 21st century. The exhibition aimed to restore the divided city, long out of the

ABOVE: A network connecting Shikoku island to Kyushu island. *BELOW*: La Défense, Paris, 1989.

international limelight, to a new glory equal to that of the 1920s, when it led all of Germany.

My idea that centralisation and decentralisation must exist in symbiosis is essentially the same as the idea behind the Berlin project. Tokyo must be developed and, through its participation in the network of international cities, all of Japan will be linked to the rest of the world.

A Man-made Island in Tokyo Bay

A major redevelopment of Tokyo is required to enable it to function as an opening to the network of international cities. This redevelopment is no more than the preparation of the access route through which one of the networks of a world on an entirely different, much higher level, will enter a network that will create a new age in every region of Japan.[2]

Millions of non-Japanese will pour into the city, and even now Tokyo does not have sufficient housing. The coastal areas are being recommended for new developments, but it is not ecologically sound to continue to increase landfill along the shore; this method also drives up land prices in adjacent areas and makes public works more expensive.

I believe it is much wiser to preserve the shoreline more or less as it is and build a man-made island off Tokyo, like Portopia in Kobe. Let us assume we are building an island of 30,000 hectares in Tokyo Bay. At its deepest, the bay is 20 metres, and it is estimated that the sludge on the bay bottom is another seven metres deep, so for an island five metres above sea level, you would need landfill to a depth of 32 metres. The amount of landfill to create an island of 30,000 hectares – approximately two-thirds the size of the present 23 wards of Tokyo – would be nine billion cubic yards. This is equivalent to two-thirds of Mount Fuji. Where could this amount of landfill come from?

First, from the dredging of Tokyo Bay itself: this would produce 4.5 billion cubic metres of soil. The other half of the total needed would be provided by excavating a Boso Canal – a canal 500 metres across, connecting Tokyo Bay with the Pacific Ocean through the Boso Peninsula. If the Boso Canal were built, the difference in the tides would mean that three or four metres of water would come rushing in and out of Tokyo Bay daily. This would cleanse the bay and increase its marine life, in a symbiosis with development.

At present, several hundreds of thousands of boats ply the waters of Tokyo Bay annually. The creation of a man-made island would disrupt their traffic, so the port of Tokyo would have to be moved to the tip of the island. At the same time, an outer Tokyo Port would be constructed at the Pacific mouth of the Boso Canal. Products that did not have to be unloaded in Tokyo Bay could be shipped from there by pipeline.

The cost of constructing this 30,000-hectare man-made island would be about 80 trillion yen. Computing the net land cost from this, 3.3 square metres would cost about two million yen. If we suppose a land-use ratio of 400 per cent, that is reduced to five hundred thousand yen, a cost that would permit the average white-collar worker to buy a condominium. In that projected cost of two million yen per 3.3 square metres, all construction and support facility costs are included: undergrounds, bridges, roads, parks, water, and energy plants. A pleasant, liveable apartment from which one could commute by underground, by car or even by boat need not be an impossible dream.

The intent of this project does not contradict the larger policy of decentralising population and technological capacity across the archipelago. It is merely a plan to improve the appalling living circumstances of Tokyo's working class, to meet the needs of the rising foreign population and to improve the business efficiency of Tokyo as an international financial centre.

The projected population for this man-made island is five million. Of that total, 1.5 million will be non-Japanese. The projected population increase for the native Tokyo population by 2025 is another 1.5 million. The remaining two million will be previous residents of 'mainland' Tokyo, lessening its population density. The completion of the man-made island will not intensify the concentration of population in Tokyo.

As far as the 80-trillion-yen construction cost is concerned, we can see that, with the enormous amount of Japanese money invested overseas, this is a far from impossible figure. Furthermore, there is a clear and certain demand for this new island. Land sells for about 12.7 million yen per 3.3 square metres today, so the profit to be had from this project is approximately 200 trillion yen. If the project were carried out by private enterprise, the capital that is now floating around in the domestic stock market and foreign bonds could be attracted by this potential profit. The tax revenues from this 200 trillion yen could be used for further redevelopment of Tokyo and the major regional cities. In other parts of Japan, the same pattern could be followed: encouraging projects based on private enterprise, and using the profits to initiate yet other projects. This would be a way to bring funds that float like disembodied spirits through the stock market and foreign investments down to earth, in Japan.

For the Japanese government, facing the challenges of institutional reform and the restoration of government finances, large-scale regional projects and the redevelopment of Tokyo are burdens too heavy to bear. It is in the country's best interests to push surplus funds from profitable enterprises into increased circulation and pursue regional development on the private level. In the future, this new strategy will attract considerable attention.

Preserving the Jumble of Tokyo's Rhizome

The new island in Tokyo Bay will provide the elbow room necessary for the redevelopment and resuscitation of Tokyo. The recent jump in land costs has made redevelopment of the present city increasingly difficult. The new land of the man-made island will be useful here, providing land of the same value in exchange for land in mainland Tokyo.

The aims of Tokyo's redevelopment will be to make the city safer in the case of a natural disaster on the scale of the Great Kanto earthquake; to increase the space per person in Tokyo's housing, currently far below the national average; and to add to the city's green spaces. If two or three million people

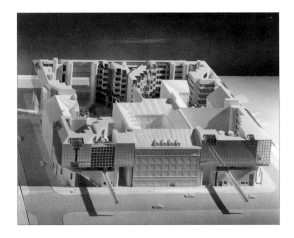

Kisho Kurokawa, Redevelopment project for South Friedrichstadt, IBA, Berlin, 1980. The plan proposed that existing structures be preserved and the old wall line of the city restored. However, part of the new street facade is lattice, and the actual buildings face inside, slanting at an angle towards an inner garden. Thus, the plan provides both a 'soft facade', which suggests diversity of human activity existent inside, and a 'hard facade', which conceals the inside and unites these varied elements into an urban order. The lattices and the 'city door' of the facade are the manner to connect the inner garden with the outside streets. The intermediate space created in-between allows for interpenetration of streets and buildings, bringing continuity and symbiosis to the buildings and city. Various facilities such as housing, shops, offices, public facilities and accommodation for elderly and handicapped people are piled up in vertical order. An abstract mirror facade suggests another dimension of space in this urban environment and another image of an invisible world.

can be drawn away from Tokyo to the new island, two loop-shaped canals can be excavated in the land that they vacate. A belt of high-rise buildings can then be constructed along both sides of these canals. These loop cities will be effective firebreaks in case of a natural disaster.

Aside from the canals' construction and their high-rise loop cities, Tokyo can be left as it is. The maze-like chaos of Tokyo is a natural rhizome that possesses the potential for becoming a city of night, a post-modern city of symbiosis. Tokyo today seems chaotic, without order. If order means the Avenue des Champs-Elysées in Paris, where the buildings on both sides of the avenue are standard in height and consistent in design, then indeed Tokyo is chaotic. While there's nothing wrong with broad boulevards and high-rise buildings, we also want cluttered maze-like districts to explore. Tokyo's attraction is in its complexity, its variety and its wide range of choices. Its constant transformation is also enjoyable. It is a city that doesn't distinguish between the wealthy, the middle class, and poor students; a city that is fun and interesting to walk through (unlike Los Angeles, for example); it also has buses, an underground and taxis, and this wide range of choice is what makes Tokyo human.

Modern Tokyo is a city in which old things and places are preserved, even if they lack historical value, but at the same time a city that is being rebuilt with the most advanced technology, the most pioneering designs and avant-garde architecture. We must not lose this source of Tokyo's attraction through redevelopment. If we supplement Tokyo with the elements it lacks and proceed pragmatically with the required changes, it may well become the most attractive and interesting city in the world by the 21st century. Aside from doubling the amount of park land and greenery and increasing the size of living space, the city should be left alone. Leaving it as it is, we can proceed slowly, taking our time with Tokyo's revitalisation.

The development of the loop cities along the canals and the preservation of the present city are a package. We could call this the symbiosis of development and preservation. There is also a need to invest in the suburban areas outside the present belt motorway number eight to foster the development of an urban network there. And we should also restore the Musashino Forest, creating a ten-thousand-hectare deciduous grounds that is a combination of castle grounds and sacred forest.

Contemporary Tokyo has three important overlapping meanings for the Japanese people: it is their greatest metropolis, the capital and the home of the Emperor who is symbolic of the nation. This degree of concentration is unnatural. The nation's capital should be transferred to the new island in the bay, which will then become a special administrative district. Kyoto will be celebrating its 12th centennial in 1994. Why not mark the occasion by building a new imperial palace in Kyoto? It could become the first imperial palace, and the present palace in Tokyo could be a second palace. Couldn't we have the Emperor spending half the year in Kyoto?

A linear motorway that would connect Tokyo with Osaka in only an hour should be built, and the functions of the nation's capital split among Tokyo,

Osaka and Nagoya. Even now several ministries – the Imperial Palace Agency, the Ministry of Education, the Agency for Cultural Affairs and the Science and Technology Agency – have relocated one or another of their divisions, and the belt from Tokyo to Osaka can already be regarded as a 'capital corridor'. One way of invigorating Hokkaido and the Tohoku region would be to run the bullet train through the Seikan tunnel, build a 'super port' in Hakadate and relocate the Supreme Court in Sapporo.

It is widely held that Japan's current huge budget surplus can only last another three decades. Now is our chance to build a new Japan for future generations. Nor do I think that Japan will end its age in the sun as just an economic giant. In the new age that is dawning across the world Japan will for the first time make its own creative contributions to world thought and culture.

Epilogue

From Coexistence to Symbiosis

I first began to use the phrase 'the concept of symbiosis' in 1979. My interest in the idea began when I was chairman of the Yokohama Design Conference, on the theme 'Towards the Era of Symbiosis', but I had been discussing 'the concept of coexistence' since the 1960s. In a book I published in the early 60s, *Toshi Dezain (Urban design)*, the section 'The Philosophy of Coexistence' commented in part:

> Isn't dualism a sickness that has taken root in all areas of modern thought and methodology? To put it impetuously, we cannot conceive of European civilisation without Christianity. European civilisation is, in other words, Christian civilisation. Christianity presupposes such dualisms as that between a good and an evil deity, the god of goodness and light and the evil material world, or the creator and his creation. This is true of Western philosophy as well. The philosophical dualism in which the fundamental principle of the universe was the separation of existence into mind and matter was already established in ancient Greece. In modern times, Descartes postulated a dualism between mind as a limited entity that depended on God for its existence on the one hand, and matter on the other. Kant, who divided existence into the thing in itself and phenomena, freedom and necessity, was also a typical dualist.
>
> European Rationalism has been the spiritual backbone that has supported the industrialisation and modernisation of society. This Rationalism is based on dualism. Our thought has been articulated from head to tail in dualistic forms: spirit and body, art and science, man and machine, sensitivity and rationality.
>
> Humanity has relentlessly pursued these two extremes, terrified of the deep chasm it has discovered between them. Without a doubt, the impressive modern civilisation born of European Rationalism is the product of the recognition of this deep abyss and the will to somehow or other bridge it.
>
> The discoveries of contemporary design, too, are based on dualism, giving us such contrasting pairs of terms as beauty and utility, form and function, architecture and the city, human scale and urban (superhuman) scale. All debates about design up to now have been pendulum-like, swinging back and forth between such extremes. The father, as it were, of functionalism, the American architect Louis Sullivan, proclaimed that

'form follows function'. From the more modest position that the pursuit of function will produce its own distinct beauty to the most extreme dictum that beauty is to be found only in function is only a difference in degree. The weight of this way of thinking in modern design is considerable indeed.

But the other side of this dualism is just as extreme: that humanity, sensitivity, beauty, are independent entities opposed to function, and that functionalism compromises humanity, represents the defeat of humanity. From this is born the dogma that only the beautiful is functional. The debate is then reduced to a simple counting of heads on each extreme side of the issue, from which no creative thinking is likely to result.

When we try to resolve problems with dualistic methods, the concept of harmony comes into play. Here is an example: in urban space, there are two scales, one human and the other superhuman, and they are regarded as antithetical. To bridge the gap between them, a hierarchy of several graded scales leading from the human to the superhuman is created, and that is how these extremes are harmonised.

If these two scales are really antithetical, there will always remain an unbridgeable gap between them, no matter how many intermediary steps are constructed. Conversely, if the gap can be bridged, that means that the two scales were never actually antithetical. As long as dualism is to be a creative logic, it will always arrive at either compromise or escape.

Our task is to move from dualism to pluralism, and from there to advance to a philosophy of coexistence.

My philosophy of coexistence began here; its roots are in the Indian philosophy of absolute non-dualism that can be traced to the Vedanta philosopher Nagarjuna, and the Mahayana Buddhist concept of emptiness.

This is the source of my present concept of symbiosis which first began to take shape as early as 1959, and has been growing and developing ever since.

The City of Symbiosis, a Way to Liberation

In the early 1960s, together with Noboru Kawazoe, Masato Otaka, Fumihiko Maki, Kiyofumi Kikutake, Kiyoshi Awazu, Kenji Ekuan, Shomei Tomatsu, and others, I laid the foundations of the Metabolist movement.[1] We borrowed the term metabolism from biology: just as living organisms have metabolisms, we believed that cities and architecture grew and metabolised. The Metabolist movement touched many different fronts and although it is impossible to summarise it in a word, it is fair to say that the issue of the symbiosis of past, present, and future, of human beings and technology – in other words, the issues of diachronicity and synchronicity – were central to it.

Also at the core of Metabolism was the tradition of Eastern thought. At the time, I remember reading with great interest Hajime Nakamura's *The Ways of Thinking of Eastern Peoples*. The work traces the evolution of Buddhism as it was transmitted from India, its land of origin, to Tibet, Thailand, China, Korea and finally Japan. He investigates the way in which the Buddhist scriptures were translated from Sanskrit and Pali into other Asian languages and explores the changes that took place in Buddhism as it encountered other peoples and cultures. His book had a very great influence on me, and through it I was directed to other sources of stimulation: the Edo-period Japanese philosopher Miura Baien, for example, and the Consciousness Only current of Buddhist thought that is one of the bases of Mahayana Buddhist philosophy. The book made me aware of the rich and unique cultures of India, Tibet, Thailand, China, Korea and Japan, about which I had previously had no clear idea. It also marked the beginnings of my commitment to Buddhist philosophy, which I had encountered at school as a teenager. I attended Tokai Gakuen in Nagoya, which is affiliated with the Jodo, or Pure Land, sect of Japanese Buddhism. This school was established in the Edo period, and even today most of the teachers are monks. The Principal of the school when I attended it was Benkyo Shiio, the head of the huge Zojoji temple complex in Shiba, Tokyo. His lectures over six years had a profound influence on my way of thinking. Only recently did I learn that the term symbiosis had been coined by Shiio in 1923. He began a Foundation for Symbiosis (Zaidan Hojin Kyosei Kai), which published religious verses on symbiosis and a manual of symbiosis. In those works we find:

> We take the truth of coexistence as our guide and concentrate on the realisation of the Pure Land, for both the sharp and the dull, the strong and the weak, hand in hand. No one exists divorced from the thoughts of those around him. All comes into existence through an assembly of causes. All things are interrelated. In accordance with this principle, it is our aim to build an ideal world, step by step.

This is the true teaching of symbiosis. In Shiio's Buddhism of symbiosis, he reads the characters *kyosei* as 'living together', or coexistence. At the base of his philosophy is the conviction that all existence not only lives, but, at the same time, is being given life by the rest of existence. Inorganic substances such as minerals are crucial for human life; if even one vital mineral is lacking, we cannot survive. Human beings live and are kept alive through their coexistence with animals, plants and minerals. Shiio calls this essentially Buddhist vision of life 'true life'.

In Buddhism, human suffering is said to be caused by two things: craving and ignorance. Craving is attachment to things and the delusions that arise from that attachment. Ignorance means not to know what our universe is, what our self is. When you think that you are living entirely on your own, you begin to cling to your own life and to fear death – in other words, craving arises. The arrogant attitude that you know everything there is to know is based on ignorance. The escape from those two kinds of suffering is called liberation, and that escape is based on grasping and living the concept of symbiosis.

Until very recently, I had no inkling of the existence of the Buddhism of symbiosis; I am deeply grateful for the fortunate coincidence that has led me back into the profound teachings of my earliest teacher, Benkyo Shiio.

The interior of a Kabuki theatre, 1743, print by Torii Kiyotada, depicts the multiple ways in which space was used. Note especially the actor's passageway through the audience and the divisions between the audience's seats which were used as paths.

Notes

I
Hanasukiya: The Aesthetic of Symbiosis

1 A tea room in Japan is, of course, a unique architectural unit where the tea ceremony and related arts such as flower arrangement are practised. However, it is also a place for quiet contemplation and the appreciation of works of calligraphy, painting and ceramics. *An* means 'hut' and is often used to describe a tea room or tea house.

2 These key terms in Japanese aesthetics are notoriously difficult to define in English. *Wabi* suggests a highly austere, severe aesthetic of a sort of sacred poverty. *Sabi* carries additional connotations of sadness and loneliness, reflection and isolation. These highly emotional 'sensibilities' — for they are not rigorously defined concepts in any sense — are more often associated with each other than accurately distinguished. They are applied to a wide range of visual, plastic and literary arts.

3 Shokado Shojo (1584-1639) took up residence in Takimotobo when he was 17. Later he became the head monk of Takimotobo, but he is better known for his tea room and collection of tea utensils, paintings and works of calligraphy, now preserved at Iwashimizu Hachimangu. Shokado is also credited as the inventor of the traditional Japanese lunch box, the *bento*. This is a rectangular lacquer box divided into four compartments for rice and various foods. Shokado was a noted connoisseur and man of taste of his age.

4 Kan'unken was built in the style favoured by Kobori Enshu. Though destroyed in 1773, it was reconstructed in almost identical fashion in 1922, and the tea room in Takimotobo

today is that reconstruction. It is often confused with another tea house designed by Shojo, which stands on the property of the Atsuda family in Kyoto and is called the Shokado. The latter tea house was built by Shojo in his last years, after retiring from Takimotobo to take up residence in Izumibo.

5 Kobori Enshu (1579-1647) was a member of the samurai class, but best known as a master of the tea ceremony. He is the founder of one of the schools of tea, and he was also commissioned by the Tokugawa shogunate and the imperial house to design major works of architecture, such as the dungeons of Edo Castle and Nagoya Castle, the central compound of Fushimi Castle, and the Sento Gosho palace, as well as many gardens and tea rooms. He introduced his personal aesthetic preference, which he called *kirei sabi*, or gorgeous *sabi*, into the tea ceremony. The private library of Horiguchi Sutemi, editor of the encyclopaedic Chashitsu Okoshiezu Shu (Fold-out Plans of Tea Rooms), contains a work called Sukiyashiki (Sukiya Mansions), which includes a floor plan with the legend 'The Takimotobo in Hachimangu shrine is built from the same plan as Enshu's Fushimi tea room.' *Sukiya* is a style of architecture characterised by a sophisticated taste that blends the formal and informal, the heavy and the light. It was strongly influenced by the evolving aesthetic of the tea ceremony and is the dominant style of non-official architecture in the Edo period. *Suki* means 'taste' or 'style' and is used in compounds such as *eabisuki* and the author's neologism *hanasuki*.

6 A *daime*-sized mat was slightly smaller than an ordinary tatami mat. It was usually the size of the space from the host's mat to the *daisu* tea-utensil stand.

7 A *kaiki* is a detailed record *(ki)* of a tea gathering *(kai)*. The *Matsuya Kaiki* is one of the most valuable of these records, as a rich historical source for the development of the aesthetic of the tea ceremony.

8 Designed by Oda Uraku, this tea room is a national treasure and survives in the Urakuen of Oyama castle town in Oyama City, Aichi Prefecture. It is said to be the *sukiya*-style portion of the retirement residence that Oda Uaku built in the Shoden'in at Kenninji in Kyoto. The name derives from Oda's Christian name, Joao, which he received upon his baptism in that faith. In 1908 the tea room was brought to the Mitsui residence, and in 1971 reconstructed at its present site.

9 Oda Uraku (1547-1621) was the 11th son of the warlord Oda Nobuhide and the younger brother of Oda Nobunaga, who ruled Japan in the mid-16th century. Born Oda Nagamasu, he adopted the name Uraku, by which he is usually known, after joining the Buddhist order. He survived the reigns of his brother and the two rulers who came after him in succession, Toyotomi Hideyoshi and Tokugawa Ieyasu, and was made a feudal lord of a moderate-sized domain. His line continued on through to the Meiji period. The names of the present Tokyo districts Yuraku-cho and Sukiyabashi derive from his mansion, which was located in those areas. He is also the founder of the Uraku school of the tea ceremony.

10 Yuin is one of the tea rooms in Kyoto's Urasenke school of tea compound.

11 Nambo Sokei was a master of the tea ceremony from the port of Sakai, near modern Osaka. He was active during the rules of

Oda Nobunaga and Toyotomi Hideyoshi. He describes himself as a Zen monk, the second-generation head priest of the Shuun'an at Nanshuji. He was the foremost disciple of Sen no Rikyu and regarded as his successor, but disappeared after the third annual memorial observance of Rikyu's death. He was completely devoted to the aesthetic expression through the art of tea of his Zen ethic of 'pure poverty'. The *Nampo Roku* is a secretly transmitted manual of Sen no Rikyu's school of tea, regarded as having been composed by Nambo Sokei. The earliest copy we have of the work is in the hand of Tachibana Jitsuzan, a senior minister of the Kuroda clan in Fukuoka fief. Because of the strange 'coincidence' that the work was discovered on the one-hundred-year anniversary of Rikyu's death its authenticity is suspect. Nevertheless, it offers an accurate record of the world of tea, and based on this work, Jitsuzan founded the Nambo school of tea. Though the Tachibana family line terminated eight generations later, the school has continued to be active in Kyoto and other areas as the Namboryu Meikyoan school.

12 Takeno Joo (1502-55) was a wealthy merchant of the port city of Sakai who made a name for himself as a leader and patron of the art of tea. He was the teacher of the great tea masters of the age, including Imai Sokyu, Tsuda Sogyu and Sen no Rikyu. With his wealth to support his innovations, he introduced the aesthetics of the linked-poetry (*renga*) gatherings which had been popular for many years, and brought Zen to the tea ceremony. He is the leading figure in the period of the evolution of the so-called *wabi*-style tea ceremony (*wabi cha*). His three followers mentioned above were also all from merchant families, and they eventually became tea masters for the samurai class and spread the art far and wide.

The major masters and schools of tea are as follows:

Murata Jouou (1422-1502)

Oda Uraku (1547-1621)　Furuta Oribe (1544-1615)　Hosokawa Sansai (1563-1645)

Kobori Enshu (1579-1647)

13 Fujiwara no Teika (or Sadaie; 1162-1241) was a distinguished poet and compiler of the *Shin Kokin Waka Shu*. He is renowned for his critical writings.

14 The full title of the anthology is the *Shin Kokin Waka Shu*, or *New Anthology of Ancient and Modern Poetry*. Compiled by Fujiwara no Teika in around 1205, it is one of the greatest of the 21 imperial poetry anthologies.

15 Robert H Bower and Earl Miner, *Japanese Court Poetry*, Stanford University Press, 1971, p307.

16 The *daisu* was a tea utensil stand used in the elaborate and formal tea ceremony of the aristocrat's mansion (*shoin*), which was practised before the spread of the much simpler tea ceremony of Murata Juko. By the time of the *wabi*-style tea ceremony, the *daisu* was usually no longer set in the much smaller tea room.

17 Murata Juko (1422-1502) is regarded as the founder of the tea ceremony. After becoming a monk at Shomyoji in Nara, he returned to lay status and began to practise the art of tea. He is not directly linked to Sen no Rikyu or his followers and descendants, but he is the undisputed founder of the Way of *wabi*-style tea. He was instructed in Zen by the famous monk Ikkyu Sojun, and he was also a curator of Chinese art and tea master to Ashikaga Yoshimasa, the shogun. He created a tea for the common people based on his deep knowledge of the tea ceremony as it was practised among the elite.

18 A record of Rikyu's life, compiled by Rikyu's first disciple, Yamanoue Soji (1544-90). Soji was also Toyotomi Hideyoshi's tea master, but he was of extremely unattractive appearance and had a sharp tongue, which eventually led to him being dismissed from Hideyoshi's service. He became the guest of the Hojo clan in Odawara (in modern Kanagawa Prefecture) and spread the Way of tea there. When Hideyoshi attacked the Hojo, Soji had his ears and nose cut off.

19 Jun'ichior Tanizaki, *In Praise of Shadows*, trans

by Thomas J Harper and Edward G Seiden-sticker, Tokyo, Charles E Tuttle Co, pp13-14.

20 Matsuo Basho (1644-94) is the most famous haiku poet. He travelled throughout Japan composing haiku and poetical prose called *haibun*, and he also contributed significantly to the aesthetics of these genres.

21 Mukai Kyorai (1651-1704) was Basho's disciple. Basho placed great faith in him and he was the editor of the collection of hiaku called *Sarumino* (*Monkey's Raincoat*). Kyorai's greatest achievements, however, were in criticism and theory of the haiku. He was born in the samurai class, but gave up his status to become a yin-yang diviner, which remained his profession for the rest of his life.

22 *Kyorai Sho* is Kyorai's masterwork, in which he identifies and discusses many of the distinctive properties of the haiku and *haibun* genres, including 'unchanging flux'.

23 Zeami (1363?-1443) was a Noh actor, theorist, director and composer. Together with his father Kan'ami, he created the theatrical genre of Noh. Zeami made his first real debut as a performer at the age of 12, when he and his father performed for the shogun Ashikaga Yoshimasu, who was much taken with Zeami. Yoshimasu showed such affection for and protection of Zeami that it was widely believed they were lovers. Zeami based his Noh on that of his father, which had a broad popular appeal, but he placed a tremendous emphasis on beauty and raised the art to great heights. After suffering persecution from Yoshima's successor, Zeami increased the intellectual content of Noh, formulating the art as we have it today.

Kaden is a systemisation of the theories of Noh that Zeami had inherited from his father. It is a practical work, dividing the life of an actor into seven periods and prescribing the correct practice for each one. Zeami composed *Kakyo* when persecution by the new shogun threatened to destroy his theatrical troupe; it contains the marrow of Zeami's thoughts. The 'flower' (*ka*) found in the titles of both works refers to the power to continue to be attractive on the Noh stage, and it is related to Zeami's key concept of the ideal of beauty: *yugen,* or dark mystery.

24   J Thomas Rimer and Masakazu Yamazaki, trans, *On the Art of the Noh Drama: The Major Treatises of Zeami,* Princeton University Press, 1984, p12.

25   Sen no Rikyu (1522-91) was born into a merchant family in Sakai, the por city near Osaka. He studied tea under Takeno Joo. When Oda Nobunaga demanded payment of a huge indemnity from Sakai, Rikyu and Imai Sogyu, were sent as members of a party to negotiate a settlement. After Nobunaga's death, Rikyu became the tea master of Toyotomi Hideyoshi. Rikyu is known as the great formulator of the art of tea; we owe the transmission of the art of tea down to the present not only to his aesthetic vision but also to his success in promoting tea among high-ranking samurai. His seven disciples, most of them of samurai origin, are called the Seven Sages of Rikyu, and he also taught tea to such well-known feudal lords as Date Masamune. Rikyu's increasing political influence may have played a part in Hideyoshi's decision to sentence him to death by *seppuku,* or self-disembowelment.

26   Furuta Oribe (1544-1615) was of samurai birth, and he served under both Oda Nobunaga and Toyotomi Hideyoshi, rising to a fairly high rank in the feudal hierarchy. Oribe studied under Rikyu, but he adapted Rikyu's style of tea, which was essentially quietist, finding beauty in stillness, to a more dynamic style that would please members of his class. He is said to have purposely broken tea utensils and had them repaired with gold. His disciples included Kobori Enshu and Hon'ami Koetsu, and a type of ceramics has been named after him. He was tea master to the second Tokugawa shogun, Hidetada, but when his involvement in plans for a *coup d'etat* in Osaka was discovered he was condemned to commit suicide, at the age of 72.

27   En'an, or Swallow Hut, was designed by Furuta Oribe and survives, designated as an important cultural property. It is located in Kyoto, on the grounds of one of the subsects of the Yabunouchi school of tea. It was

destroyed by fire in 1864 and rebuilt three years later. The 'crawl-in entrance' (*nijiriguchi*) is at the southeast corner, under eaves over an earthen floor. A three-mat guest area is bracketed by the host's mat by an area for retainers. This area for retainers, separated from the guest area by two sliding doors, is a unique feature of this tea room and represents a layout favoured by the samurai class.

28   Bruno Taut (1880-1938), the German expressionist architect, moved to Japan in 1933. He extolled what he called 'emperor art', by which he meant Katsura Detached Palace and Ise Shrine, as opposed to 'shogun art', referring to the Toshogu shrine at Nikko. His writings include the book *Nippon.* Taut left Japan in 1936 to teach in Istanbul. The German architect Walter Gropius (1883-1969), began with industrial architecture based on the techniques of modern industry, and, while advocating progressive and rational architecture, sought a unification of the hand crafts and the industrial arts. While director of the Bauhaus, he assembled many creative personalities, such as Wassily Kandinsky, Oskar Schlemmer, Paul Klee and Laszlo Moholy-Nagy, and sought to create a unified design for Modern architectural space. He and his writings form one of the bases of the Modern Movement.

The Katsura Detached Palace was originally a 17th-century country villa of the Hachijo no Miya family. There are four sections to the main house, and four pavilions, several belvederes and a Buddhist chapel arranged throughout the gardens. A combination of *shoin* (palatial) and *sukiya* styles, it is regarded by many as the finest example of residential architecture in Japan.

29   The Grand Ise Shrine is located at Ise in Mie Prefecture and is one of the two or three most important shrines in Japan. It is associated with the imperial deity, the Sun Goddess Amaterasu. Made of unpainted Japanese cypress wood, it has a bold and simple design suggestive of South Pacific architecture. Ise Shrine is dismantled and rebuilt every 21 years, always following the same special Shinto architectural style, though some changes have crept in over the centuries.

30   The Toshogu Shrine at Nikko serves as the mausoleum of Tokugawa Ieyasu, the founder of the Tokugawa shogunate, who ruled Japan from 1600 to 1868. It was completed in 1636, and the shrine buildings and gateways are highly decorative and ornate.

31   Okamoto Taro (b 1911) is a painter, sculptor and designer of monuments. Born into an artistic family, he spent his youth in Paris, studying at the Sorbonne. After his return to Japan he fought in the Second World War in China, and when the war was over became active not only in the art world but in politics and as a writer and critic. His sculptures include the *Tower of the Sun* at the Osaka Expo and the sculptures decorating the Children's Castle in Aoyama, Tokyo. His writings include *Nihon Saihakken (Rediscovering Japan)* and *Wasurareta Nihon: Okinawa Bunka Ron (Forgotten Japan: A Theory of Okinawan Culture).*

32   The Jomon period, from about 10,000BC to 300BC, (Japan's Neolithic period), is characterised by the dynamic and dramatic clay figurines and pottery that have been discovered dating from that time. 'Jomon' means rope patterns, which are one of the commonly found decorative techniques on Jomon pottery. The following Yayoi period, from about 300BC to 300AD, was when rice production was first introduced to Japan. Its pottery is much simpler and more austere and delicate.

33   Toshodaiji was founded in 759 in the western sector of Nara by the Chinese monk Jianzhen, and Todaiji was built between 710 and 784 in the eastern sector of the same city by Emperor Shomu.

II
Transcending Modernism

1   Gilles Deleuze (b 1925) is professor of philosophy at the University of Paris. His philosophical method is characterised by a rejection of the theories of consciousness of traditional metaphysics and a focus on will and desire, from which he proceeds to analyse

modern society. In *Anti-Oedipus*, co-authored with Felix Guattari (see below), he postulates the two principles of schizophrenia and paraphrenia in contemporary society. According to Deleuze, the 'modern intellect', which seeks to know all, ignores the fact that life itself is inherently anti-hierarchical. In modern capitalist society, the desire to see all existence as orderly has become an independent entity that intervenes between people and is reborn as a feeling of pressure and anxiety.

Felix Guattari (b 1930) is a psychoanalyst at the Borde clinic. He has also been in the forefront of the development of a new, revolutionary psychoanalysis in the face of the largely British-American reaction against psychoanalysis in general.

2 Jacques Lacan (b 1901-81), under the banner 'Return to Freud' established a structuralist psychoanalysis by interpreting patients' non-intellectual accounts on the symbolic levels of metaphor and suggestion. In Lacan's thought, the signifier – that which transmits meaning – is given precedence over the signified – the content of meaning – and the former is represented by S while the latter is represented by s. In other words, for Lacan it was not the content that was important but the symbolic expression of content, its linkings, its condensations, its displacement as an event. He placed less importance on the individual and more on the unconscious call from the S; here it was the language functioned, and it was in this dimension that the human being was created. Lacan's seminars were attended by many contemporary intellectuals, including Guattari and Louis Althusser, and his ideas had a great influence on the post-structuralist movement.

3 René Girard (b 1923) found the image of the scapegoat at the core of human culture and also developed a theory of culture as the 'imitation of desire'. According to Girard, desire cannot exist on the level of the individual. He offers the love triangle as an example. In a love triangle, the desire of B for C is linked to B's awareness that A desires C. In this triangle of desire, a reciprocal imitation of desire is carried out, and this paradigmatic relationship extends infinitely to encompass the entire world until it produces a violent confusion, exposing all groups of human beings to danger. In reaction, the natural defence mechanisms of these groups are activated and the reciprocal imitations of the groups of human beings are transferred to a relation between the group and one individual, and that individual's relations to other individuals. This individual becomes a scapegoat and the symbol of the evil which has brought chaos to the group. At the same time, he is a symbol of the group's salvation. The scapegoat possesses an ambivalent significance. Girard points to Jesus Christ as an example of the scapegoat. He also seeks to liberate contemporary society from this scapegoat phenomenon.

4 Jacques Attali (b 1943), professor of economic theory at the University of Paris, has been active in the French Socialist Party since Francois Mitterrand became president in 1981. Transcending the traditional boundaries of economics through his research into semantics, cultural anthropology and sociology, he has attempted to deconstruct orthodox economic theory into new paradigms.

5 Claude Lévi-Strauss (b 1908) held that we must observe phenomena not from an established theory but from the perspective of their own structure. The system of distinctions among phenomena is their structure; existence is the system of relationships among different things. Lévi-Strauss applied these ideas to the study of anthropology, especially kinship relationships and mythology. He is sharply critical of the modern notion of the self as a discrete entity, and refuses to accord a higher value to the entity of 'civilisation' than to the entity he calls 'the unknown'. He discovered so called 'uncivilised thinking', that is, non-rational thought, and revealed that the equation of thinking with rationality only applies within the context of European culture; he went on to criticise the principles of substance and existence, based on rationality, as an oppressive ideology.

6 Yamaguchi Masao (b 1931) has, from the 1970s, been investigating new ways of perceiving the problems of linguistics and cultural anthropology. Among his concepts is that of the core and the periphery. Yamaguchi claims that a culture develops more from the power of its periphery, which energises the culture as a whole, than from a concentration of power in its core. The core forever tries to reject the periphery, and the periphery continues to stimulate and enliven the core. The ambivalence of the relationship between core and periphery is to be found in all binomial relations: the sacred and the profane, heaven and earth, order and chaos, man and woman, regulation and freedom.

7 CIAM was founded in 1928 at Las Sarras, Switzerland. The Athens Declaration outlined the social principles of city planning.

8 Le Corbusier (1887-1965) was born in Switzerland, but was active as an architect in France. He is also famous as a painter and writer. In architecture, his work spanned many areas, from residential housing design to city planning. He was also a major theorist of Modern architecture and set forth its five principles: the *pilotis,* independent skeleton structures, unobstructed interior space, self-supporting walls and rooftop gardens.

9 Jan Mukarovsky was a Czech dialectical thinker of the 1930s. Mukarovsky held that while a structure possesses a tendency toward integrity that preserves its continuity and establishes regularity it also possesses factors that seek to destroy that integrity. A structure is forever repeating a cycle of stability, upset and restoration. The internal integrity of a structure is preserved by the opposition of the forces of harmony (affirmation) and conflict (negation), but Mukarovsky places more the greater emphasis on negation. In other words, the dominant structural elements are renewed through the introduction of negation of tension into the system, and the subsequent upset of the system's balance. In this model, structure is always in the midst of reformation.

10 Maurice Merleau-Ponty (1908-61) was a French philosopher and essayist. He began as a political realist akin to Sartre and evolved into an existential idealist. His thought is characterised by an enthusiasm and a fascination with visible, tangible reality.

11   Paraphrased by the author.

12   See Chapter VII for a further discussion of the Consciousness Only school of Buddhist philosophy and the *alaya* consciousness.

13   William Morris (1834-96), the English poet, painter, craftsman and social reformer established the manufacturing and decorating firm Morris, Marshall, Faulkner & Company in 1861 and then embarked on the production of room interiors, stained glass, metalwork and wallpaper. He was opposed to industrialisation and sought to bring beauty to daily life through the handicrafts. As a poet and artist, he promoted medievalism in the midst of the Gothic revival of the 19th century and believed that was possible in the context of socialism.

14   Peter Behrens (1868-1940) was a German architect who was a leading influence in the emergence of Modern architecture. His style evolved from Art Nouveau to a highly modern purism. Gropius, Le Corbusier and Mies van der Rohe worked in his office in the 1920s. Tony Garnier (1869-1948) was a French architect who pioneered the use of reinforced concrete and is known in France as the father of Modern architecture. Auguste Perret (1874-1954) started out as an engineer and, together with Garnier, developed reinforced concrete into an acceptable building material. His later style had neo-classical affinities. Le Corbusier and other famous architects worked in his atelier.

15   Arthur Koestler (1905-83) was imprisoned as a spy in 1937 during the Spanish Civil War. He claimed to have experienced 'the third reality' in prison. Koestler writes in *The Holon Revolution*: 'The third reality cannot be explained on either the perceptual or conceptual levels. It is like a magical meteorite perceived by primitive man streaking across the round dome of the heavens, and it is when we have occasion to gain access to that level that we encounter occult phenomena ... Just as we cannot feel the pull of a magnet with our skin, we cannot hope to understand this ultimate level of reality through language. It is a text written with invisible ink.' Koestler's essay,

'The Tree and the Candle', was published in *Unity Through Diversity* – a collection of papers published to commemorate the 70th anniversary of the birth of Ludwig von Bertalanffy, the originator of general systems theory.

16   David Bohm (b 1917) is an American physicist. He has suggested that both mind and matter have an 'implicate order', which links the two. Bohm uses the image of a drop of ink in a glass of water. If we stir slowly, the ink will spread out until part and whole are completely inseparable. This is the world of implicate order. If we could slowly stir the water backwards, the ink would slowly separate from the water and return to its form as a single drop, becoming a part again, a distinct phenomenon. According to Bohm, this is the process through which atomic particles are formed, as well as mental process and nerve impulses.

17   Suzuki Daisetz (1870-1966) is perhaps the best-known populariser of Zen in the West. According to Suzuki, the total self-identity of 'I am I' is the state of non-time and is equivalent to the emptiness of Buddhist philosophy. In that state, the mountain is the mountain. I see it as it is; it sees me as I am. In other words, my experience of seeing the mountain is identical to the mountain seeing me. From this, Suzuki moves to the conclusion that absolute subjectivity is identical to absolute objectivity. That which is inside me is at the same time that which stands opposed to and outside of me. Human beings and nature, God and nature, are one, and the many and the one are also one. In this way, Suzuki arrives at an absolute monism.

18   Miura Baien (1723-89) was a doctor by profession, but studied a wide range of subjects, from Confucianism to traditional astronomy to mathematics. The originality and profundity of Baien's trilogy marks him as a universal philosopher who transcends all genres and his age.

19   By Professor Hiroto Saigusa of Tokyo University, in his *Philosophy of Miura Baien*, 1953.

III
Edo: Precursor of the Age of Symbiosis

1   Shitamachi, the 'low city' or 'downtown', is now east central and northeast Tokyo. It was traditionally where townsmen and craftsmen lived, as opposed to the feudal lords and their entourages, who lived 'in the hills', the Yamanote area. The Shitamachi district preserves more of the old character of Tokyo-Edo than other parts of the city.

2   Yamagata Banto (1748-1821) was a scholar of the merchant class. He was adopted at 13 by his uncle and moved to Osaka, where he became the manager of a rice business. While carrying on his trade he also studied Confucianism, astronomy and Western science, or Rangaku, and wrote *Instead of Dreams*. That work is divided into 12 sections, on astronomy, geography, mythology, history, government policies, economics and other subjects. The section on astronomy is especially well-known. Banto's achievements as an economist and a thinker rank him with his contemporaries in Europe, America and Asia.

3   Shizuku Tadao (1760-1808) was a scholar of Western science, or Rangaku, who translated many Dutch works in addition to his own writings. His main work is *Reki Sho Shin Sho*, a translation from Dutch of an original English commentary on Newton's *Principia*. The theory of the Earth's movement appears there, and Tadao's appended theory of the origin of stars rivals the Kant-Laplace hypothesis.

4   Ino Tadataka (1745-1818) is famous as a cartographer, although until he was 50 he was the manager of a brewery. It was only after retirement that he began to study astronomy, geography and mathematics and began drawing maps. In 16 years starting from 1800, he spent 3,736 days travelling around Japan and charted 43,708 terrestrial miles, taking hundreds of thousands of readings. His maps are accurate to about a thousandth of a degree. Ino's maps became the standard maps of the country during the Meiji era.

5   Joruri is Japanese puppet theatre, also called Bunraku. In the Joruri theatres, serious

dramas were enacted for an audience of adults. The large puppets were eventually operated by three puppeteers dressed in black and visible from the waist up. The drama was accompanied by a ballad narrative called Joruri, which gave its name to the theatrical genre.

6 The dates of Toshusai Sharaku's birth and death are unknown, but he was active in the late Edo period. His output of more than 140 prints is concentrated between May 1794 and January 1795; after that we know very little more of him. Various theories about his true identity have been suggested, but there is not enough evidence to confirm any of them.

7 The Rimpa school of painting started around 1600 by Sotatsu, also associated with his contemporary Hon'ami Koetsu. The paintings of this school are characterised by their decorativeness, delicate shading and colouring and the abstraction of their layout and design. Though the Rimpa painters were keen observers of nature, their work is highly stylised. Sotatsu was active in Kyoto from 1600 to 1640. Hon'ami Koetsu (1558-1637) was widely admired for his calligraphy, pottery and lacquer designs, and encouraged Sotatsu by giving him many painting commissions. Ogata Korin (1658-1716) is known for his gorgeous screen paintings in rich colours against gold grounds. Ogata Kenzan (1663-1743) was a potter as well as a painter, and combined the rigour of the Chinese literati style of painting with Japanese decorativeness.

8 Kumadori make-up, in contrast to the make-up of Peking Opera, for example, is based on the muscles of the face, abstracted in stylisation. It is said to have been influenced by the iconography of Buddhist images, especially those of fierce guardian deities such as Fudo Myoo.

9 Suzuki Harunobu (?-1770) was the originator of the multicoloured woodblock print, or nishiki-e. In addition to his prints of beautiful women (bijinga), he designed many scenes of loving couples and sights of daily life about town. He is often regarded as having introduced the sophistication of aristocratic art into the

woodblock print, but his role in commercialising the print is probably even more important.

10 Fukugawa still exists, though no longer a red-light district. As a brothel district, it had a reputation for a lower (and cheaper) class of courtesan than its rivals in Yoshiwara and Shinagawa. Many courtesans took male professional names and they developed a refined and satiric dandyism that Edoites enjoyed immensely.

11 Kobayashi Rekisai (1884-1959) was a maker of miniatures, including tiny, perfectly crafted ink boxes, incense stands, dressers, samisens and other furniture and accessories.

12 Maki-e is a process in which mother-of-pearl, gold dust and other decorations are embedded in lacquerware, creating beautiful painterly designs.

13 Komon means small crest or design. Edo komon is characterised by a repeat pattern of tiny motifs, produced with a paste-resist dyeing technique.

14 In the shoin style of residential palace architecture, several large buildings are linked by elevated, roofed corridors. The main building is open to the south, and the typical shoin layout forms a U, with a garden including a pond enclosed in its middle. The design details of shoin-style architecture are relatively formal and elaborate.

15 The Flying Cloud Pavilion is located in the southeastern corner of the Nishi Honganji temple compound. It is said to have originally been part of Toyotomi Hideyoshi's Juraku no Tei palace, which would mean Hiunkaku was built in around 1586 or 1587, although another theory suggests it was built in the early 1600s. It has an unconventional design, containing shoin-style rooms, a steam bath and a famous tea room.

16 The soan style refers to the simplest and most austere type of tea house or tea room design, in which the structure is modelled after a hermit's hut. Simple, homely materials are used in a style that is at once rough and

highly sophisticated.

17 From the tenth century in Japan a theory was current that stated that Buddhist deities truly existed and Shinto deities did not; what appeared to be a Shinto deity was only the manifestation of a Buddhist deity in Shinto form. This doctrine was an attempt to establish the pre-eminence of Buddhism over the native religion. It resulted in a duplication of deities: a multivalence of the sacred.

18 The Civilisation prints showed scenes of the latest Western inventions (railroads, steamboats, curling irons), fashions, and even scenes of Westerners and Western capitals. The Yokohama prints specialised in scenes of Westerners and their activities in the port of Yokohama, where a Western settlement had been established.

IV
Rikyu Grey, Baroque and Camp Ambiguity and Ambivalence

1 Hishikawa Moronobu (1618?-94) began as a fabric painter and later became popular as a print maker depicting the lives of the flourishing merchants' culture of Edo, including scenes of the courtesans of Yoshiwara, Kabuki actors and daily life. His works did much to shape and publicise the contemporary worlds of design and fashion.

2 For Fujiwara no Teika, (see chapter I, note 13) the Gu Hi Sho is a work of Teika's middle years, concerned with poetic theory, though some question its provenance. The ideas of closely and distantly related verses were especially important in anthologies and sessions in which poetry was composed by several poets in turn.

3 Robert H Bower and Earl Miner, Japanese Court Poetry, Stanford University Press, 1971, p307.

4 J Thomas Rimer and Masakazu Yamazaki, trans On the Art of the Noh Drama: The Major Treatises of Zeami, Princeton University Press, 1984, pp96-7.

5   Eugenio D'Ors, *Lo Barocco,* Aguilar, sa de Ediciones, Madrid, 1943. Translated into English from the Japanese edition, Keizo Kanki, trans *Barokko Ron,* Bijutsu Shuppansha, Tokyo, 1971, pp24-5.

6   Giacomo della Porta (1540-1604), an Italian architect and painter whose career spanned the Renaissance and the Baroque periods. He studied with both Michelangelo and Vignola, and it was as Vignola's successor that he was entrusted with the completion of St Peter's, in which he collaborated with Domenico Fontana. His facade for the Il Gesu Church was also a completion of a Vignola project, and he used the same design for the facade of the Sta Maria dei Monti Church. He is also known for his work on the interior of the Farnese Palace.

7   Baldassare Peruzzi (1481-1536) was active both as a painter and an architect. In 1503 he came under the influence of Bramante and worked for him on St Peter's, and he designed the first stage setting using perspective in Rome. His last work, the Palazzo Massimo alle Colonne in Rome, is regarded as the first mannerist building.

8   Nicolas Poussin (1594-1665), a French painter, deeply influenced by Raphael and Titian, spent most of his life in Rome. The carefully calculated and measured, even architectural compositions of Poussin's paintings had a great effect on later painters, and in the 19th century, he was regarded as the model of Classicism.

9   Herbert Read (1893-1968), the English poet and critic, published *Education Through Art* in 1943. He stressed the idea that works of art were expressions of the highest truth of the universe. After the Second World War he wrote several political works coloured strongly by anarchism.

10   William Empson (1906-84), the English poet and critic, aimed for a merging of feeling and intelligence in his works, which are metaphysical in substance and lyrical in tone, often cast in traditional forms. As a critic he worked from the perspectives of psychology and semantics, and his writings have had a great influence on the methodology of some of the New Critics. *The Seven Types of Ambiguity,* Penguin Books, New York, 1977 (pp5-6 cited here) is a seminal work of modern poetic criticism.

11   Kunio Yanagita (1875-1962) sought to uncover the unwritten history (the traditional accounts of the people) that lay beneath written history (documentary history). To accomplish this, he travelled to villages all over Japan surveying and recording the customs, beliefs, ways of life and ceremonies that had been transmitted down to the present. In that transmission which he called 'folklore' (*mizoku*), he found that all past and present ages existed side by side in abbreviated form. Yanagita also pointed to this folklore as an important key to studying history.

12   Aldo van Eyck (b 1918) the Dutch architect, was one of the founders of Team Ten, and was very active in new architectural movements in the 1960s. Louis Kahn (1901-74) was an American architect born in Estonia. His main works include the Museum of Fine Art at Yale, the Richards Medical Research Center at the University of Pennsylvania, the laboratory buildings for the Salk Institute, the Institute of Management at Ahmedabad, the Kimbell Museum of Fine Art and the Center for Research on British Art at Yale. The British architect James Stirling's (b 1926) major works include the Leicester University Engineering Department, the Cambridge University History Faculty, the National Museum of Art at Stuttgart and the Arthur M Sackler Museum of Art at Harvard.

13   Buber's thought is paraphrased from a Japanese translation of his essay 'The Question to the Single One', in *Between Man and Man,* Macmillan, New York, 1974.

14   Charles Jencks (b 1939) is an American writer on and professor of architecture. His main publications include *The Meaning of Architecture, Architecture 2000, Modern Movements in Architecture, Adhocism, The Language of Post-Modern Architecture* and *The New Moderns.*

15   Charles Rennie Mackintosh (1868-1928), the Scottish architect and designer, was the leader of the Glasgow School of Art Nouveau. First recognised in continental Europe, he was a pioneer of Modern architecture. His best-known design is the Glasgow School of Art, and his work is characterised by a decorativeness and craftsmanship free from past styles.

16   Otto Wagner (1841-1918), was professor of architecture at the Vienna School of Art from 1841 and played a leading role in the birth of Modern architecture, both as theoretician and working architect. He held that artistic creativity must spring from the actual conditions of daily life and advocated a functionalist style. His best-known works are the Karlsplatz station of the Vienna subway and the Savings Bank building in Vienna. He placed considerable importance on the social role of architecture.

17   Jacopo Pontormo (1494-1557), an Italian painter of the Florentine school, worked on the border between Classicism and Mannerism. His work is often so sensitive that it seems overwrought. Fiorentino Rosso (1494-1540) was an Italian painter active in Florence. His works are highly exaggerated and dramatic, placing him firmly in the category of the early mannerists. Caravaggio (1573?-1610), perhaps the foremost painter of the Italian Baroque, throughout Italy and beyond. His compositions are marked by dramatic contrasts of light and dark and sculpturally depicted figures.

VII
The Philosophy of Consciousness Only

1   This is articulated in the Upanishads, a group of sacred texts that have been appended to the Vedas, the ancient texts of the Brahman religion in India. One of the most striking teachings of the Upanishads is that each human being possesses an absolute self (*atman*) identical to the great universal self (*Brahma*), and that the two can be unified through religious practice. The Upanishads are also the first Indian texts to offer a theory of *karma*, or deeds and their results.

2   The *alaya* was conceived of as a stream of continuity, but in orthodox Buddhist philosophy it is said to be 'empty' – that is, have no substantial existence. The concept of the *alaya* is a recognition of process apart from substance.

3   Nagarjuna lived in the second century in southern India. Of Brahman birth, he converted to Mahayana Buddhism. The central concepts of Nagarjuna's writings are the 'mean' and emptiness. Emptiness means that no phenomenon has substantial existence; and the mean refers to the Middle Way between all dualistic extremes, such as illusion and enlightenment, or non-existence and existence.

4   Maitreya (not to be confused with the Boddhisattva of that name) was a Buddhist scholar of fourth-century India. Asanga, his pupil, also lived in the fourth century, and taught that the stream of the *alaya* consciousness could be purified, transforming our consciousness into enlightenment itself. Asanga's brother Vasubhandhu was the most prolific writer of the three and with him the philosophy of Consciousness Only reached its completion. His doctrinal innovations included distinguishing the sense of self from the *alaya* consciousness and his encyclopaedic listing of the afflictions that pollute the human mind.

VIII
The Symbiosis of Man and Nature

1   Yoshida Kenko, *Essays in Idleness*, trans Donald Keene, Columbia University Press, New York, 1967, p10. Kenko (1283?-1352) first served Emperor Gonijo as a poet and in various official posts, but at about 30 he retired from secular life to become a monk. In his 40s he composed *Essays in Idleness*, in which he ably expressed the essence of the Japanese aesthetic. Kenko had a broad range of acquaintances, aristocratic and common, religious and lay, and including members of the rising samurai class. While his work laments the passing of courtly values, it also portends the changes that were soon to occur in Japanese society. The sensibility that Kenko

formulates in *Essays in Idleness* combines the quiet splendour of court life depicted in *The Pillow Book of Sei Shonagon* with the strongly Buddhist colouring of *A Tale of a Ten-Foot-Square Hut* to define the aesthetic consciousness of the new age.

2   Noboru Kawazoe (b 1926) is an architectural critic and the director of the Kawazoe Research Institute. His main writings include *Tami to Kami no Sumai* (*The Dwellings of the People and the Gods*), *Kenchiku to Dento* (*Architecture and Tradition*), *Seikatsugaku no Teisho* (*A Proposal for a Science of Lifestyle*), and *Toshi Kukan no Bunka* (*The Culture of City Space*).

IX
The Philosophy of the Karakuri

1   K Atsumi, 'New Concept – BIOMATION – Its Revolutionary Impact on Industry and Society', *Proceedings of Discoveries International Symposium*, OSU, 1982.

X
From Post-Modernism to Symbiosis

1   Jean-François Lyotard *The Post-Modern Condition: A Report on Knowledge*, trans Geoff Bennington and Brian Massumi, University of Minnesota Press, Minneapolis,1984. Lyotard (b 1924) is a French philosopher, a professor at Paris University and Director of the International Institute of Philosophy.

2   Michel Foucault (1926-64) was a French philosopher, the author of such works as *The Order of Things* and *The Archaeology of Knowledge*. He was preoccupied with identifying the forces that underlie human institutions, and carried out studies on the treatment of the insane, criminals, and the history of human sexuality. In *The Archaeology of Knowledge* he suggests that different ages recognised different styles of knowledge.

3   Giambattista Piranesi (1720-78), the Italian architect and engraver, was active mostly in Rome and produced many views of that city, but he is best known for *Imaginary Pris-*

ons, with its fantastic and macabre variations on Roman architecture.

4   Antonio Sant'Elia (1888-1916) argued for a new architecture free from all past conventions, and exhibited his ideas as sketches in the 1914 Nuove Tendenze group exhibition under the title *New City*. His concepts were visionary, and though his work had few links to contemporary modern architecture, many of his ideas uncannily were realised decades later. He died in the First World War at the age of 28.

5   Ludwig Mies van der Rohe (1886-1969), the German-born architect and leader of the purist school of Modern architecture, succeeded Walter Gropius as director of the Bauhaus, was a pioneer of furniture design. In 1937 he emigrated to the United States and became a leading exponent of geometrical, abstract Modern architecture.

6   Roger Caillois, *Man and the Sacred*, trans Meyer Barash, Greenwood, 1980.

7   Gilles Deleuze and Felix Guattari, *A Thousand Plateaus*, trans Brian Massumi, Athlone, London, 1988, p25.

8   François Marie Charles Fourier (1772-1837) was a French social reformer and economist whose vision of a new society exercised considerable influence on later anarchists such as Kropotkin. In Fourier's ideal society, the central government merely facilitated transactions involving goods, and people were organised into mostly agricultural co-operatives called phalanxes. Each phalanx consisted of about 1,600 people, who lived in common buildings called phalansteries.

9   Edward Robert de Zurko, the American architect active in the 1950s, was professor in the Department of Architecture at the Rice Institute, University of Texas.

Little is known of Vitruvius except that he is the author of the celebrated treatise *De Architectura*, 27BC (?). In that work, Vitruvius reveals himself as strongly Hellenistic and it was closely studied by Renaissance architects such as Bramante, Michelangelo and Vignola.

Leon Battista Alberti (1404-72), the Italian humanist and architect, was active in the early Renaissance. His theories of architecture, set forth in the work *De Re Aedificatoria*, were quite influential, and his church of San Francesco at Rimini is based on them.

Andrea Palladio (1508-80), the Italian architect who gave his name to the neo-classical Palladian style, was, with Vignola, one of the most important theorists of his time. His love of Roman architecture and strongly classicist styles are reflected in the church of San Giorgio Maggiore and the magnificent Sta Maria della Salute in Venice.

10   Claude-Nicolas Ledoux (1736-1806) was a French architect active during and after the reign of Louis XVI. His designs are original and sometimes fantastic, based on simple geometrical forms.

Karl Friedrich Schinkel (1781-1841) was a German architect who revived Greek architecture in the early modern age. He was also a stage director and a fine painter of Romantic landscapes.

Horatio Greenough (1805-52) was an American neo-classical sculptor and architectural theorist, whose ideas presaged the development of functionalism.

11   Jean Baudrillard proclaimed in his *Consumer Society* that Capitalism had reached a dead end and we were entering an age in which symbols will be exchanged instead of goods. In subsequent works he has emphasised that we have reached the end of the age where symbols and their content are regarded as of equal value, and entered one of simulation, where symbols without content will be the medium of exchange. Baudrillard's conclusion is that views of economy and government based on production and labour will collapse, to be replaced by views of society based on consumption.

12   Yoshimitsu Morita (b 1950) is one of the leaders of Japan's 'New Wave' cinema. He first attracted wide attention with *No yo na Mono*, and went on to work in a variety of genres with great success. His next major work was *Kazoku Geemu*, followed by a film version of Natsume Soseki's novel *Sorekara*.

13   Ferdinand de Saussure (1857-1913) was a Swiss linguist who has had a fundamental influence on modern thought. In his incomplete *Research on Anagrams,* begun in his last years, de Saussure began to move from the study of the common code that has been the object of linguistic study so far (*langue*) to 'speech as action' (*parole*).

14   Keigo Okonogi (b 1930) is a psychiatrist at Keio University Medical School. *Moratortiamu Ningen* earned him popular recognition, and he has written several other books on topics of wide interest, including *Katei no nai Kazoku no Jidai* (*The Age of Families Without Homes*) and *Jikoai Ningen* (*Self Love*).

15   Gaston Bachelard, *The New Scientific Spirit*, trans Arthur Goldhammer, Beacon Press, 1985. The English translation is based on the Japanese edition of the book.

XI
Towards the Evocation of Meaning

1   English version based on the Japanese translation by Yasuo Kobayashi.

XII
The Symbiosis of Redevelopment and Restoration

1   *Asahi Shimbun*, 6 Jan, 1987; 9 Jan, 1987; 16 Jan, 1987; 15 March, 1987.
2   New Tokyo Plan, 2025. The City of Symbiosis; see pages 202-205.

Epilogue

1   Masato Otaka (b 1923) is an architect and the director of the Otaka Kenchiku Sekkei firm. His main works include the redevelopment of Sakaide City in Kagawa Prefecture, the Bunka Kaikan in Chiba Prefecture, the Prefectural Government Building in Tochigi Prefecture, the Gumma Prefectural Museum of History, the Fukushima Prefectural Museum of Art, and the redevelopment of Motomachi in Hiroshima City.

Fumihiko Maki (b 1929) is an architect and the director of the NAME firm. A graduate of Tokyo University, his main works are the Toyota Memorial Lecture Hall at Nagoya University, the Kumatani campus of Rissho University, the Daikanyama Housing Complex, the library of the Hiyoshi Campus of Keio University, the Spiral building, and the Kyoto National Museum of Modern Art.

Kiyofumi Kikutake (b 1928) is an architect and director of the Kikutake Kiyofumi Kenchiku Sekkei firm. His main works include the Izumo Taisha building, the Kyoto Community Bank, Aquapolis, the Tanabe Art Museum, and the Kauruizawa Takanawa Art Museum.

Kiyoshi Awazu (b 1929) is a graphic designer and the director of the Awazu Design Institute. He is a professor at Musashino College of Art and a member of the planning committee for the National Ethnological Museum in Osaka. His writings include *Dezain ni nani ga Dekiru ka?* (*What Can Design Do?*), *Gaudí Sanka* (*A Tribute to Gaudí*), and a collection of his works.

Kenji Ekuan (b 1929) is an industrial designer and the president of the GK Industrial Design Institute and the head of the Kuwasawa Research Institute. He was a special consultant for the design of the exhibits at the Tsukuba International Science Fair and the producer for the Japan IBM exhibit. His major writings include *Dogu Ko* (*On Tools*), *Indasutoriaru Dezain* (*Industrial Design*), *Makunouchi Bento no Bigakau* (*The Aesthetics of the Box Lunch*), and *Dogu no Shis* (*The Philosophy of Tools*).

Shomei Tomatsu (b 1930) is a photographer. In the 60s, his work focused on street scenes in Tokyo and he is regarded as the founder of that genre in Japan. He received the Ministry of Education special prize for his work, including *Taiyo no Empitsu* (*The Sun's Pencil*) and *11:02 Nagasaki*.

Kisho Kurokawa
New Tokyo Plan, 2025

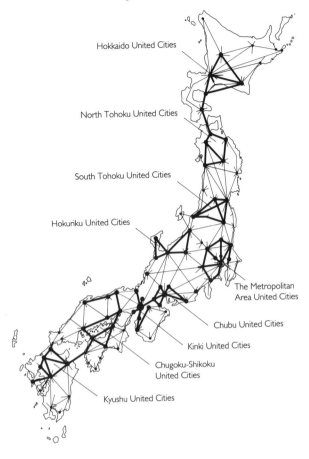

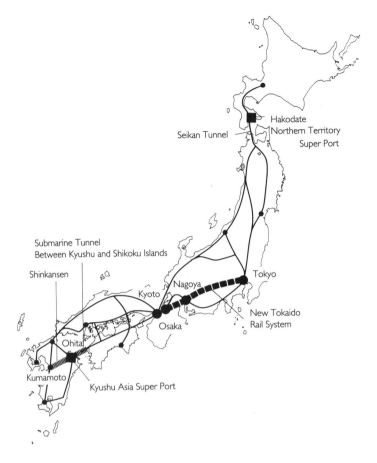

PROPOSAL 1

A drastic priority investment by the public must be made for the large metropolitan areas of Osaka, Kyoto, Nagoya, Fukuoka, Hiroshima, Kumamoto, Ohita, Sendai and Sapporo to accelerate the formation of united cities in each of these districts to urge the progress of a well-balanced network system throughout Japan.

PROPOSAL 2

By the year 2025, a large scale project must be carried out in rural areas for the formation of an efficient network system connecting large cities throughout Japan. The most urgent projects are: the New Tokaido Rail System, the Submarine Tunnel between Kyushu and Shikoku Islands, the Local Rail System connecting the large cities, the Kyushu Asia Super Port, and the Hakodate Northern Territory Super Port (Excluding the projects which are under research or planning).

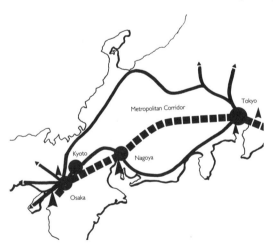

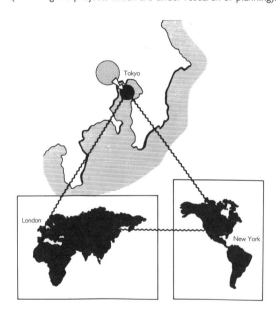

PROPOSAL 3

The formation of a Metropolitan Corridor and partial dispersion of the functions of the capital city: the New Emperor's Palace will be constructed in Kyoto and the Imperial Household Agency and the Agency of Cultural Affairs are to be moved to Kyoto. It is necessary to review the possibility of moving important ministries to Osaka and Nagoya. The new railway system (linear motor car), will be constructed between Osaka, Kyoto, Nagoya and Tokyo, forming the Metropolitan Corridor with a unified information system.

PROPOSAL 4

Tokyo will develop into one of the three large international financial centres of the world along with London and New York. The status of Tokyo in the information network system will be more important. Naturally, this will change Tokyo into a city where people from all over the world will be working and living. To adjust to this change, a large scale redevelopment of present Tokyo and the construction of the new island in Tokyo Bay to contain a population of five million will be carried out.

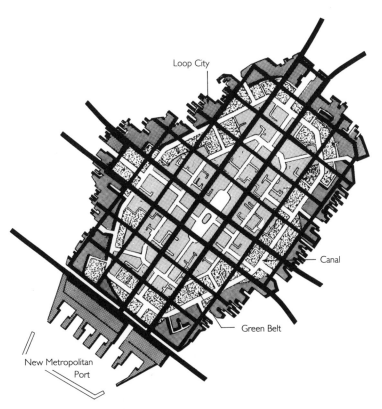

PROPOSAL 5
Construction of the New Island in Tokyo Bay.

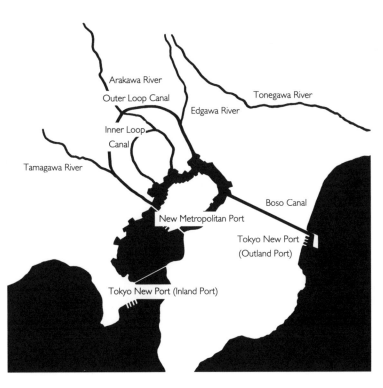

PROPOSAL 6
Construction of the Boso Canal and the Tokyo New Port.

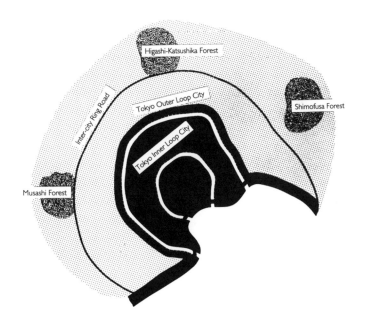

PROPOSAL 7
Redevelopment concept for Tokyo with the application of the Loop City and the Loop Canal.

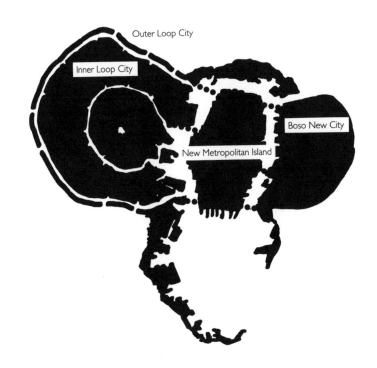

PROPOSAL 8
The concept of the Twin City by the construction of the New Boso City.

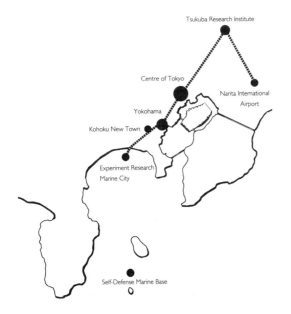

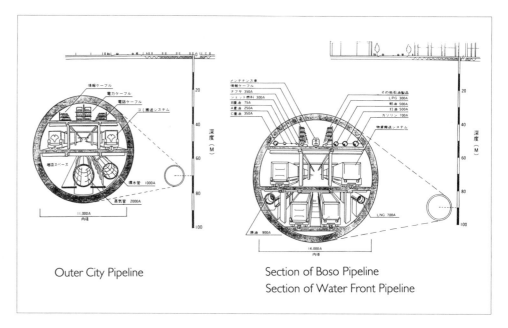

PROPOSAL 9
The construction of an Experimental Research Marine City and Self-Defense Marine Base in Sagami Bay.

Outer City Pipeline

Section of Boso Pipeline
Section of Water Front Pipeline

PROPOSAL 10
Tokyo Capital Area: Proposal of an Underground Pipeline System.

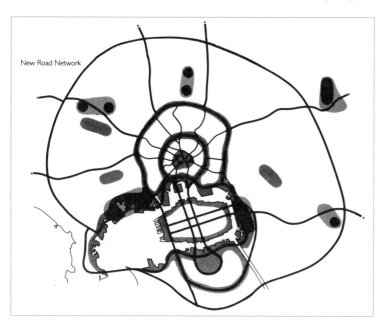

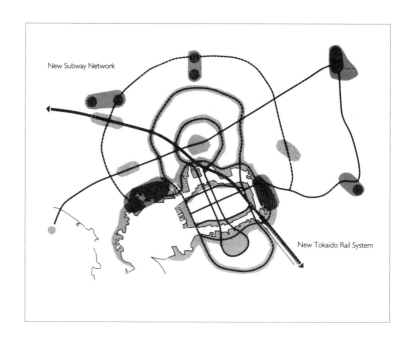

PROPOSAL 11
Aiming to improve the transportation network of the capital area, we propose the construction of the Tomei, Chuo, Tohoku, Kan'etsu and other motorways into two or four layered multi-level motorways which are to be located in the central loop and the exterior loop, and at the same time to construct the loop subway between the Kanjo Line No. 8 and the Chuo Line. The new capital island and the new city on the Chiba side will be connected by the subways and motorways to the old city centre of Tokyo.

PROPOSAL 12
For the realisation of these proposals, the establishment of a general policy and organisation, which will not be restricted by sectionalism or the government and public, is necessary, and a drastic alternation of rules and regulations and the alleviation of regulation must be challenged. Furthermore, these projects should not only be released to domestic demand but released overseas as well.

MID-RISE HOUSING UNITS ON THE NEW ISLAND IN TOKYO BAY
The housing district is composed of various types of housing units including high-, mid-, and low-rise. Yacht harbours are close to the housing units, creating the landscape of the City Canal. Each building will be designed by different architects of the world, becoming a place of architectural competition.

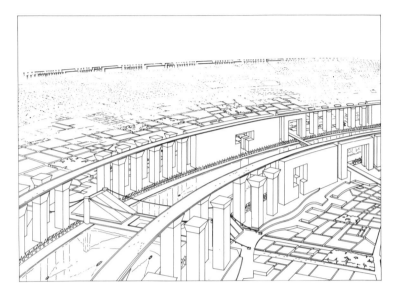

LOOP CITY
The redevelopment of Tokyo will be concentrated on the realisation of an Outer Loop City and an Inner Loop City (along Kanjo Line No. 8). These two Loop Cities will form the protection belt for disasters while, at the same time, implying the transformation of the city from the radiated structure to the Loop structure. It implies the city's transformation into a city without a core, a city of the 21st century.

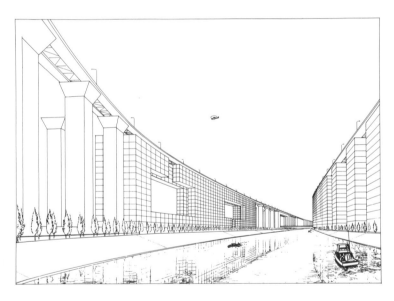

LOOP CANAL
Loop Cities are constructed on both sides of the Loop Canal. The Loop Canal implies the symbiosis of the artificial and the natural. Furthermore, it was meant to aim for the relocation of the landscape of the canal in the Edo period (symbiosis of the historical and the modern). Motorways run on the roof of the Loop Cities and the subways, underground corridors and information pipelines run beneath the Loop Cities.

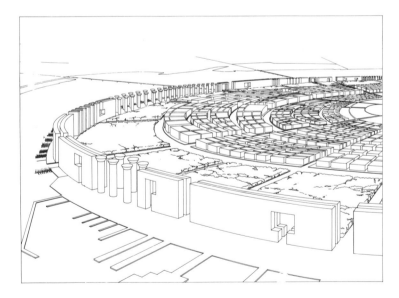

THE NEW ISLAND IN TOKYO BAY
The New Island in Tokyo Bay composes the Loop Core (where its centre is at the rim of the Loop), becoming the city without a centre. Rings of Loop Canals are constructed on the New Island in turn, becoming a composite of Loop Cities.

Kisho Kurokawa, Hiroshima City Museum of Contemporary Art, Hiroshima, 1988, overall plan. Situated in the Hijiyama Art Park, on the ridges of a hill, 60 percent of this Museum is below ground in order to preserve the green. All the buildings are connected with points and axial lines like a constellation to set a network of facilities within the park. In order to enhance the sense of symbiosis and integration of the park and the buildings, semi-outdoor, intermediate, spaces were provided at several locations.

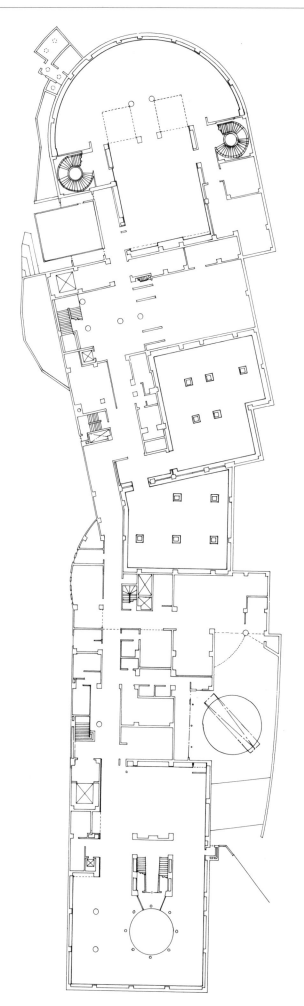

List of Illustrations

ADDENDA & CORRIGENDA

A number of inconsistencies exist within the text which include various interpretations of Japanese terms. We apologise for the mistakes and provide a list below:

Contents and Chapter I throughout: Hanasukiya should read Hanasuki.

Page 9, line 10: Toyota should read Toshiba.

Page 21, caption: Murano Shouo should read Takeno Jouo and tea master should read shogun.

Pages 22 and *23* captions: Oyama should read Inuyama.

Page 23, caption: Hana suki should read Hanasuki.

Chapter V throughout: Al-Sarir should read As-Sarir.

Pages 96 and *97* captions: 1967 should read 1976.

Page 104, line 30: Nanazawa should read Kanazawa.

Page 130, caption: Sazaedo should read Nikko.

Page 131, caption: should read Yanaka Kannoji Five-storeyed Pagoda.

Pages 148 and *173*, captions: please ignore word Sawara.

Page 175, caption: third floor should read first floor.

Page 194: Murata Jouou should read Sen no Rikyu (1522-1591).